VO

Tales and Techniques of a Voice-Over Actor

HARLAN HOGAN

ALLWORTH PRESS
NEW YORK

© 2002 Harlan Hogan

07 06 05 04 03 02   5   4   3   2   1

Published by Allworth Press
An imprint of Allworth Communications, Inc.
10 East 23rd Street, New York, NY 10010

Illustrations by John Sandford, Kurt Mitchell, and John Hayes

Cover design by Mary Belibasakis

Page composition/typography by Integra Software Services Pvt Ltd.,
Pondicherry, India

Back cover photograph by Brian McConkey

ISBN: 1-58115-249-3

Library of Congress Cataloging-in-Publication Data: Hogan, Harlan.
VO: tales and techniques of a voice-over actor / by Harlan Hogan.
p. cm.
Includes bibliographical references and index.
ISBN 1-58115-249-3
1. Television announcing. 2. Radio announcing. 3. Voice in motion
pictures. 4. Voice-overs. I. Title.
PN1990.9 .A54 2002
791.45'028--dc21
2002011722

Printed in Canada

Contents

Acknowledgments

Thanks to the great people at Allworth Press, Nicole, Michael, Jamie, Birte, Elizabeth, Jenna, Kate, and Tad, and to Karl Winkler of Neumann, USA, for allowing me to feature the sexy Neumann M-147 microphone on the cover.

Thanks to my family: "Bill," Marjorie, Marilan, Jamie, Graham, and Lesley Hogan.

Thanks to the insanely talented illustrator, John Sandford—and to artists Kurt Mitchell, John Hayes, and Arlo Bryan Guthrie.

And thanks to my friends, coconspirators, and all-around good sports who shared their stories, advice, and friendship: Gerry Souter, Steve King, Al Mitchell, Chuck Cohen, Gaylord Villers, Joel Cory, Brad Bisk, Sheila Dougherty, Richard Hawksworth, Robin Rutledge, A. J. Tyson, Jim Stephen, Joan Sparks, Jim Parks, Nancy Kidder, Todd Kijanka, Anne Gartlan, Mike King, Pete Stacker, Jamie Marchi, Mike Matheson, J. Eric Seastrand, Jeff Klinger, Chris Harlan, Jay Marks, Rick Elliott, Margaret Travolta, Marie Burke, Mike Miniskun, Stacey Christie, Mickey Grossman, Kit Woods, Beau Weaver, Jay Rose, Jeffrey Fisher, Steve Schatzberg, and a boatload of other people who will either be irritated—or relieved—that I didn't mention them.

One more thing. A special thanks to all of you who promised to purchase a leather-bound limited edition of this book for a low, low $175 plus tax, shipping, and handling. These sure-to-be collectible, autographed volumes are new and improved, come complete with a guaranteed certificate of authenticity and a coupon good for a free Whopper at participating Burger Kings. Best of all, this edition is strictly limited to the number of volumes I can manage to peddle in the next ten years.

INTRODUCTION

"When I was born I was so surprised I didn't talk for a year and a half."—Gracie Allen

The abbreviation "VO:" on a script technically stands for voice-over, a disembodied voice heard "over" pictures, film, or video. However, in the last ten years its accepted definition has broadened to include voice performers as well. I suspect that's because the term "announcer" conjures up negative thoughts of old-time barrel-chested basso profundos, right hands cupping their ears, unctuously oozing,

> **Ladies . . . are you using the most modern-day wash solution on your husbands' white shirts?**

Today, even the word "announcer" seems contrived—artificial and remote. It conjures up a parental figure *telling* us what to do, *telling* us what to buy, instead of a voice that sounds like a trusted friend *giving* advice, *giving* suggestions.

Anonymity is the stock in trade of voice-overs, as it is for others in media production: directors, editors, jingle writers, and recording engineers. The late Lorenzo Music, best known as the voice of Garfield the cat, enjoyed being this kind of secret celebrity. In an October 22, 1998, *New York Times* article, he said, "I like being famous *and* anonymous. I can walk down the street and nobody comes up to me."

I've always thought of myself as a kind of "verbal typesetter." Instead of Helvetica Bold and Arial Light, my stock-in-trade is intonation, tone, and emphasis. Like any good typesetter, if I've done my work well, I should be transparent, not really noticed, and unremarkable. This requires checking your ego at the door, though, and resigning yourself to the fact that, 99 percent of the time, no one will notice your work at all. Jingle composer Dick Reynolds of Comtrak, one of the top advertising music houses on the planet, put it well: "When I die, just bury me under an announcer, since that's where I spent my career."

As for me, when I get booked for the final session, I've pledged my wife and kids to employ another film abbreviation for my gravestone—MOS.

When German-born film director Luthar Mendes was the darling of Hollywood in the early days of motion pictures, he would scrawl "MOS" on his scripts and clapboards to indicate the scene was to be shot "Mit Out Sprache," without speech. Just as trendy then as it is now, the film community universally adopted his sophisticated-sounding abbreviation for all its silent scenes. So, I think my future epitaph, HARLAN HOGAN—MOS, has a very nice, oh-so-trendy and oh-so-sophisticated sound to it.

But before I get stuffed permanently into that final, claustrophobic "announce booth," I figure it's time to answer some of the questions I've been asked about my career over the years. Most people wonder how in the world you get a job "just" talking for a living, and many more wonder how they, too, might become a voice-over. Take, for example, this high school student living somewhere just outside of Tulsa, who was researching for her career term paper and sent me this e-mail:

> **Dear Sir:**
>
> **1. So how did you become a voice-over?**
>
> **2. How much do you make?**
>
> **3. Did you need any training?**
>
> **4. How can I get to do voice-overs?**

Not many years ago, I doubt that she, like me at her age, even knew that there were people who made their living doing voice work. If I gave it any thought when I was seventeen or eighteen, I'm sure I figured those voices on commercials, training films, and movie trailers must belong to somebody working at a radio or TV station. (That is, if I thought of it at all, being a little preoccupied with bad grades and the heady lure of cars and girls.) I do remember writing my career term paper on funeral directing, as much to shock my friends and parents as out of genuine interest. Besides, all the good subjects like cartoonist and Indy car driver were taken.

So, I was sympathetic to this young lady's career questions, and firmly resisted my natural urge to answer her e-mail tersely:

> **1) So how did you become a voice-over?**
>
> *Dumb luck.*
>
> **2) How much do you make?**
>
> *A lot some years, barely enough in others.*
>
> **3) Did you need any training?**
>
> *Yep, but I'm still not sure in just what.*
>
> **4) How can I get to do voice-overs?**
>
> *That's the question I try to answer every day.*

Instead, I decided I'd write this book for her.

THE WORST VOICE IN THE WHOLE THIRD GRADE—TALKING ROBOTS, TALKING ROCKETS, AND THE RECORDIO

"And I've never forgotten any of those people, or any of the voices we used to hear on the radios"
—Woody Allen, *Radio Days,* Orion, 1986

I don't believe in psychics, astrologers, or fortunetellers. But I love their chutzpah.

I'm not sure why I was lucky enough to become a successful voice-over performer, but an astrologer would be. Simply by gleaning a few random factoids of my oh-so-ordinary childhood, he would skillfully weave a tale in which I, a terminally shy kid from the south-side Chicago suburbs, was ordained by the stars to give voice to ad campaigns, Web sites, and training films everywhere. Any astrologer worth his or her salt would explain how the conjunction of the planet Pluto with the constellation Taurus in my chart would all but guarantee I'd one day perform voice-overs for Disney and Ford. A crystal gazer could have clearly seen all of the amazing people and events that would help shape my career. The Tarot reader, dealing her deck onto the table, would reveal my neatly organized career path, card by card, instead of the haphazard half-shuffled journey it's been.

In fact, I have always been fascinated by sound. I don't know why. My grandparents had an apartment on 79th Street in Chicago, and though at age four I was just barely tall enough to reach the old-fashioned talking-tube intercom in the downstairs entry hall, I found it, somehow, well, magical.

When stereo phonographs came out in 1958 I'd happily sit for hours listening to records—sound effects records. Invisible basketballs dribbled from speaker to speaker, while other kids were outside in the bright sun actually playing ball. Unseen automobiles screeched to a stop narrowly missing my dad's pride and joy, his genuine Naugahyde recliner.

While my sister was falling off her clamp-on roller skates onto the unforgiving cement sidewalk outside our house, I remained unscathed inside, transfixed between the two gray- and silver-flecked cloth-covered speaker grilles as ghostly roller skaters glided by, crisscrossing the living room. Anyone foolish enough to disturb my reverie would immediately be coerced into taking my place in the precise center of our living room.

"Just listen to this!" I'd hiss, shaking my head with wonder, "Does this sound real or what?" Steam and diesel locomotives would roar past the coffee table and fade into the distant footstool. "That," I'd inform my captive audience, "is known as the Doppler effect!" Usually the effect was demonstrated a second time, as my hapless victim ran screaming down the hallway.

A few years before, my preoccupation with sound led me to eviscerate one of my favorite toys, Robert the Robot, just to figure out what mechanism made him talk. Long before battery-operated, computer-chipped, made-in-China talking toys, Robert could repeat this little doggerel when you turned the crank on his back:

I am Robert Robot, Mechanical Man—guide me and steer me whenever you can.

And like so many others kids in the 1950s, after the lights went out I stealthily got out my Rocket Radio, a plastic, three-inch-long, rocket-ship-shaped AM radio receiver. By attaching a tiny alligator-shaped clip to almost anything metal, which served as an antenna, radio stations mysteriously whispered in my ears.

I felt quite smug, knowing my parents had no idea that I was wide-awake upstairs. I lay there, quietly laughing at the cornball humor of Homer and Jethro on *The WLS Barn Dance*, or humming along to the big band sounds from the Tip Top Tap high above Chicago's Allerton Hotel. Sometimes, on particularly lucky star-filled nights, I barely made out the faint voices of Station KMOX from faraway St. Louis, Missouri.

But most of all, I remember the first time I heard my own recorded voice.

Everybody had cautioned me: "You'll hate the sound of your own voice, Bobby." (I'll explain later how the Teamsters forced me to change my name from Robert to Harlan. . . .) Warnings aside, I was really curious to hear what I sounded like. Maybe I had a future at WLS or even KMOX. So I was excited when I found out that my third-grade field trip would be to Chicago's Museum of Science and Industry. In the "Science of Sound" exhibit, I would get the chance to actually hear how I'd sound "on the air."

Our first stop in the museum was the Whisper Room. It's an ellipsoidal chamber with two small platforms a little over forty feet apart. You stand, facing away from your partner, and whisper into a tall acrylic parabolic dish. Amazingly, without the aid of amplifiers or electronics, the other person, facing his or her dish, hears you perfectly.

In a burst of nostalgia during the Christmas holidays last year, I stopped by the Museum of Science and Industry with my twenty-one-year-old son, Jamie, and dragged him to the Whisper Room. That's right, it's still there. He found it just as fascinating as it was back in 1937, when the exhibit first opened.

Barbara Trent was my assigned buddy on my 1955 school outing. Holding hands as we were *forced* to do on field trips, we left the marvelous Whisper Room and trooped over to another display—the one where you could hear your own voice. For me, of course, this was the big moment. I was ready. Surely I'd sound like a younger version of those wonderful voices on my Rocket Radio.

Manfully (at least in my mind's eye) I released my sweaty hand from Ms. Trent's, stepped up to the microphone and—

Nothing.

I froze.

Like tens of thousands before me, I couldn't think of a single thing to say. Sure, we have recording devices almost everywhere today. But even now, if you stick a microphone in most people's faces, the majority will blurt out, "Testing 1-2-3," or worse yet, recite: "Mary had a little lamb." It's almost a tradition dating back to 1877 when Thomas Edison said the same thing—"Mary . . ."—as he tested his new invention, the phonograph. Me? Well, I followed his example.

What played back was just plain awful. Words cannot describe how much I sounded like an adenoid-ridden eight-year-old, giggling through, "fleece as white as snow." This was actually worse than my Grandmother's preoccupation with the dangers of BB guns and how they'd "put your eye out." We kids all knew that was pretty remote. But when everyone had told me that I'd hate my voice—wow, for once they knew what they were talking about! It was the equivalent of, "you'll put your ear out." I didn't speak for two years.

Okay, maybe not two years, but I was uncharacteristically quiet all the way home on the bus.

That God-awful sound reverberated through my tin ears all the way to junior high, when for homeroom, I got Mr. Jones by default, predestination, or just plain luck. Tall and balding, Mr. Jones also taught speech and drama. He ran a Rainbow Cone Ice Cream stand in the summer and had a mysterious middle initial, "Y." Best of all, he had his own personal, professional tape recorder in his classroom.

Now, other teachers at the time had tape recorders, but they were usually Wollensaks—cheap, bulletproof, reel-to-reel standard-school-issue machines with a sound quality just slightly better than a public telephone.

John Y. Jones, however, owned an Ampex 601 tape recorder! It was a professional quality machine and enticing just to look at, swathed in dark brown leather-like vinyl, with glowing meters and knobs—lots of knobs. I had an almost irresistible urge, when he wasn't looking, to spin each one up and down just to see what in the world they all did. Ampex advertising of the day claimed, "At last, true Ampex performance in a twenty-six-pound miniaturised [the British spelling] professional package." This was serious and very expensive gear in 1958, costing as much as $995 for the two-track model, plus $195 for the ten-watt portable speaker and amplifier. In comparison, clunky, garden variety Wollensaks were priced at less than $200. Mr. Jones also possessed a professional Shure Brothers microphone on a—get this—shiny, adjustable microphone stand. To me, this was CBS, NBC, and ABC all wrapped up in one, right in my homeroom!

After years of teaching hormone-raging preteens, Mr. Jones had become adept at finding ways to keep his homeroom busy, always busy. I'm sure it cut down on the number of fistfights and hair-pulling contests. So he'd often dig out old radio scripts and record us playing the parts and making the sound effects on his Ampex 601.

Most of us had never heard a real old-time radio drama. Sony had begun selling the first transistor radios the year before and the radio programs we listened to consisted mainly of disc jockeys spinning the Top 40 and newsmen rambling on about current events. When I was little, I do vaguely remember my mom listening to *The Romance of Helen Trent* soap opera on our wine-colored Motorola radio in the kitchen. That was as close to the Golden Age of radio drama as I can remember. Fact is, I actually thought the program was about our neighbor, Barbara Trent's mother.

From the moment Mr. Jones began recording us, I was hooked, and as I look back, I find it amazing that I ever went home. The sight of those two clear plastic reels turning and those voices—not just any voices, but our voices—blaring through the speakers was mesmerizing.

Mr. Jones encouraged me to try out for a few school plays and I landed my first speaking role in the school operetta. My one and only line was, "Good morning, I've brought the contracts." A small part, perhaps, but I remember my mom's unprejudiced praise of my performance even today: "You were the best one!" Luckily I only had to pretend to sing during the curtain call. It's a skill I'm still unable to grasp. But those fifteen seconds in front of the footlights and an audience was all it took. A full-fledged ham was born.

Meanwhile, I pleaded, wheedled, saved, connived, and conned my parents to "please, please, please, please, *please*" get me a tape recorder for my eighth-grade graduation. God love them, they did. Of course there was little money for a luxury tape recorder, certainly not an Ampex, or even a tinhorn-sounding Wollensak. But they found an affordable machine at Goldblatt's Department Store.

The Recordio was arguably one of the worst-sounding tape recorders ever built. It made even a Wollensak sound like high fidelity (there's a lost phrase). But I just loved it. So much so that when my parents, my sister Marilan, and I went to Canada that summer, I took my beloved, fifty-five pound Recordio along.

Hauling a behemoth-sized tape recorder had an unexpected advantage in a foreign country. I carefully removed the four screws holding the top of the Recordio to the case and stuffed it full of firecrackers, legal in Canada but very illegal in Illinois. My parents found the firecrackers. I'm not sure if they were more shocked by the fact I'd smuggled them over the border, or by my frank admittance that I'd planned to sell them to my friends at a profit so I could buy more magic tricks.

I think it was at that moment that my dad's fears were confirmed. I was, indeed, some alien life force invading his home. I swear I heard him mumble something to the effect of, "What hath God wrought," but I could be wrong.

Mom was aghast, but she hunkered down, redoubling her efforts to be tirelessly supportive and encouraging. Her enthusiasm for whatever Marilan and I were up to, or into, still amazes me today. From baton twirling classes for Marilan to sewing cloth bags for my myriad magic props, she was interested and very forgiving—with the possible exception of the firecracker incident. That one really pissed her off.

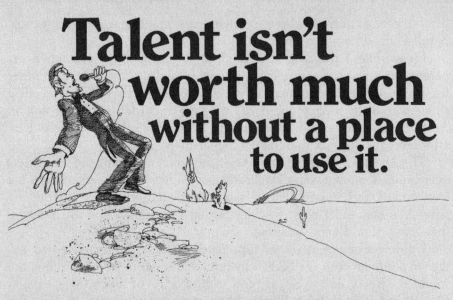

Talent isn't worth much without a place to use it.

Techniques of a Voice-Over: Talking Inside the Box—Training, Technique, Tools, and Talent, or, the Four *T*s of Voice-Over

"Just because your voice reaches halfway around the world doesn't mean you are wiser than when it reached only to the end of the bar."—Edward R. Murrow

I have a whisper room of my own now. No, not the kind we climbed all over at the Museum of Science and Industry. This one is a small, soundproof booth, handmade in Morristown, Tennessee. It's just big enough to hold two people, assuming they like each other, and I record much of my work in it. Now when I whisper, my voice can be heard anywhere in the world. The digital revolution in audio production is alive and well here at home. Using the Internet and ISDN phone lines, I'm able to telecommute anywhere.

For example, I just finished narrating a video for Rockwell Automation this morning. Rockwell is located in Ohio and its client is in Hong Kong, but I never left home. By next weekend the video, with my voice, will be playing continuously at a trade-show kiosk in Hong Kong. Yesterday, China Steel sent its footage via digital phone lines, complete with the original Chinese narration, to me here in Illinois and to Rockwell in Ohio. Today, the producer in Ohio and I were able to simultaneously watch the video as I timed my new English narration to fit the original Chinese precisely. The entire session was done live and in real time via ISDN. The technology is an amazing thing.

Recording equipment, like so many electronic devices, has become smaller and smaller and more and more affordable, so voice-overs can live just about anywhere and in a sense, "e-mail" themselves to the production center. Of course, there's a ying and a yang to this. It's easy to feel isolated without face-to-face interaction. And, although it lets a Midwest-based talent compete in L.A., New York, and other markets, it also lets other voice-overs invade *my* space. But when your commute is down the stairs to clean the kitty litter, start the coffee, and stroll into the whisper room, it's hard to imagine a better job.

I suspect many readers would like to join me. Not in my whisper room, but as voice-over actors. How? Well, as you'll learn in the main chapters of this book—the "tales"—I'm living proof that there's no one surefire career path to voice-over success. Well, maybe one, but that involves becoming a major movie or TV star first. If you accomplish that, then voice work will roll in all on its own accord. Personally, I've been holding my breath waiting for that to happen for the last twenty-five years, and so far, no cigar.

So, instead, here in the Techniques of a Voice-Over sections, you and I can talk about the realities of the voice business—how to get into it and stay in it with newcomers, old pros, and even the unfairly dreaded wanna-bes. Hey, we all were wanna-bes at some time, so the least I can do is point you in the right direction, as so many generous performers did for me.

If you're curious about the business, you've probably wondered what a typical voice-over recording session is like. They usually go something like this.

With a swoosh, the airtight door on the soundproof booth clicks shut. A "second" (audio engineer in training) stands next to the Sennheiser 416 microphone and with a twist aims it toward my lips. "Got it set on 'Harlan Height,'" he says familiarly. I glance at the script on the copy stand. On the paper are printed six words for American Family Insurance, just six words.

Through the glass, John Binder of Another Country Studios smiles and gestures to my "cans." I fit the headphones tightly over my ears. The door to the booth closes shut once more, and the second leaves.

I'm alone with six words.

My producer is Tom Thiede, a principal with Blue Horse Advertising. We've worked together for years. Tom nods and says over the talkback mike:

"You know the drill, we've got four 4.6 seconds. Here's picture."

Twenty-nine and a half seconds of film fly by on the tiny video screen near my copy stand.

John says, "We're rolling on take 1."

It's wonderful footage of people happy with their lives and their life insurance, lovingly directed by Danny Levinson of Moxie Pictures. The American Family Insurance logo fades up, and as the music swells, I say my six words.

"All . . . your . . . protection . . . under . . . one . . . roof."

"Cut," says John.

"Perfect," says Tom.

"Easy," say I.

And believe me, each and every one of the thousands of voice-overs I've performed in over twenty-five years has gone just as smoothly as that.

Well, maybe a few.

Well, one.

Truth is, long before any voice-over is lucky enough to land a session this easy, with an equally easygoing producer like Tom Thiede, they'll need a few basics, what the corporate types are fond of calling a skill set. I've named this voice-over skill set the Four *T*s: Training, Technique, Tools, and Talent.

Training includes your background and education—not just in acting or voice acting, specifically, but in business, broadcasting, and advertising, too. Technique is your skill set in front of a microphone—interpreting copy, reading it in time, and taking direction. Your tools include everything from your voice demo and self-promotion to the performing unions and your agent. The final *T* is the toughest to define and impossible to create—talent. Talent is the fuel that drives the engine, of course, but without the other *T*s it's only raw ability—unshaped and unrefined. Simply put, talent isn't worth much without a place to use it, but combine natural talent with technique, tools, and training, and you've got the recipe for a successful career as a voice-over actor.

But if talent is the God-given ability you can't buy or fake, how do you know if you have it? Let's turn that question around. How does a producer decide if you have the talent to record his or her voice-over? Simple, they use a little test called the audition.

So let's clear our desks, boys and girls, for a pop quiz. This examination will be multiple choice. In fact, the multiple choices you make in your performance and interpretation of this script are exactly what might or might not get you the job.

Today's exam is from a national TV commercial voice-over for Sears. This is *real* copy and *real* direction (despite my twisted imagination, even I could never make this up). If you're already a working voice-over, it's likely you'll recognize the script, since it was sent to agents all across the country. Even if you aren't a voice-over newcomer, wanna-be, or pro, you might enjoy auditioning this script—who knows? You just might possess the most elusive of the three *Ts*—talent.

Agency direction:

The voice for this spot should be younger, probably thirty-something. It should be honest and real and not too zany like a Steven Wright or Mark Fenske. If the voice were music it would sound more like the Dave Matthews Band or Brian Ferry. Angie Harmon, formerly on *Law and Order*, would be a good start as a description for a female voice. Self-assured, with a brassy tone. George Clooney, if he could talk with more enthusiasm and speed, would be a good example of the quality we seek in a male voice.

Well, alrighty then. That's what they want. I'm not sure if I'm any of the things described but, of course, neither is George Clooney. By the way, did you notice how it took almost a hundred words to describe this commercial? Stunning when you realize that the actual script contains only thirty-three.

So, give it whirl, reading it out loud, please.

VO: *This Saturday Sears says thank you. We're taking 10 percent off everything, even the sale prices. Which means, you can save anywhere from 10 to 40 percent throughout the store. During The Customer Appreciation Sale only at Sears.*

Now, read the script out loud again, but this time, grab a watch and time yourself.

Great, you probably read it in around eighteen to twenty seconds the first go-round, *but* this is a fifteen-second commercial, so let's try it again.

Got it down to fifteen seconds? Good, but I probably should have warned you: Although the *total* commercial time is fifteen seconds, editors like to leave about seven frames of video or film at the front and back of a spot, so there's a slight pause between commercials. Bottom line: You lose another half-second.

Oh, and don't forget to add appropriate emphasis on those important client words: "save," "sale," "thank you," and, most importantly, "Sears."

Try it again. This time you've got precisely fourteen and a half seconds. In time? That's great.

Whoops, there are just a few more things we'll need before you're done. Read the script once more:

- On time,

- with appropriate emphasis,

- and make your voice honest, real, not-too-zany,

- with a Dave Matthews band musicality,

- self-assured and brassy,

- with enthusiasm, and speed.

  VO: This Saturday Sears says thank you. We're taking 10 percent off everything, even the sale prices. Which means, you can save anywhere from 10 to 40 percent throughout the store. During The Customer Appreciation Sale only at Sears.

Perfect! "That's a wrap."

2

STUMBLING THROUGH SCHOOL—RONALD REAGAN, RADIO, AND A WHALE OF A ROOMMATE

"Don't you see?! We're actors—we're the opposite of people!"
—Tom Stoppard, *Rosencrantz and Guildenstern are Dead*

It's only in retrospect that you see the obvious: the connections, emerging patterns, and noncoincidences that send you whirling off in one direction or another. Back in my junior high homeroom I was lucky enough to find the first chink in my armor of shyness. It's my contention that most actors are shy. That's why we embrace the idea of being someone else. Someone not shy but brave and suave, and, well, *anything* but shy.

Resisting the urge to retreat back into my shell, I considered my options as I entered high school. Marching band was out of the question due to my lack of musicality. The school newspaper unfortunately required some ability at grammar and spelling. The brightest and most popular kids headed the student council, and I met neither of those qualifications. So I poured myself into performing magic and decided to try out for the freshman play.

Robert "Sam" Phillips taught speech and directed our high school plays. Sam demanded serious dedication to his productions. Long before the word "ensemble" acting became the rage, he created an atmosphere where there really were no big or little parts. Everybody built sets, moved props, hung lights, and sold their fair share of tickets, or they were gone. Sam's shows were so good that once in a competition at the University of Illinois, a downstate judge criticized our production of *Auntie Mame* for being "too professional." Sam's gift to T. F. South High School was a rich tradition of theater excellence. His gift to me was his assurance that despite my mediocre grades, there was sure to be a college somewhere that would welcome me. In fact, it was his alma mater (and Ronald Reagan's as well), tiny Eureka College. Actually, tiny may be too small a word for Eureka.

Freshman registration day was a scorcher, and we didn't have air conditioning or even a radio in my dad's Chevrolet Impala. As my mom and I drove onto the diminutive but very pretty ivy-covered campus, there was a "hootenanny" going on. Folk songs were the rage then, foreshadowing the political unrest of the Sixties, and sing-along hootenannies were the height of chic, at least in central Illinois. We strolled over to hear "The Hydraulic Banana Singers." Three very talented folk singers, one just shy of midget status, one thin as a rail, and one, John Bryan, actually weighed an eighth of a ton and played a mean five-string banjo. I admired John's bravura and humor on the stage, and afterward I told John how much I liked the group's music and name. He asked if I had a roommate for the semester. I laughed and said, "I do now."

We became fast friends, and pulled every stupid stunt freshmen can—from completely filling one dorm room with crumpled paper balls to spending the better part of a weekend hiding all the possessions of our dorm's resident bad boy, Walt Putback, and forging a note from our housemother telling him his belongings had been shipped home.

In the spring, John introduced me to his hometown of Bloomington, Illinois, home of Illinois Wesleyan University, the university's acclaimed theater department, and the local radio station WIOK. The station had not one but three Ampex 601 tape recorders, two huge turntables, three production rooms with shiny Electro-Voice and Shure microphones, scads of headphones—and my roomie had a friend who worked there.

Two life-altering events occurred simultaneously, when John's friend Jay said those three words kids like us feared more than any others: "I got drafted." We grimaced, sympathized, and silently thanked our lucky stars we had student deferments, at least for the moment.

"Hey," Jay said. "I've gotta sell my motorcycle, and the station's looking for a replacement. My shift's from five to midnight. You guys ought to audition."

I auditioned for the radio station and Illinois Wesleyan's Theater school, and got into both. Despite my parents' misgivings, I also bought Jay's Honda motorcycle. John proved himself just as good-natured as always, easing my guilt with his heart-felt congratulations at taking what might rightly have been his job. John went on to have a very successful career in journalism, got a master's degree in English, and today works at the *Los Angeles Times*.

Naturally, my first shift on the air was flawless. As the record ended and I switched on the microphone, I no longer felt the temptation to repeat, "Mary Had a Little Lamb." Instead, I managed to croak out, "Nancy and Frank Sinatra on WIOK," started a prerecorded commercial, and thought to myself, "Hey that was easy!" Nanoseconds later the program director, station manager, and sales manager of WIOK were all in the control room, glowering.

"What did you say?" demanded John McDermott, the nearly seven-foot-high station manager.

I'd only said six words. What could possibly be wrong? "Uh . . . ," I managed.

"He said 'Doubya,'" replied Henry Zang, the station sales manager, tugging at his clip-on tie, and then cleaning his black-rimmed glasses with the tail of his rumpled J. C. Penny's white shirt. Goateed program director Thom Brown slowly and silently nodded assent.

"Uh . . . ," I repeated.

"Hogie," said McDermott, "It's double U, double U, not 'doubya,' double U eye oh kay. . . . Got it?"

"Right!" I said.

"And by the way, Jim won't make it back from his remote, so you gotta do the news at fifty-five."

"Got it!" I said.

The United Press International printer was in the hallway just outside the control room, spewing out an endless stream of yellow paper with purple inked stories from around the world. I glanced through the window at the Barbra Streisand record, making sure it was still playing, and checked the control room clock that read 4:52. I had three minutes to figure out what to read from the UPI machine. Welcome to the radio world of "rip and read."

I started to panic until I saw the headline: "Five-Minute News Summary." "Perfect!" I thought, ripped it off the teletype, and barely made it back to the booth to "back announce" Ms. Streisand by once again mentioning the name of the song and then saying that the news was just a minute away over the last bars of music.

I flicked on the Ampex 601 to play a thirty-second commercial for Howard Johnson's and with trembling hands quickly managed to put a huge record onto the unoccupied turntable. I turned the volume control, or "pot," down to the "cue" position as my predecessor Jay had taught me, so that the sound wouldn't go on the air, and "cued up" the next commercial from the thirty or so prerecorded spots on the record. Cueing up meant rotating the disc back and forth to find the exact beginning of the commercial. Who would have expected that many years later DJs would make a career out of that same basic movement—"scratching" records.

I feverishly grabbed another record containing the music that introduced our newscasts and slapped it down in place of the Streisand record and just managed to cue it up before the commercial on the other turntable ended. Breathless, I flipped on the microphone to start my first live newscast. Looking back I realize I was perfect—perfectly awful.

"Ripping and reading" news stories without prereading or rehearsing them is a learned art, and one I had never practiced. On top of that, UPI printouts utilized tons of abbreviations, and translating those on the fly was another skill I hadn't mastered. I reported in my most serious tone that "General Mac Murty was struck at an *R R* crossing and was *D Oh A* at the hospital . . . . He had served the *US* in *W W* Eye Eye." Then I confidently informed my listeners that an East German pilot had defected by flying his plane over to West Germany. Unfortunately, I reported that he'd "defecated" over West Germany. The phone lines at WIOK lit up like a Christmas tree.

I spent the next three days practicing "double *U*," "double *U*," "double *U* eye oh kay" over and over and over, and read the *United Press International Manual of Terms and Abbreviations* cover to cover. Somewhere deep inside, I knew this wasn't going to be quite as easy as I'd thought.

The following weekend I was scheduled for my first "God" shift. Most radio stations have religious programming on Sunday mornings, and WIOK was no different—hence the name: God's shift. Even though I had to get up early, my 6:00 A.M. to noon time slot was easy, consisting only of reading the station sign-on announcement, delivering two newscasts, and introducing tape-recorded programs of a variety of ministers and choirs.

As the strains of "The Star Spangled Banner" faded, I announced with a perfect double *U* that, "WIOK radio 1410 is on the air" and introduced *The Light and Life Hour*.

The tape rolled on the Ampex 601 to my left and I heard

rouh efil dna thgil eht neeb sah siht ogacihc morf . . . .

For a moment I thought that this must be a program from one of those religions that talk in tongues. Pretty strange way to start the show, I thought. Then it dawned on me, as a single phone light began to flash, that the tape was playing backward! I stopped the tape, cued up the first record I could grab and answered the phone. Well, I thought, I guess there's at least one soul up early enough to call in and complain.

"Hello, WIOK," I cheerfully answered in my best announcer voice.

"This is Harry."

"Harry who?" I asked.

"Harry at the transmitter."

I hadn't met Harry the station engineer yet but I'd heard stories. He lived at the remote transmitter site in the middle of an Illinois cornfield south of town. He was, basically, a self-appointed semihermit. I knew enough to know that he didn't really qualify as a human listener.

"It's tails-out, you know that, don't you?" he said.

"I guess so . . . what'll I do?"

"Get an empty reel from the production room," he calmly instructed. "You do know where that is?"

"Sure," I answered with more confidence than I actually felt.

"Then fast forward the tape onto the empty reel, reverse the reels, and you can play it. 'Course you'll be off a few minutes all morning."

"I'll shorten my newscast," I said. "Thanks for the help. How come they didn't rewind this at the production studio, or at least label it?"

"Saves time after they high-speed duplicate it, and cuts down on print-through noise, though I'm sure you don't know what that is, and I'm quite sure it's clearly labeled," Harry said brusquely.

"Nope, I'm looking at the box right now it says, 'Light and Life Hour, property of Disciples of Christ Church, recorded at Genesis Recorders.' Nothing says it's backward."

"Tails-out," he corrected. "What color is the tape?"

"Brown," I responded.

"No! Not the recording tape," he shot back. "The header tape—the little piece of sticky tape that holds the loose end onto the reel."

"Oh, it's blue, Harry."

"Then it's labeled properly," Harry said sanctimoniously. "Don't they teach you guys anything? Blue header tape means the tape is wound tails-out, red means it's heads-out."

"You're not kidding me are you?" I asked.

"Everybody knows it," Harry said matter-of-factly.

Well, not everybody, I thought.

"Thanks again for the help, I'll try to remember."

"You're welcome, kid. Here's a tip: 'Red *head* and the blue-*tail* fly.' You'll never forget."

I never did.

Little by little, lesson by lesson, I caught on. Soon, I could rip and read the news, instinctively translate UPI abbreviations, edit recording tape without slicing my fingertips off, and was even privy to the unwritten code, "*Red*-head and the blue-*tail* fly."

Fall approached, and it was time to register for college classes. As I stood dutifully in line, I got my first glimpse of . . . Dr. Ficca. He was seated at the end of one of those eight-foot-long folding tables that usually spend their entire lives in the school cafeteria. Today, an endless ribbon of tables had been furloughed to snake its way around the Illinois Wesleyan University's Fred Young field house.

Framed by the garish green and white HOME OF THE TITANS banner, and a posterboard sign scribbled with TH. DEPT., Dr. Ficca didn't look menacing. He had, however, the unmistakable aura of a man very bored with sitting in this gymnasium dealing with schedules, class conflicts, and housing screw-ups. Instead, he belonged in—and to—the Theater. That's what made Dr. John Ficca the new top dog of Illinois Wesleyan University's McPherson Theater and precisely the right man for the job.

I was terrified.

I had auditioned for his predecessor, Dr. Tucker, and won acceptance into the department. But after the ten-thousandth person tells you how lucky you were not to have auditioned for Dr. Ficca, you can't help developing a little angst when the time comes to meet him. And the time had come. My thoughts began to spiral out of control. Would he, could he, make me audition all over again? Who knows? I might have to audition right there, right then.

"Gee, Dr. Ficca," I imagined saying, "I'm not really prepared."

"Not prepared!" he would boom so everyone within earshot could hear. "A *real* actor is always prepared. You, sir, are dismissed!"

As I approached the "Th. Dept." table, he looked up over his black-rimmed reading glasses at me as I handed him my stack of registration papers, transcript, and schedule.

"Mr. Hogan," he said, not a question, exactly, and not exactly a statement either. I fought back the urge to look around to see if my father had somehow magically appeared behind me, since "Mr." was a title I'd not heard much at age nineteen.

"Yes, Dr. Ficca," I said.

"It says here you're transferring in from Eureka College, but I don't remember you auditioning for me."

"Oh God," I thought, "here it comes, one day at Wesleyan and I'm out."

"I auditioned for Dr. Tucker," I managed to squeak out.

Again came the glance over the glasses.

"Are you any good?" he asked in a flat tone of voice.

Am I any good? *Am I any good?* Am I any good? The question ran through my mind, careened off the back of my cranium, and stuck somewhere between the left and right hemispheres. Alarm bells sounded in my ears, my left brain shouted to the right, "Dive! Dive!" This was a trick question, of course. No, this was the trick question of all time. If I say yes, I'll be branded as cocky—worse yet, a troublemaker. If I say no, how could I be worthy of IWU's acting program? I'd been voted best actor at Eureka, but as I've mentioned, it was a very, very, small school. He peered up at me, and I lamely smiled down and said, "I'm pretty good."

Pause.

Glasses off.

Slight smile.

Deep frown.

"Then you'll never make it," he said.

Long pause.

"Gulp."

Glasses on.

"Mr. Hogan," the good doctor confided, "you've chosen the most competitive, difficult, demanding, infuriating, and vicious way to try to make a living on earth, and if you're not *really* good then you'll never make it. See you in class."

The truth sometimes hurts, but it's always the truth.

Now, after over twenty-five years of making my living as an actor, I realize Dr. Ficca was right. He did, however, leave out one important detail. The most competitive, difficult, demanding, infuriating, and vicious way to try to make a living on earth is also the most fun.

From the 1989 Harlan Hogan Production Calendar—John Hayes, Illustrator

Techniques of a Voice-Over: Coining a Phrase—Spinning Words into Gold?

"It's always a crap shoot, always will be a crap shoot."
—James Earl Jones, *AFTRA Magazine*

It's absolutely true. Performing voice-overs is nothing less than spinning words into gold, each glittering phrase of copy weaving a tapestry of financial success. This verbal largesse is wrought without any effort, study, or expense on the part of the performer.

And if you believed that paragraph, I've got this great bridge to sell you.

It's become an urban legend. "I know this friend of my cousin, Maureen . . . well, her kids did one voice-over for McDonald's, and the residuals put both of them through Harvard!" The fact is there are some people who have made considerable amounts of money for just one or two commercials, especially back in the 1980s, but people also win the lottery too, and just about as often.

So, despite the fact that you did so marvelously well on our Sears audition in the last Techniques of a Voice-Over section, it's really important that you understand the economic realities of voice work before we tackle the Four *T*s—Training, Tools, Technique, and Talent—in detail.

Here are the facts, as of the new millennium. A union radio commercial pays roughly $298.70 if it plays in Chicago for thirteen weeks. A television voice-over session fee is $375.95. If your commercial then plays in a major market, like Chicago, you'll earn an additional $239.55. That $615.50 allows an ad agency to run your spot an unlimited number of times for thirteen weeks. Your earnings increase to $1,180.50 if the commercial airs in New York and Los Angeles as well. If you're lucky enough to have a commercial playing on the TV networks, you'll earn even more—a residual fee—paid on a declining scale every time it plays. Industrial/corporate voice-over narrations earn approximately $345 for the first hour of recording, at scale (union minimum). In 1999, Screen Actors Guild members earned $677.3 million dollars in TV commercials alone. Just remember, though, that that money is spread out over a lot of performers, many of them highly paid celebrities.

What will it cost you to grab a share of those millions? Well, your expenses will most likely include union dues, perhaps a Web site, and certainly a voice-over demo. Don't overlook the costs of parking, auditioning time, and agents' commissions. How about some promotion, too. My mailing list contains well over five thousand names. If I send a postcard to each person to promote my Web site, for example, that's over $1,200 in postage alone, and at least another $800 to print and design the cards themselves. If you decide to send your voice-over demo to the whole shebang, the mind and pocketbook reels.

I'm not attempting to discourage anyone; the business will do that on its own. But please don't buy into the *Just buy my book, just take my course, just let me produce your voice demo and you'll make hundreds or thousands a minute*. . . . Nonsense. There's no magic bullet. Training, experience, talent, and hard work can't be replaced.

Dick Moore of AFTRA (The American Federation of Television and Radio Artists) says that of the eighty thousand members the union represents, no more than a hundred people do most of the voice work. This quote from Screen Actors Guild Web site is just as sobering: "Despite the popular image that all actors are rich, most Screen Actors Guild members earn less than $7,500 per year from Screen Actors Guild jobs."

Here's one more example, just in case the "urban legend" of easy money hasn't already faded from your memory banks. If—and this is almost unheard of-an actor had a radio commercial running on *all* the radio networks, and on *every* single radio station in the *whole* county, *and* on the Internet for the maximum contract length allowed by AFTRA—twenty-one months—that actor's total fees would come to approximately $8,635. Not bad, but hardly four years' tuition at an Ivy League school. In fact, it comes to right around $13.70 a day, and doesn't include those pesky state and federal taxes and agent's commissions.

Voice-over is a *business*, and the real work is getting the work. That work is done outside the voice booth. It's really no different from any other endeavor. Being a voice-over takes a serious investment of time and money.

But maybe, just maybe, you'll beat the odds and carve out a lasting career in voice-overs and spin a few words into gold along the way. My friend Russ Reed certainly did.

Russ, one of the all-time best voice-overs ever, was seated across the desk at a mortgage company from the "loan officer" who couldn't have been more than twenty-five years old. A young rabbit in charge of the lettuce.

Russ has forgotten more about voice acting than I'll ever learn. He cut his teeth on the radio soap operas as a kid, and has been doing voice-overs ever since. There's a lot to be said for longevity, and Russ has said it all.

One fact that most actors get used to is that it's usually a very bad idea to put "actor" as your occupation on credit applications. Even though you might have great credit and a high income, computers and loan committees somehow manage to equate the word "actor" with "bum," and most financial institutions don't generally loan large sums of money to bums—at least not bums who aren't sports or movie stars.

So, of course, the loan officer was not at all prepared for Russ Reed. After pawing through and being very impressed with Russ's financial data, he said, "Well, Mr. Reed, we certainly won't have any problem getting you a mortgage!"

"Fine," said Russ, who is the most soft-spoken and gentlemanly person I know. The "officer" then ran through a few stock questions: address, social security, occupation.

"Voice actor," Russ said proudly.

Perplexed, the young man said, "Really?"

"Yes," said Russ.

"Any other sources of income?"

"Do I need any?" asked Russ.

"Oh no, no, I'm just . . . you mean, you make this much money just talking?"

"Son," Russ said, leaning across the desk with a slight smile, "I'm very good at it."

INDIANA AIRWAVES—BIG TIME IN THE SMALL TIME, BUT DICK CLARK NEVER CALLED

"You ought to have a job on the radio announcing the time."
—Alfred Uhry, *Driving Miss Daisy*, Warner Brothers, 1989

For three years, radio helped pay my college bills, but I was still enamored with the possibility of a career as an actor. As graduation approached, I felt forced to make my first real career decision. Go with my heart of hearts and risk becoming a full-time actor? Or stick with the sure thing— broadcasting?

Terrified, I sent out a few résumés and "air checks" (recordings of myself on the air) and was relieved when a job offer came in.

The temperature had reached parboiling in my 1963 Beetle. When I stopped in a gas station just outside of Indianapolis, the attendant eyed the United Press International decals prominently displayed on both of the rear windows. I'd already figured out the power of the press. Those decals, which I'd found jammed behind the WIOK radio UPI teletype, had already gotten me into concerts, state fairs, and prime parking spaces. Here in central Indiana, I was about to discover the power of fame too, and its cost.

"So, just head up north through Pendleton and Lapel (pronounced with that Indiana twang: Lay- Pel), keep your eye out for Louise Street (inexplicably pronounced lou-wise), and that radio station's right there next to the tracks . . . you a newsman?"

"DJ," I replied, quickly adding, "and the new program director!"

Station management knew that for young up-and-comers, titles were as good as gold, actually even better, since handing out titles instead of cash could actually improve the bottom line. Titles cost a station nothing and kept kids like me happy. The attendant didn't even grin at my audacity.

"1470 . . . 1470 . . . 14," I thought as I eased out the clutch, flipped on the radio, and spun the dial up and down the AM band. When the needle hit 1470, an announcer's voice blared out loud and clear across the cornfields.

"Tonight, it's WHUT [*always* pronounced "WHAT" at W H U T radio] Nut night at the Putt Putt! We'll be broadcasting live from the Putt Putt miniature golf center, come see all your favorite DJs live and in person! Get your own 'I'm a WHUT NUT' bumper sticker. Win 45s from Anderson Music on the bypass, and everybody gets an autographed eight-by-ten photo of their favorite WHUT Disc Jockey!!!"

Man, this was the big time! WHUT was going to be my new radio home. I had a title, a serviceable car, my college degree, and I was going to be famous!

And I was.

At least in Anderson, Chesterton, Lapel (remember, it's *Lay*-Pel), and even Fowler, Indiana. For a couple of years, "Best of luck on your Graduation . . . Bob Hogan, WHUT," was scribbled in countless high school yearbooks by me at the countless sock hops and record parties I emceed. You see, the DJs at WHUT were quite famous, at least within the transmitter tower's broadcast radius.

It was heady stuff to be recognized on the street, and though we knew it was only in central Indiana, each of us, I'm sure, figured our fame was bound to spill out onto the canvas of the Midwest, and then the world. Naturally, we were also paid very little for the privilege of fame.

Radio was always notorious for low pay. Instead of salary, many stations arranged "trades" for their DJs. Gasoline trades, tire trades, movie trades, and appliance trades were commonplace. The station gave an advertiser free commercial time, and in return an employee got a certain amount of goods and services in trade. For a while I even had a pizza trade.

The WHUT station owners had figured out an even more profitable pay plan than product trades. They'd pay very little salary but make us locally famous; we could then supplement our small weekly stipend by performing every weekend as live disc jockeys. Week after week as I tried to scrape together enough money to pay my bills, the thrill of being on the air and semifamous began to fade.

Our live appearances paid the lofty sum of $35 to $50, and the competition among us to get those bookings was stiff. Dick Lange was the station engineer, assistant manager, and morning drive-time jock. He was also in charge of assigning the weekend DJ gigs. The obvious conflict of interest was not lost on the rest of us as he plucked the prize assignments for himself. Dick was truly the rabbit in charge of the lettuce.

Meanwhile, I married my high school, and later college, sweetheart, Jayne Milazzo. She joined me in Anderson clutching her new diploma.

After a year or so of making collection calls for Indiana Bell, she was having her doubts about her career choice as well. Collection calls were secretly monitored back then, and she was called in on the carpet when the twelfth deadbeat of the morning remarked: "You can shove your phone up your ass, Missy!" "Oooh, I certainly hope it's one of our new Slimline models, sir," she shot back. Great comeback, but snappy one-liners weren't appreciated at the arch-conservative Anderson, Indiana, phone company.

I was still hoping my Indiana fame might begin to spread a little— like to the nation—and for the briefest of moments I thought it had.

Let me set the record straight. I was on *American Bandstand* talking to Dick Clark, or at least my voice was. Dick and I never actually talked. But I was on the show. Really.

WHUT was Anderson, Indiana's ABC news affiliate. One afternoon our news director, Dave Butler, popped his head in the control room during my air shift and asked, "Frisch's?"

"Sure," I replied. Frisch's was the Indiana incarnation of the Big Boy restaurant chain, and just about every day Dave, Jay Benoit (WHUT's other newsman), and I would enjoy a gourmet repast sitting in Dave's shiny black Buick as he constantly reminded us to keep the ketchup off the upholstery.

On the way to Frisch's Big Boy, Dave said, "Hey, Dick Clark's gonna call you Friday."

"And Raquel Welch," I replied.

"No, really, here." Dave handed me a letter from the ABC Network saying that WHUT would be featured in an interview on *American Bandstand.*

"Please have your head disc jockey, or program director, available for a call at 2:30 Friday the 11th."

"You are the program director, right?" Dave asked with a touch of sarcasm.

"Yeah," I said, already feeling nervous.

"Well, if you'd rather, I can just give this to Dick Lange. He's our 'head' disc jockey, I think. . . ."

"Gimme that!" I shouted.

I grabbed the letter out of Dave's hands, as Jay in the back seat laughed so hard he almost choked on his fries. I studied the grease-stained letter, holding it up to the sun's light through the windshield to check the authenticity of the ABC letterhead, making sure it wasn't a Dave Butler hoax. Dave smiled and wiped his chin. We shared a lot in common. We both enjoyed magic and practical jokes, we both thought his friend from Ball State University in nearby Muncie, Dave Letterman, was hysterically funny, and we both just loved giving Dick Lange a hard time.

"I'll do it," I said.

I didn't sleep much Thursday night. In just a few hours—"8-7-6-5-4-3-2-1"— THE Dick Clark would be calling me.

I arranged for another DJ, Steve Cash, to handle my show from 2:00 to 3:00 P.M. so I'd have plenty of time to prepare for Dick. "Gee, do I call him Dick? Mr. Clark? Mr. Clark, sir?" I even wondered if that was his real name. Steve Cash's real name, on the other hand, was Cashdollar, but I'd felt—and it was the prerogative of the lofty program director to change a DJs name—that Cashdollar sounded too theatrical, too made up. This, during an era when disc jockeys were routinely named "Purple Haze" and "Sherwood Forest."

At 1:30 P.M. the receptionist buzzed the control room. "You've got a call from New York." It was an hour early. My mind froze for a second, and then I realized Dick—I'd decided on calling him Dick—was in New York, an hour ahead of Anderson, Indiana.

"Shit!" I said. "Tell him to hold on." I ran to the newsroom, "Jay, you gotta help me out," I pleaded. "Just run the board for a few minutes, Dick's on the phone."

"Dick? My, my, aren't we the familiar one," he chided, his cherubic face breaking into a broad grin. Speechless, I stared at him.

"No problem," he said, heading for the control room. "But I'm not saying anything."

"Sold," I agreed, realizing that he wanted to preserve his image as a serious newsman, not a fill-in DJ.

I ran to the production room, had the presence of mind to flip on one of our ancient Magnecord tape recorders to preserve my moment in the network sun with Dick, and answered the phone, "Bob Hogan."

The voice was unmistakably from New York—and unmistakably not Dick Clark's.

"Okay . . . uh . . . Bob? I'm Dick's producer Jerome. Now then, on the show Dick's gonna say something like this: 'We're talking with ABC affiliate W . . . W . . . W whatever, with Bob uh . . .'"

"Hogan?" I helped.

"Right, right," he agreed, " . . . and then he'll ask you: What's this week's big hit in, in, in . . . "

"Anderson?" I ventured.

"Right, and then you say—hang on, I gotta record this—are we rolling? Okay, we're rolling, so what is it?"

I was stunned, no Dick Clark on the phone, just Jerome whoever recording my words to be played back on the show later. I stumbled thorough my answers: hot song, up and coming song, etc., etc.

After my "conversation with Dick," I walked the long corridor back to the control room in a daze.

"You owe me," Jay said as he relinquished the chair.

"Thanks, the fries are on me tomorrow," I said.

"How was your pal Dick?" Jay asked, as he scurried back to the comfort and sanctuary of the newsroom.

"Oh, just great," I lied.

I came home to visit my parents the next week, and it seemed as if all of Lansing, Illinois, was abuzz with the news that I'd been on *American Bandstand*. Well, at least all of Lansing, Illinois, who had any contact with my mother. Come to think of it, that was most of Lansing, Illinois.

While I was home I also went to see Dr. Heichel, my optometrist since fifth grade, for some much-needed new glasses. "Bob, I was watching *American Bandstand* with my kids last week, and we heard you! So . . ." he added conspiratorially, "What's Dick Clark really like?"

"Just great," I managed. "He sounded to me just like your everyday, ordinary guy. . . ."

Soon Jayne and agreed that though it had been fun to be recognized as local—very local—celebrities, we were tired of the pseudo-fame game and of Indiana. It seemed everyone else I knew had a *real* job paying *real* money. I was bored spending weekends shouting into a microphone and spinning records at birthdays, bar mitzvahs, and sock hops. If fame was its own reward, then maybe it was time to do something anonymous and, hopefully, fulfilling. Naturally, I had no idea what that might be.

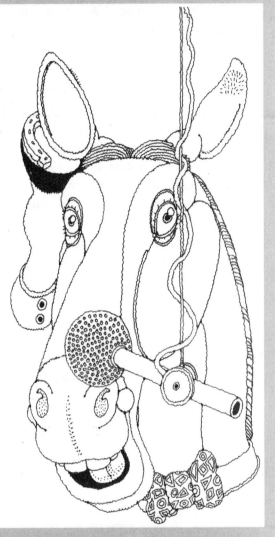

TOP TEN WAYS TO KNOW IF YOU, TOO, SHOULD BECOME A VOICEOVER

10. Enjoy standing in tiny, soundproof, airless rooms

9. Think Joan D'Arc had right idea

8. Actually believe people say things like: *"These are hearty chips, Honey!"*

7. Can resist urge to throw easel through glass and strangle producer

6. Well-stocked with environmentally friendly hairspray so headphones don't muss hair

5. Have open account at Acme Premium and Novelty Company for obligatory trinkets left at every session

4. Able to imitate Stallone at *least* as well as most eighth graders

3. Perfect strangers who call you on Saturday mornings with investment opportunities always tell you- *"You've got a great voice!"*

2. Figure if Mr. Ed can make it.. **hey**- why not you?

1. Skilled in proper placement of silverware at day job

From the 1992 Harlan Hogan Production Calendar—John Sandford, Illustrator

Techniques of a Voice-Over: Free and Not-So-Free Voice-Over Classes— From "Wanna-Be" to "New-Be"

"Faith is believing in things when common sense tells you not to."— George Seaton, *Miracle on 34th Street*, Twentieth Century Fox, 1947

If I haven't discouraged you wanna-bes too much about a career in voice-over, that's great. If I haven't discouraged the new-bes and old pros either, that's even better.

Learning and improving is a step-by-step process. Often the smallest and seemingly inconsequential steps are the most important of all. I'm a firm believer in the concept of Kaizen, the Zen philosophy that advocates constant and gradual improvement. Kaizen teaches us to take one lesson, and one session, at a time. Step by step (sometimes baby steps), we can achieve mastery.

So, assuming you have the raw talent to pursue this business, then the next *T* we need to discuss is training—and where to find it. The obvious answers: acting schools, voice-over classes, workshops and coaches, books (even mine), and universities aren't necessarily the only or the best answers. Voice-over work is related as much to advertising and broadcasting as it is to acting and performing. You really need a conglomeration of training to become a professional.

The vast majority of working voice-over pros have a background in acting or radio and TV—and often both. I believe you must have at least some experience and training in performance, onstage or on the air, to become successful as a voice-over performer. There are, I'm sure, some exceptions, but so far I haven't met any. You'll also be going into business for yourself, so any background and knowledge you have in marketing, promotion, and even—dare I say?—bookkeeping, will prove very valuable.

Before you rush out and hunt down an acting school, broadcasting class, or voice-over workshop, consider this: There are free classes you can take almost everywhere to get you started in voice-over work. There are classes in advertising, recording, acting, marketing, radio and TV, film and video production, and casting.

These free classes often masquerade under the pseudonym "Intern Position Available." In exchange for your time as an intern, or just as a volunteer, you'll get real insight and training in these industries. You'll make some valuable contacts and have some honest credits to put on your résumé. Don't think interns are all just college-age kids either.

It's true that some interns are treated as slave laborers, and I'll be the first to tell you to "walk" from any job—paid or unpaid—if you are being taken advantage of. But everybody has to pay his or her dues in one way or another, and often interning or volunteering is a small price to pay for a "behind-the-scenes" experience.

There are other benefits as well. Helping out or working even part-time in a local radio station, for example, will most likely give you access to professional recording gear, invaluable when you are ready to make your first voice demo. In addition, stations are always in need of voice performers for the commercials they produce in-house. These commercials have little or no budget, so the odds are high that you'll have ample opportunity to get real voice-over performing experience almost immediately. Obviously, at this point, you'll be happy to work for free.

Advertising agencies also often record "mock" commercials for client approval, and believe me, they are desperate for voice talent willing to perform just for the experience. Be absolutely sure, however, that you are just recording "scratch tracks" that will never actually go on the air—if they do, even though you might consider yourself a rank amateur, you deserve to be paid.

Casting directors and talent agencies are constantly looking for interns too. The benefits of investing your time there should be obvious. Think of the inside track and inside knowledge you'll have when it's your turn to start auditioning, or to start finding an agent.

Interning in a recording studio is probably the best choice of all. You can be the proverbial fly on the wall, watching and learning from the professional voice talents performing there. When the time finally comes to create your first voice demo, it's likely you'll be able to get plenty of help from your coworkers—the studio engineers. The conversation might go something like this: "Hey, Mister 'Let's-Have-the-Intern-Go-Get-Us-Lunch,' after all the free spots I've done for you guys, and all the coffee I've made, the least you can do is record my voice demo. . . ." Never underestimate the power of a good guilt trip.

On a whim, I e-mailed twenty or so top voice-overs from all across the country and asked them, "Has anyone ever asked to intern with you?" Almost unanimously, they said no. But, every single voice-over did say they would mentor a person if they felt he or she was serious about the business.

Don LaFontaine is often called the "King of the Movie Trailers" and with good reason. You've heard his "Voice of God" on practically every coming attraction in your life. Don's method of mentoring newcomers is to invite them to ride along with him in his chauffeur-driven limo from session to session. Talk about a priceless education in voice-over from an amazingly unselfish man. Let's not forget that some of those newcomers will go on to be Don's competition.

One top female voice-over, who shall remain unnamed, said—with her tongue planted firmly in her cheek—she'd take on an intern: "If the candidate was of the opposite sex, at least six feet tall, had some clue as to conversation and was willing to stay for breakfast."

The simple fact is, the vast majority of voice-overs are bright and generous people willing to help serious newcomers.

Beau Weaver, a marvelously talented voice-over based in Los Angeles, reminisced, "When I was trying to get into commercial broadcasting, I started hanging around radio stations (at age twelve!), getting coffee for the on-air talent, answering phones, telling them how great they were. Was I an intern? No. But I got a lot of help and guidance from them."

Beau took a small step into the world of voice-overs by volunteering his time in exchange for learning. The Kaizen philosophy recommends the same approach for newcomers. Instead of focusing all your energies on the sometimes-overwhelming goal of becoming a full-blown voice-over performer, just take one or two small steps in the general direction. Those first tentative steps might include joining Toastmasters, performing a "bit part" in community theater, or simply reading books aloud to your kids.

Beau also has these words of advice and encouragement for you: "I have had lots of help along the way, but my most valuable tools, perhaps even more than natural talent, have been persistence and consistent hard work. I did the work required to get myself prepared, then I simply *refused to go away*. Eventually, the industry gave up and let me come in to play, and for this, I am grateful. If you love this stuff, don't let anything stop you."

Beau's right. Discouragement is easy to find, encouragement just as difficult to get, and reality—almost impossible. So if you are still interested in a career as a voice-over actor, here are my ten realistic low- and no-cost ways to begin your training.

1) Read an entire newspaper out loud every day.

2) Listen—really listen—to TV and radio commercials. Take notes on the style and sound of the voice-overs you hear. Which do you like? Which do you loathe?

3) Tape-record yourself and then listen—really listen—to *your* style and sound. If you don't have any ad "copy," just pick up any magazine and read a few advertisements out loud. Now, reread your copy faster

and slower and with different emphasis and pauses. Do you like what you hear?

4) Listen to voice talent demos. If you don't have access to any, just surf the Web. Many individual performers and virtually all major voice agents have Web sites with audio samples you can "audition."

5) Ignore anyone who tells you, "You have a great voice," or, "You have a lousy voice."

Listen to yourself and judge for yourself. If it seems that everyone you know says, "You ought to be doing voice-overs . . . ," stop just a moment and consider the source. Are these same people ready and willing to hire you for voice-over work?

6) Act, build sets, work lights, or just sell tickets at a community or professional theater.

7) Volunteer to read for the blind or to kids at the local library.

8) Study *all* aspects of performance, from acting to singing, dance, and movement.

9) Read. Read every book and magazine you can on voice-over, acting, auditioning, advertising, self-marketing, public relations, and broadcasting.

10) Make a commitment to become a working professional voice-over; then back that commitment up with a serious investment of your time, your talent, and your money.

Feel you're ready to change from a wanna-be to a new-be? Then it's probably time to sign up for some of the voice-over classes and workshops conducted in most metropolitan areas. It's likely they won't be listed in the yellow pages, so start your search by calling a local recording studio or an ad agency. You can also log on to the performing unions at *www.sag.org* or *www.aftra.org* for a list of all the local offices of the Screen Actors Guild and American Federation of Television and Radio Artists. Even though you aren't yet a member, most offices have a lobby bulletin board chock full of classes and seminars. Theater-oriented bookstores like Act One in Chicago, The Drama Bookstore in New York, and Samuel French in Hollywood and Studio City have similar bulletin boards.

College and university theater departments may also know of, or offer, voice, broadcasting, and acting programs. Industry-specific newspapers and magazines like *Backstage* or The *Voice Over Resource Guide* contain many ads for voice-over classes, workshops, and coaches, although most are located in larger cities. Online, *www.backstage.org* has a very nice resource section listing coaches, schools, and demo producers. And, at least one voice coach offers personalized coaching via stay-at-home teleconferencing.

Many newcomers decide to work with a voice-over coach for individual training. Some coaches will also help you make a voice demo. Coaches—though not absolutely necessary—can be a worthwhile investment, but you need to do some homework before you plunk down your hard-earned money. Interview the coach and make sure you'll feel comfortable with his or her style. Always, always, ask for the telephone numbers of at least two of the coach's current students whom you can contact. Any legitimate voice-over coach will be happy to provide that kind of credential. Keep in mind that the top voice-over coaches charge thousands of dollars just to produce a voice demo and hundreds more per hour for class and individual sessions, so you must do your homework.

How? Simple. The same way you'd shop for any major purchase—ask questions. If you know any working voice-overs, by all means ask them for recommendations. If not, the Web is a marvelous resource, as my wife pointed out just yesterday.

"Honey," she said as I was writing this, "I've got a great idea."

"Wonderful, but I'm almost through with this Techniques section so if . . ."

"I really don't need two cars."

That was a good enough idea for me quit tapping the keyboard.

"Why don't we sell both cars and buy just one."

"No argument, sweetie; it'll save us a lot on insurance alone."

"Okay, bye, I see you're busy."

"Justa second," I shouted as she hastily retreated down the hallway and into the dining room. "What are you thinking of buying?"

For a brief moment I thought her muffled reply was "bummer!" and wondered what was wrong. Then it hit me.

"Did you say Hummer?"

"They're cute!"

"They're huge! You might as well duct tape together the two cars we already have and just drive them; they'd be about the same size."

"C'mon, Harlan, give me two good reasons why we shouldn't get a Hummer."

"One, I don't know anything about Hummers, and two, they're huge!"

"You already mentioned size, so that doesn't count."

"Why don't you give me three good reasons we should buy a gigantorus truckus." I figured upping the ante to three reasons might stop her in her tracks.

"Harlan—one, I can haul the dogs and cats around with room to spare. Two, you can haul all your recording crap around with room to spare. And, three, think how much my parallel parking skills will improve just through sheer necessity."

Hard to argue with logic like that, but I still had one ace-in-the-hole rejoinder, "I still don't know anything about Hummers."

She had just three words for me, "Log on, buddy."

A quick Internet search and we learned everything we needed to know about these exotic machines—what to look for and what to avoid—plus a few tips on parallel parking.

I suggest you do the same kinds of Internet searches when looking for voice classes and coaches. Tell you what, I'll start the process for you right now. Fire up your computer and head on over to *www.HarlanHogan.com* and click on the "VO: Tales and Techniques of a Voice-Over Actor" button. There, you'll find a regularly updated list of voice-over classes, workshops, and coaches—fair enough?

Remember, though, that your training won't stop the day you book your first gig. As any professional actor—on- or off-camera—will tell you, your education in this business never ends. Even the most successful voice-overs continue to train, sometimes at workshops where advertising agency writers, producers, and casting directors are present to "work out" with the talent.

One note of caution: Don't attend workshops, lessons, and seminars where potential employers are in attendance, thinking that you'll necessarily have a greater chance of being hired by them. It's possible that your work may be noticed, and might lead to a job, but if the class is being touted as a quick way to get hired by the "teachers," forget it. It's the classic "bait and switch" scam with writers, producers, and agents as the bait.

Sometimes it does seem as if the old "casting couch" has been replaced by the "casting class." The unspoken pitch goes something like this: *Attend my workshop and hey, guess what—I'll see your great talent and be sure to include you in all my casting calls, auditions, and sessions. Just sign here.*

I ran into an old friend and very experienced actor I hadn't seen in a while at an on-camera audition recently. "Hey, where have you been hiding?" I asked.

"I gave L.A. a whirl for the last year," he replied.

"And . . . ?"

"And, here's the stats: five important auditions, one important booking, and *forty* casting director's classes."

"So you lost money," I sympathized.

"Big time . . . but the classes were the only way I could get in to meet them." Another reality check, I'm afraid.

So, ask those questions: What's the fee? How many students are in a class? What are the instructor's credentials? Who are any past or present students that are working professionally? One last suggestion: Ask if you can "audit" a session first before actually signing up.

As important as training is, however, don't become a professional student. Learn what you can, but then get out there, distribute your demo, start auditioning, and get to work.

In *True and False: Heresy and Common Sense for the Actor*, David Mamet laments the proliferation of professional acting students, that ever-growing group of actors who *never actually perform*. Instead of stepping into the spotlight to entertain an audience, they just flit from workshop to workshop and class to class.

In the movie *Stage Door*, Kaye Hamilton's character tells Katherine Hepburn's, "You're an actress if you're acting. But you can't just walk up and down a room and act. Without that job and those lines to say, an actress is just like any ordinary girl trying not to look as scared as she feels." I couldn't agree more.

The older I get, the more I realize every bit of knowledge you acquire can help you as a voice-actor—everything, not just the obvious, specific training. Yep, I'm turning into one of those (God forbid) adults. Worse yet, one of those adults who spout advice.

I don't know about you, but I remember all the times in high school when I would justify my lack of understanding with this comforting self-reassurance: "I'll never need to know this stuff. No one is ever, ever, ever, ever going to walk up to me on the street and say, Hey, jerky, *I'll give you a thousand bucks if you can prove* $a^2 + b^2 = c^2$."

On the other hand, after my two disastrous attempts to make a living in the computer industry—which we'll relive in all its gory detail in chapters 4 and 5—I was equally convinced that all my training in computers would be about as useful to me as an actor as the Pythagorean Theorem. Wrong, wrong, wrong.

My mother, with her always unbridled enthusiasm, cheerily prattled out the old Adult 101 line, "Well you never know when it'll come in handy!"

God, I hate it when adults are right.

"Harlan? It's Linda Phelen at Shirley's. Got an on-camera audition for you at ten. Wear a business suit. Oh, do you know anything about computers?"

The script was filled with phrases I'd had to learn when I was a computer salesman: COBOL, Fortran, tree-like hierarchies, even sys1(.)jobque—pronounced, by the way, as "sis one dot job que," which no other actors knew, I'm told. Bill Wildhage, of Arthur Andersen, booked me not only for that script but for well over a hundred on-camera and voice jobs over the years.

"You are the only actor I know who always sounds like he actually understands this stuff," he told me once.

I'm sure he was right, but then, so was my mother.

NO SALE—COULD THERE BE A WORSE COMPUTER SALESMAN?

"Only one thing counts in this life: Get them to sign on the line,
which is dotted."—David Mamet, *Glengarry Glenn Ross*,
New Line Cinema, 1992

"Mr. Patel, you've got exactly thirty minutes to complete this aptitude test; I'll set this timer and check back every ten minutes." This was a scene out of Brecht. I was administering a test to prospective computer trainees. It was a test designed to evaluate mathematical and logical abilities, abilities that I, the test administrator, totally and completely lacked. Mr. Patel and I had met at the movies.

My new boss, Jerry Murray, was a member of Mensa. He looked for all the world like the actor John Lithgow and was just as flamboyant and energetic as Lithgow's hilarious character Dick Solomon on NBC's *Third Rock from the Sun*.

Jerry seemed to be just what the Honeywell Institute of Information Science needed to turn its troubled computer training school on its ear. Part of his plan, if there was a plan, was to hire me—now an ex-radio jock. I could do a pretty good standup presentation, and I could put the arm on broadcasting friends to get either myself or Jerry interviewed on the air about the wonderful future of computers and our equally wonderful computer courses. The fact that I knew nothing about computers seemed not to matter a whit.

My wife Jayne and I had moved back to Chicago. I'd answered a vague but intriguing ad in the *Chicago Tribune* and found myself working for Honeywell, then the second-largest maker of computers in the world. I, of course, thought they only made thermostats, as did 99 percent of the public. That conception proved to be a major stumbling block in enrolling students in our computer institute. Honeywell, like GE and Univac, eventually threw in the towel and conceded victory to IBM.

We tried everything to get smart students to sign up, from visiting college campuses to attending Indian movies at a north-side Greek Church, where I'd met Mr. Patel. Actually, we met a lot of Mr. and

Mrs. Patels (the "Smiths" of India) and other bright, educated folks who lacked computer training. We developed a good rapport with them, and a taste for the exquisite street vendors' curry with our movies, instead of popcorn.

I was required to attend three nights of torture each week at the Honeywell Institute as well. I graduated six months later, actually understanding what a tree-like hierarchy is and how to program computers in COBOL. This was knowledge I was convinced would do me absolutely no good in the future. I eventually proved myself no psychic.

The institute faltered, despite all the great movies we saw, and I was offered another job at Honeywell as a computer salesman. So, I tried my hand at it—and "tried" was the operative word. I simply hated it. I despised making the obligatory cold calls in my sales territory in the far western suburbs of Chicago. Over and over I tried to conquer my shyness and go from office to office aggressively peddling my wares, but it just wasn't in me.

Instead, I got increasingly depressed, increasingly fat, and increasingly facile at creating daily excuses to avoid making sales calls:

- Mondays—Weekly sales meeting. Silly to waste the afternoon driving all the way to territory.
- Tuesdays—Account activity reports due Wednesday. Necessary creative writing takes most of day—no time for sales calls.
- Wednesdays—Visit territory. Enjoy Golden Wheel Pancake House "Farm Hand" breakfast, but almost 11:00 A.M. by time of first call, prospects off to early lunch—beat traffic home.
- Thursdays—*Bozo's Circus*. Local magician friends appear on Thursdays—too late in day to drive west.
- Fridays—Honeywell salesmen meet at Spinning Wheel restaurant—expense account food, camaraderie, live lingerie show.
- Saturdays—Celebrate getting through another week.
- Sundays—Gnawing feeling in the pit of stomach returns.

Despite my ineptitude, and excuses, I did mange to make one sale, only to have it torpedoed by the office technician, Frank (at least I think his name was Frank) whom we all called "Pocket Protector."

I *had* sold a computer memory upgrade to Babson Brothers, a major manufacturer of milking machines and one of the few Honeywell Computer customers we had in the suburbs of Chicago. The manager of data processing had finally gotten his company to part with the thousands and thousands of dollars needed to upgrade from—ready?—32 to 64 kilobytes of main memory. I know it seems laughable today, with gazillion-gigahertz Pentiums practically given away. But be kind; this was a long time ago.

The big day finally came for Frank to install Babson's new memory. He showed up at my client's with his attaché case full of tools, his black nerd glasses, and a pocketful of pens.

"Where's the new memory?" my client asked.

"Right here," Pocket Protector grinned, holding up a jeweler's needle-nosed wire cutter.

"What?"

"Watch closely," he replied as he strolled over to the dining-room-table-sized central processing unit. Opening the side access door, Pocket Protector repeated, "watch closely."

Reaching inside, he snipped a red jumper wire. "There ya go. Reboot this puppy, and you've got twice the real estate."

The phone call was not pleasant. "Bob, you mean to tell me that I've had 64 K in my machine all along, just sitting there?"

"Uh, yeah," I replied, "but you only bought a 32 K machine so they put in a jumper and—"

"You listen to me, son," he interrupted. "I'm calling our lawyers and then IBM . . . got it?"

I got it.

I don't know what ever happened to Pocket Protector, but I suspect he's probably in charge of our cable TV system.

In the midst of all this angst I got more and more addicted. Addicted to the only drug that had consistently made life fun and exciting for me—the theater.

For seventy-two years, Western Springs, Illinois, has been home to one of the finest community theaters in America. The Theatre of Western Springs mainstage rivals any professional theater. Designed by James Hull Miller, it features an intimate audience-stage relationship, and state-of-the-art lighting, sound, and seating for 414. A second theater space seats 125 and houses workshop, experimental, and children's theater productions, as well as classes for over four hundred young drama students. More than a dozen ambitious productions—from Shakespeare to Simon—are mounted during the season by over three hundred active adult volunteers, and the shows are all consistently sold out.

I spent virtually every evening at the theater, getting my fix. In addition to acting in plays like *Mr. Pickwick*, *Three Sisters*, and *Rosencrantz and Guildenstern Are Dead*, I ran sound, hung lights, designed the set for *The Biggest Thief in Town* with my wife, and even costumed *Spoon River Anthology* with my all-male crew.

I also knew my time at Honeywell was running out, based on my abysmal sales record. I dreaded the days—and lived for the nights at the theater. But the responsible, adult voice in my head said, "You can't just chuck it all and go be an actor."

So, chock full of computer and sales training, I answered another ad in the *Chicago Tribune*. They needed someone to teach and sell the secrets of giving good business presentations, and I figured that would be me.

From the 1983 Harlan Hogan Production Calendar—John Sandford, Illustrator

Techniques of a Voice-Over: Storytellers of the Electronic Age—Ask the Right Questions, Tell the Right Story

"The voice means nothing. The voice is nothing. Nothing, nothing, nothing."—Daws Butler, Voice of Yogi Bear, Huckleberry Hound, Quick Draw McGraw, Elroy Jetson, Cap'n Crunch, and Mr. Cogswell

What the brilliant Daws Butler was making abundantly, totally, and completely clear is that voice work is all about interpretation of the script, not the sound of your voice. If people tell you you've got a great, or interesting, or unusual voice, that's nice, but you've got to know what to do with it. Great voice-over actors have a combination of an interesting voice and the ability to interpret a script in fresh, believable ways. It takes natural talent and learned techniques.

Don Kennedy, a master of celebrity imitations, once asked me how I approach a script. I was flattered and dumbstruck. Not silent, mind you, which wouldn't be me, but I could only mumble some platitude or other. Don, a product of those great Catholic schools of the 1940s where everything, including life itself, had hard and fast rules, and guessing that someone named Hogan must have the same Irish Catholic upbringing, said, "It's all the parts of speech, right?"

"Uh, sure" I mumbled.

"Thought so!" Don said: "So you do what *I* do—recognize the nouns, adjectives, verbs, on the fly, and mentally construct the right reading."

It's a scientific approach, certainly, and one that had obviously worked for Don, but to me it was as alien as the formula for yeast. It also smacked of the dreaded task we faced in grammar school—diagramming sentences—but instead of a blackboard, you use your gray matter.

"No, I see the words and just know how it ought to sound, Don," I said.

Truth is, I don't know, or care much, whether it's a noun or a pronoun, but something in my mind knows how it ought to *sound*. And with luck it comes out of my mouth that way.

Years ago, when I was listening and studying the voice demos of top voice-overs, it suddenly struck me. Every one of those performers knew how to *interpret* a script. They somehow made all the words make sense—believable—even when human logic would dictate that no human anywhere would actually say those lines. Some of the talents did have amazing voices, deep and rich, or clear as a bell. But for the most part, it wasn't their voice-quality that was intriguing, it was the way they worked with the script to make the words their own.

We voice-overs are the storytellers of an electronic age, not that far removed from our ancestors who huddled around a bonfire in their caves, listening to tales of that day's hunt re-created by the shaman. Today, we're selling products on radio and TV, explaining how to perform a complex series of tasks on a corporate video, entertaining the kids as cartoon voices, or just keeping you company while you're on hold. No matter what, we have still have a story to tell, and our ability to deliver that story by adding just the right emphasis, just the right rhythm and cadence, just the right touch of humor, or seriousness, to our voices is what sets the pros apart. A voice-over isn't about how you *sound*, but how you make the listener *feel*.

Can you learn "just the right" interpretation?

Well, maybe the question should be, is there only one "just right" interpretation? I'd suggest you to listen to any Frank Sinatra or Barbra Streisand recording. Their phrasing and interpretation of lyrics is so often "wrong," so "different" that you shake your head in wonder, but they both *sound* so "right."

Study, practice, experience, and confidence all can help you master interpretation. I'm not just talking about "hitting" a particular word in a script. I mean making the words, penned by a stranger, your own. Naturally, that stranger, the copywriter, will also have his or her idea of how you should interpret the script. Taking direction from the copywriter and producer, heeding it, and still bringing your own unique personality to the script is the ongoing challenge and reward of voice acting.

I've had plenty of people try to teach me to play music, golf, or ski. Somehow I just never get it. But that's okay with me. We all have natural abilities and mine lie elsewhere. In Robert Pirsig's soul-searching masterpiece, *Zen and the Art of Motorcycle Maintenance*, he postulates that you can't define quality (or ability, in this case) but you know it when you see it (or hear it). I think that's true. No book, at least not mine, can teach you how to interpret a script, but a good coach and a good book can point you in the right direction and get you asking the right questions. In the last Techniques section, we brainstormed the process of finding the right voice coach. In my opinion, the right book is James Alburger's *The Art of Voice Acting*. Buy it, read it, and reread it; you won't regret it.

Sometimes, I'm sorry to say, no amount of interpretative skill will make a script sound believable.

The call I got one chilly Chicago morning was flattering. It was from a writer who'd left Chicago to join a hot agency in Minneapolis. He remembered me and called, panic-stricken: "Harlan, we've got a spot for a new upscale Gallo wine, and you're last my last hope."

"If that's true, you really are in trouble, Terry," I laughed.

"We've auditioned in L.A. and New York," he added, "and everybody sounds too 'announcery.' Can you be at Audio Recording Unlimited at 10:00 tomorrow?"

Later, at the studio, Terry held the copy close to his chest as if it were a secret. "Now before you look at this, I want to set the scene okay?"

"Fine," I said.

"You're at this party. You spot this beautiful woman. She smiles. You smile and she comes over to where you are. Just as you are about to experience a fantastic wine, you offer her a glass and then say. . . ." He indicated the script still clenched to his breast.

"Okay," I replied.

Terry slowly started to relinquish his hold on the copy but stopped to remind me, "Everybody who auditioned this sounded like an announcer. Remember, you are just a *real* guy at a *real* party talking to this *real* . . ."

". . . and beautiful," I added.

" . . . and beautiful," he agreed, "woman."

Slowly the holy grail was handed over, and the first six words told the story, explaining why everyone else sounded more like an announcer than a real living human being talking to another, albeit beautiful, human being. The six words?

"Introducing, two new wines from Gallo."

Sometimes casting can't solve an impossible problem; if you want the words to ring true, you've got to write true.

I did my best.

It wasn't good enough, either.

What Terry feared, rightfully in this case, was that the voice-over would sound like many radio and TV announcers who just spew words onto the airwaves to some huge, impersonal mass called "the audience." Announcers like these just aren't believable because they are not talking to individual listeners—the audience of one. Worse yet, they usually concentrate on how they *sound*, not how a listener will *respond*.

These announcers are masters of emphasis. They "hit" the sell words, raise their pitch to underline the salient copy points, growling, shouting, and whispering in an attempt to "cut through." Hand or headphone pressed tightly to their ears, they swoon to the rapture of their own perfect diction. Talking, always talking, to a different audience of one—themselves.

Announcers—I sometimes call them "pronouncers"—are the antithesis of voice-over actors. Announcers tell, but never ask. Voice-overs—the really good ones—ask questions first and then use the answers to guide them to the right interpretation. Their part may be labeled "Announcer," but that doesn't mean they sound or think like one. Successful voice actors instinctively ask themselves:

- Who—what individual living, breathing, human being—am I talking to? A friend, my child, my lover, or my enemy?

- Who—what individual living, breathing, human being—am I? A friend, a child, a lover, or an enemy? I might be the next door neighbor, or the serial killer lurking around the corner. Maybe I'm an idiot or a genius, a toy or an alien, or a combination of them all. Ironically, the answer is, sometimes, *I'm an announcer*! The script just might demand an old-time parody of an overblown announcer!

- Once you have a firm grasp of just who this character you're portraying is, and whom you're talking to, it's time take another look at the script to discover: What are you trying to accomplish? You can think of even the shortest script as a story, with a beginning, a middle, and an end—an "arc." Sometimes, the best way to start is to first look at the end of the script. Nine times out of ten, the end of the script— the call to action—will answer the question.

Often, with "price and product" advertising, the "plot" is simple: "great *prices* on *product X*, so hurry in now." But even with that kind of dead-nuts-simple, spokesperson type of copy, you can contribute something special by choosing a unique attitude and delivery. On the other hand, "long form" scripts like audio books, narratives, documentaries, and dialogue commercials usually have much more complex plots that will give you lots of clues to character and situation interpretation.

Scripts frequently have some indication as to character to guide you, but they often contain just a few suggestions—or worse, conflicting directions. Remember the scatter-shot direction for the Sears audition we did in the first Techniques of a Voice-Over section? So you must "climb inside" your character's head and figure out who and what this person in all about and what he's trying to accomplish. As Dame Judi Dench cautioned actors in the December 15, 1991 edition of the *Sunday Times*, "Unless you know your character's mind it's a hollow sound you make."

Nancy Cartwright, the voice of Bart Simpson, in her book *My Life as a Ten-Year-Old Boy*, writes that the only description of Bart she got when she auditioned was: "Personality—Devious, underachieving, school-hating, irreverent, clever." Nancy obviously asked herself all the right questions about Bart and made all the right choices.

The right questions coupled with the ability—and willingness—to take direction from the writer or producer, can lead to the right answers and be reflected in your interpretation. Real pros can just glance at a script and, based on years of experience, ask and answer the requisite questions in seconds, whether they are auditioning a script or recording it for real.

Standing in Magic, Inc., on Chicago's near north side one Saturday afternoon, I watched as Vic Torsberg, an old-time vaudeville magician, demonstrated a trick deck of magic cards for two teenage magicians. Even though I knew the secret of the deck, I was transfixed by his mastery. His unique approach to the timeworn "Svengali Deck" was nothing short of amazing. After years of experimentation and experience, and after countless performances, Vic had perfected his own interpretation and handling of this commonplace trick. He'd taken a standard prop and asked himself if it could possibly be more than just a tired old amateur's trick, and he succeeded in making it his personal masterpiece of magic.

I was fascinated by the brilliance of his performance, as were the kids. When he finished his final miracle, the teens said, "Man, that was great. How much?"

Vic smiled at them with a twinkle in his veteran performer's eye and said, "Boys, the deck will cost you a buck fifty—the routine, twenty-five years."

5

AN ACCIDENTAL ACTOR

"They can't fire you if they can't find you."
—Charles Kuralt, CBS Television

Death comes in around third on most people's fear list. Giving a speech? It's consistently chosen as number one.

But giving a good presentation is critical in many jobs, especially advertising. So J. Walter Thompson, one of the country's biggest advertising agencies, developed an in-house training program. Dubbed "Communispond," it became so popular that J. W. T. began offering the course to the public. They needed someone who could do a good presentation, could sell a little, and wasn't too expensive. They needed me.

This was my first glimpse into the workings of a major advertising agency. On my second day, the phone rang. It was Les Pinto, the agency's in-house audio engineer located on the twenty-seventh floor of the John Hancock building.

"I hear you worked in radio?"

"Yeah, right out of college," I answered.

"Good. Can you come down to the studio in ten minutes?"

"I guess so," I mumbled, not sure what he wanted.

What he wanted was another voice for the "J. W. T. in-house players," people within the agency who could do a halfway decent job on-mike recording "scratch tracks" of proposed radio and TV commercials for presentations to clients.

Later, professional voice-over actors would be hired to do the final tracks if the spots were green-lighted by the sponsor. "Free" voice talent was a much-needed commodity, and I discovered for the first time that there was a world full of commercial voice actors who were, amazingly, making a living out there.

Les was impressed enough by my scratch tracks for Gillette that he asked if I was interested in making a little extra money. Of course I was. If you ever went to a drive-in movie in the 1970s, I'm embarrassed to say you probably heard my voice.

Every Friday afternoon, at precisely two-thirty, I made up a new lame excuse to leave the office, jumped in the elevator, dashed down the escalator two steps at a time, and raced along Michigan Avenue to Sound Studios. By three o'clock I ripped and read as many drive-in movie announcements as I could during my one-hour gig. Glenn, the producer, gave me a ride back to the John Hancock building, where I performed the escalator two-step again, ran to the elevator, and then casually strolled back into my office. Most weeks I got away with it.

While I was hard-selling everything from "Don't forget to visit our refreshment stand!" to "Save big on late model cars with low-low sticker prices!" a gospel group recorded their Sunday morning show in the next studio. Dressed in their choir robes, they swayed, clapped, and sang their hearts out for the glory of God: I could see but not hear them through the studio glass. That choir taught me everything I know about concentrating on a script and ignoring distractions.

Years later while I was recording an audition for Charles Stern, a highly respected voice agent in Los Angeles, and hoping he would represent me, his engineer sent a loud sixty-cycle tone into my headphones in the middle of my reading. Being paranoid (I am an actor, after all), I wasn't sure if auditioning for Charlie was like the *Gong Show*, and you were through at the sound of the tone. On the other hand, maybe it was just an accident. So I read on, ignoring the screaming whine in my headphones.

When I finished, Charles said: "That was a terrific read. Sorry about the distraction. Can't believe you just kept going."

"What distraction?" I thought to myself. Shit, I'd cut my teeth reading copy while pretending there weren't twenty-five gospel singers swinging and swaying before my eyes.

Those Friday afternoon sorties into the studio made me feel like I was an honest-to-God paid voice-guy, if only for a few bucks a week. It wasn't quite enough cash to convince me that I was sure to strike it rich as an actor, though, so I continued to enjoy the perks of the regularly employed, like an occasional free lunch. One, in particular, came with some unexpected encouragement.

It was a pretty expensive meal at the chic and fashionable Gordon's restaurant on Clark Street in Chicago, but WGN radio was paying for it. This time I was the rabbit in charge of the lettuce, and the WGN "account executive" wanted me to part with practically all of Communispond's advertising budget for commercials on his station.

I really liked this guy, whose name was also Robert. Robert-from-WGN was quite handsome, and in the course of our lunch admitted to me he was moonlighting as an actor in a Chicago dinner theater at night. I didn't mention my own dinner theater experience back in Anderson. Somehow "Peaches Pancake House and Dinner Theater" didn't sound too impressive. But I admitted that I wanted to carve out a career as an actor too.

"Here's the best part," he confided. "I did some plays at Burt Reynolds's dinner theater down in Florida last year, and next week I'm going to L.A.! Burt's arranged some auditions for me." Jealous does not even begin to describe my feeling at that moment.

"You can do it." Robert said, "The hardest part is taking . . ."

"Excuse me." The business-suited maitre d' was addressing me. "You look familiar."

I smiled as I studied his face, in a vain attempt to return the favor.

"I'm Gordon Sinclair," he said.

"The restaurant owner," I thought, impressed. "I'm Bob . . ."

He cut me off, "Bob Hogan! Of course, WHUT radio!"

Sometimes even Central Indiana fame does spill out onto the canvas of the Midwest. It seems Gordon had worked for General Motors in food service in Anderson, Indiana, when I was a DJ there.

"Well, I'm impressed," said Robert-from-WGN. "You're famous."

"Was," I said, "was . . . and only with expatriate Hoosiers."

"Oh, I'm sorry, I've lost my manners. Gordon Sinclair, this is Robert . . . ," I froze on his last name.

"Robert Urich," he grinned.

"The soon-to-be famous movie star Robert Urich," I added impulsively. And, after his first sitcom, *Bob & Carol & Ted & Alice*, forty-plus movies from *Lonesome Dove* to *Magnum Force*, the long-running *Spenser: for Hire* TV show, and a star on Hollywood's Walk of Fame, the late Bob Urich certainly was.

Despite Bob's encouragement and example, I still wasn't quite ready to take the plunge, and so I made one more career hop, taking a job as an Advertising Manager before free-falling full-time into voice-over.

I'd never seen or even heard of a Patek Phillippe watch until I met Richard M. Rodnick, my new boss at Advanced Systems Incorporated, or ASI. But I didn't need to know the measure of Dick's financial wherewithal to recognize the depth of his knowledge. Together, we were going to turn around its sluggish sales and marketing department.

I rewrote all the advertising and catalogs for our line of video programs. A new color logo was designed to capitalize on the fact that our videos were no longer just black-and-white. We bought ad space in the major trade magazines and had a professional exhibit built for trade shows. Dick believed in doing things right, or not at all. One way or another, he got my department the money we needed to position ASI as the leader in the computer training field.

Before long, I figured out a pretty smart scam at ASI. I realized that none of the executives, including Dick, were ever at the plant during the week. They were out on sales calls and high-powered lunches and God knows what other executive-type things. But being the good workaholics they were, everybody was in on Saturday morning. So on weekdays I began making the rounds of ad agencies, attending acting classes, even performing professionally in a play, long before anyone caught on. I got my day job work done on evenings and weekends, and was always hard at work in my office every Saturday morning. The executives all smiled at me, and were dutifully impressed by my industrious attitude. If they only knew it was all part of my upcoming "great escape."

Polishing up the techniques I'd used at Honeywell, I'd managed to get myself on a talk radio program promoting a show I'd written and was performing in, called "An Evening with Harry Houdini and Friends." Everything was going great. I just hadn't counted on the car radio.

Mitch Morris, President of ASI, drove a sleek black Mercedes. It had every amenity, from soft leather seats to a Blaupunkt radio. This radio, unfortunately, was tuned to WBBM AM, where he was surprised to hear his advertising manager happily chatting about his new play and budding acting career.

My intuition told me to go in to work the next day, even though it was a weekday. Dick Rodnick was sitting in my office. He neither smiled nor frowned; he just looked serious. I knew something was up. He nodded toward the hallway, and I followed like a puppy dog who's guilty of peeing on the rug. We walked past the executive offices and out the front door. I thought for a moment that he was going to escort me to my car and ban me from the building. "Let's get some coffee," he said opening the doors of his white Lincoln Continental.

We drove a block in silence, and then he glanced over at me and smiled that warm smile of his and said, "I'd turn on the radio, but I'm afraid you might be on it."

"Not today," I replied, feeling the warm blood rush to my cheeks despite the nip in the air.

At the restaurant Dick warmed his hands over his cup of coffee. "Look, I know you do plays and stuff, and Mitch just filled me in on the magic show. What I've got to know is this, Bob. Is this acting stuff a hobby—or your heart's desire?"

"Heart's desire, Dick," I blurted out, surprising myself.

"Bob, I think that's great," he said.

"You do?" I whispered, a little stunned.

"Hell, yes! You don't know it but I once played professional high-stakes bridge in Europe when I was your age." He glanced enigmatically at his solid gold watch. "Playing high-stakes bridge is my heart's desire. 'Course, it's no way to raise a family."

I nodded.

"Look, I'm not going to lecture you, and I know you realize an acting career isn't going going to be easy, but I want to make sure you've planned this out."

"Well," I hesitated, wondering how candid I should be. I figured the worst that could happen was that I'd get fired, and I was well on my way to the unemployment line anyway. I knew that if Mitch Morris or his right-hand honcho, Al Albert, had anything to say about it, I'd probably be let go today.

"I've got my headshots and résumés printed, I'm in a film acting workshop every Monday night, and I'm driving down to Anderson, Indiana, next weekend."

"What's in Anderson?" Dick asked.

"Former radio life, and a real good friend who's gonna let me use the station's production studio to produce a voice demo."

"Sounds good. All right, I've got a plan for you of my own."

And like the incredible businessman, and now confidant, he'd just become, he made me an offer I couldn't refuse.

"I'll cover for you while you get started as an actor. I'll expect you to do all your work, but you can do it when you want. Keep coming in Saturdays," he grinned, and added: "Good thinking on your part. I can probably buy you six months to a year, until we run out of excuses. Sound okay?"

It sounded like music to my ears. And so, together, we muddled along for almost eight months, until I finally left. When I think of the great gifts I've been given in my life, I think Dick Rodnick's gift—the gift of time—was one of the greatest. Seven months into our secret arrangement, though, his "gift" began to run out. On a cloudy Friday afternoon in the Detroit airport, I found myself flying back to Chicago after my grandmother had died. My grandmother had, in fact, passed away—although at the time I used that excuse, she'd been gone five years. See, I had to skip work at Advanced Systems for the day, this time to fly to Detroit to appear as a magician in a corporate film for Walker Mufflers. I needed an excuse, and her death was the first one I came up with. All went well on the shoot, and as I was walking to the airport gate, confident that I'd pulled off this booking without jeopardizing my day job, I saw a face that looked all too familiar.

"Oh, my God—it's-Al-Albert," I thought. Al was the sales manager for ASI, and to say we weren't friends would be the understatement of the year. He was getting closer and closer, though he hadn't noticed me yet. There was no escape; I had to go straight ahead into security, and he was walking right toward me.

Suddenly, inexorably, our eyes locked, he stared with an obvious shock of recognition. This was the defining moment, my Academy Award performance, and though there are no witnesses, I'm here to tell you when they opened the envelope for "Best Actor in a Leading Role in the Detroit Metro Airport," my name was written all over it.

I concentrated with all my might not to show the slightest recognition—and I did it!

Al Albert searched my eyes, eyes that looked blankly back at him for a second and then, blithely moved on to the security guard. Eyes that did not belong to Bob Hogan, cheating on his company, pursuing his dream of being an actor on a clandestine gig. Eyes that regarded him as an uninteresting, unimportant, unfamiliar stranger.

As I passed through the security gate I felt relief, and a little apprehension. Did I fool him? Would I get to work next week and find a pink slip on my desk?

At home I found sympathy flowers on the loss of my grandmother from ASI. Guilt, Guilt, Guilt. On the following Monday, Al Albert strode into our weekly sales meeting and said: "I was in Detroit on Friday and I saw you!"

My heart stopped. I felt a cold clutching hand in the pit of my stomach.

"Well, not you . . . but your double! I'm telling, you, Bob, this guy looked exactly, well not totally, but almost exactly like you."

I dodged that bullet, but out of the corner of my eye I saw Dick Rodnick wince. We both knew the ice was getting awfully thin. In less than a month, I quit.

From the 1982 Harlan Hogan Production Calendar—John Sandford, Illustrator.

Techniques of a Voice-Over: Radio and TV Voice-Overs—The Skills, the Opportunities

> "I have always believed that writing advertisements is the second most profitable form of writing. The first, of course, is ransom notes."
>
> —Philip Dusenberry, Copywriter

"Mr. Hogan?"

"Yes?"

"Mr. Hogan, thanks so much for coming in for jury duty, but you wrote under 'occupation' that you are a 'Radio and TV Announcer?'"

It was just a little white lie; my voice does appear on radio and TV, even though I don't "work" at a particular station. I knew, of course, that broadcasters are usually excused from serving on juries, and I wasn't all that excited about spending days or weeks in the jury box.

"Well, perhaps you didn't realize, we don't generally seat members of the media on juries," the bailiff went on.

"Really?" I said, in my best surprised-and-slightly-disappointed voice.

"So, you're dismissed, but thank you for coming."

I fought back the urge to say something corny and patronizing like, "Well it's my duty as a citizen. . . . " Best to just get out while the getting was good.

"Mr. Hogan?"

"Yes," I stopped mid turn.

"What station are you on?"

Mind whirling, I felt that ever-too-familiar knot in the pit of my stomach. Dissolve to soap opera, Harlan hauled off to prison, manacles clanking, I wave a teary goodbye to my now destitute wife and children, all because I lied to an officer of the court.

"Well, actually, ma'm, I'm on all of them."

Unlike radio and TV staff announcers and DJs, freelance voice-overs like me are heard on, but usually not directly employed by, broadcast stations. But if stations have staff voice performers, then what are the opportunities in the broadcast market for voice-over actors?

Although a sponsor can, and often does, buy time on a broadcast station and have that station's on-air performers voice their commercial, the vast majority prefer to "preproduce" their advertising with performers like me. It's all about control and the desire to cut through the clutter of the hundreds of commercials on the air. Advertising agencies and sponsors with enough budget choose to cast just the right voice for their commercial, one that will sound unique on the air as opposed to the familiar sound of the staff voices. Preproducing gives the client control over the tone and sound of their commercial, a control they don't have when the copy is sent to the station for the next available staff member to read.

The fact is, very few broadcast outlets also have staff members capable of performing believable dialogue commercials, and that's another reason advertisers prefer to preproduce their commercials. In fairness, it may not always be a lack of acting talent on the part of the station staff. How do you manage to get a regular listener to suspend disbelief, when the part of "Dad" sounds for all the world like the news anchor, the "Wife" the drive-time traffic reporter, and their twelve-year-old son, the all-night disc jockey? So, we freelance voice talents get hired, usually by the advertising agency to provide the unique voices and performance they want.

It's the same situation for TV commercials, where production costs are astronomical compared to radio. With the exception of down-and-dirty local cable TV ads, most advertisers produce their television commercials using professional voice-overs. In 1980 Michael J. Arlen wrote a fascinating book called *Thirty Seconds* that chronicled the making of a TV commercial. Although it's out of print now, you may find it at your local library, a used-book store, or online. Arlen's book is a perfect introduction to the entire process—and often craziness—that goes into making a television commercial—from the creative concept to casting, filming, and screen.

There is also other work for freelance voice-overs in radio and TV—promo work.

Promos like "Tonight on News Center Seven, a story you won't want to miss . . . ," and "See how the dead are living, Unwrapped—The Mysterious World of Mummies, only on The Learning Channel. . . ." Or even James Earl Jones's famous three-line promo: "This is CNN."

The promo field is dominated by a handful of very talented men and women. All are masters at bringing life and excitement to the copy and are inevitably able to "bring it in" on time, even if they only have five or ten seconds to do it in. Promo voice-overs are often under contract to specific radio and television stations, agreeing to a certain number and length of sessions—called "windows"—each day or week, so station promo work offers regular employment with regular pay. The downside is that a performer has to be available to record at certain, agreed-to times. Often, promo voice-overs miss important auditions, and even sessions, because of that commitment.

The world's largest trade association for promotion in electronic media is Promax, and you can learn at lot by visiting their site at: *www.promax.org.* Promax membership, although expensive, does include an annual directory that's invaluable when prospecting for clients. NAPTE (National Association of Television Program Executives) also publishes a guide, listing over 1,700 television stations in the United States and Canada, and can be found at *www.napte.org*, as does SRDS (Standard Rate and Data Service) at *www.srds.com.*

Even though the book *TV: Sex, Lies, and Promos* by Deidre Hanssen and Joel F. Gottlieb is primarily written for those seeking a career as *producers* of television promotions, reading it is a great way to get a behind-the-scenes look at this segment of the industry—well worth reading. I found their definition of a voice-over, from the perspective of two veteran promo producers, particularly interesting: "He or she of the golden tones who makes the promos come alive and thus convinces you to watch the show. Many crave this gig, few are good enough; the best 'voices' are millionaires."

Most promo announcements are recorded via high-speed ISDN telephone lines. If you decide to pursue promos, you'll either have to book a recording studio equipped with ISDN equipment—codecs—like those made by Telos and Musicam, or invest in a home studio setup. The investment can be sizeable. ISDN codecs alone run several thousand dollars, and you'll need a soundproof booth, top-quality microphones, and other equipment.

If you can book enough station "windows" each day, though, your audio equipment will soon pay for itself. Maybe you'll become one of those "millionaire" voices and hire a full-time staff—butler, maid, and housekeeper who vacuums, dusts, and does *your* windows.

6

RECORDER'S REVENGE

"I'm putting my money where my mouth is."
—Warren Buffet

Rolf Brandis was a film director with the Fred Niles Studios, a huge, one-time roller rink that had been converted into soundstages. Today, it houses Oprah's Harpo Studios. Every Monday night, Rolf conducted a film-acting workshop in a small space off LaSalle Street, and while I still had my day job at ASI, I enrolled. After a few months of attending classes, he handed me a scrap of paper with a phone number scrawled on it.

"Call her tomorrow, at five."

"Got it," I said.

"Exactly at five," he cautioned.

"Got it," I said.

"After work, but before she leaves."

"Got it," I said, and started to walk away. Rolf returned to whatever he was doing in preparation for class.

"Rolf?" I said. He tugged on his beard, pushed his round gold-rimmed glasses up on his nose, and looked impatient.

"Who should I ask for?"

"Shirley!" he said. "She's expecting you to call, and precisely at . . ."

"Five o'clock . . . got it. Rolf?" Now he really looked impatient. "Shirley . . . ?"

"Hamilton! If you don't embarrass yourself, she might just be your agent."

Rolf returned to stapling together scene sheets, and I left, calling out, "Thanks!"

Shirley Hamilton was the leading agent in Chicago. On Rolf's recommendation, she'd agreed to see me. I was, of course, petrified.

Shirley had her offices on Michigan Avenue, and as I took the elevator up, I checked and rechecked my bag: demo tape, videotape of ASI programs I'd done, résumés, and headshots. My watch read 4:45, so I was right on time.

I made a quick stop in the hallway bathroom and was startled to find two young men exchanging clothes. I tried not to stare as one man carefully took off his business suit and the other put it on. Grinning, they took pity on me. "We're actors," one man said. "We've both got an audition here, and we share this suit."

I met with Shirley, Linda Phelen, and several other women in her office as soon as they were done with the last audition of the day. Things were winding down, and after some small talk she said, "Well let's hear your reel," and pointed to, of all things, a Wollensak tape recorder.

I still hated Wollensaks. They sounded awful, were difficult to thread, and reminded me of high school. I opened my tape box and somehow, with trembling hands, managed to thread the tape onto the machine. I pushed "play," the wheels spun, and—nothing.

No sound save the slight clicking of the reels as they turned. "Idiot!" I thought and stopped the recorder. I checked the volume control, rewound the tape, and tried again. Shirley seemed relaxed.

Nothing.

Trying again, I noticed that Shirley seemed tense.

Nothing.

"Maybe you should come back another time, dear, with another tape." She started to get up. I scanned the tape path frantically, looking for something to fix.

Nothing.

I hit "rewind," crushed, defeated, hyperventilating.

This piece-of-shit tape recorder was about to rewind my career before it had even started. And then I saw it.

A tiny bit of red tape, stuck on the playback mechanism. A bit of header tape, the kind normally used to secure the loose end of a reel-to-reel tape to the hub when it's off the player. The old familiar, "red head and the blue-tail fly" header tape had made its home directly on the playback head.

"Hold it!" I said, catching Shirley in mid rise. "I've got it." I held up the offending half inch of tape in triumph. I threaded the tape in a blur, pushed "play," and my demo played just like it did at home. Well, not quite. Even my well-worn Teac tape recorder at home sounded better than her damned Wollensak.

For many months after the Wollensak's revenge, Shirley would call me whenever it acted up. No problem. I was happy to help. Actors love calls from their agent, even if it's just to help them fix their decrepit tape recorder.

As I got to know her, I began to see her as a female incarnation of Chuck Jones's whirling-dervish-like Tasmanian Devil cartoon.

Shirley was a whirlwind of activity: on the phone, off the phone, pulling headshots from files, recording auditions, off to lunch, seemingly seconds later, back from lunch. People banter around the word "original" a lot, but believe me, Shirley was an original. Of course, with all that pent-up energy, she did have a reputation for a bit of exaggeration, and a habit of jumping to conclusions.

That mix was a volatile cocktail and the recipe for great "Shirley stories." Everybody has one. Here's mine.

It was nearing the end of another hectic week. A music production house called Shirley frantically seeking a "Barry White" sound-alike. They'd already auditioned a number of black actors, but hadn't quite found the sound they needed and were running out of time.

"Oh! I have just the man," Shirley squealed. "I just signed him this morning. I can have him at your place in an hour."

Shirley's perfect choice showed up promptly, dressed in an expensively tailored suit.

"Oh Baby, Baby . . . My Baby, Baby," he intoned over and over, sounding much more like Colin Powell than Barry White. A few minutes after he left, Shirley made her follow-up call.

"Well! Isn't he just perfect?" Shirley asked.

The producer commented on what a nice, professional man the actor was. Unfortunately, he said, the man was totally and unequivocally wrong for the part.

"Shirley, the guy sounds like an accountant."

"What!" Shirley almost screamed. "That's precisely what makes him perfect. You told me, specifically you wanted a black man who sounded *very white*!"

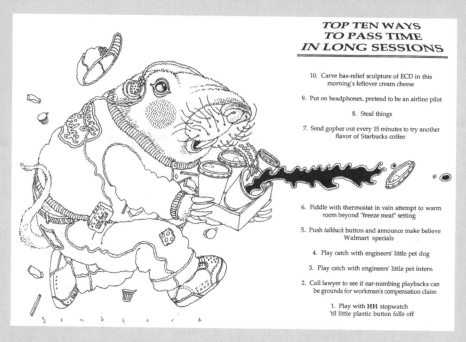

From the 1992 Harlan Hogan Production Calendar—John Sandford, Illustrator

Techniques of a Voice-Over: Long-Form Voice-Overs—The Skills, the Opportunities

"It is difficult to produce a television documentary that is both incisive and probing when every twelve minutes one is interrupted by twelve dancing rabbits singing about toilet paper."—Rod Serling

Long-form voice-over work such as documentaries and audio books arguably demand the most of a voice-talent. Narrative work requires storytelling skills, of course, but also acting, timing, cold reading, and expert pronunciation abilities.

The sheer energy and strength of voice it takes to read hour after hour is often overlooked by voice-overs used to commercial work. The mental concentration required for long-form work is likewise not to be underestimated. I've watched some seasoned commercial voice-overs fall apart after a few hours in the booth, heads aching, throats raspy, and perspiring heavily.

There is also the requisite skill, the ability to "cold read," or what radio and TV announcers call "rip and read," that you must possess. I learned to rip and read because I had to when I worked on the air. It's may sound cliché, but somewhere right now, as an announcer is reading the 4:30 newscast, the door is quietly opening on the control room, and a hand is silently slipping a late-breaking news item onto the desk: " . . . and this story, just handed me . . . " happens every day on the air, and you'd better be able to get the words right—sight unseen.

If you are booked for long-form narration and you have any say in the matter, ask to have your copy typed in upper- and lowercase, not all uppercase. Why? Because your mind will subconsciously register the *pattern* of the sentences, which helps you make instant decisions and changes in your delivery. Also, punctuation and paragraph breaks are more obvious to your eyes in upper- and lowercase type. Scripts in all uppercase look more like a solid block of text, with few visual clues as to emphasis and pauses.

Personally, I read ahead with my peripheral vision, and I can do that much better when the script is upper- and lowercase. But, judge for yourself—try reading the prior paragraph aloud when it's all uppercase and single spaced.

IF YOU ARE BOOKED FOR LONG-FORM NARRATION AND YOU HAVE ANY SAY IN THE MATTER, ASK TO HAVE YOUR COPY TYPED IN UPPER- AND LOWERCASE, NOT ALL UPPERCASE. WHY? BECAUSE YOUR MIND WILL SUBCONSCIOUSLY REGISTER THE *PATTERN* OF THE SENTENCES, WHICH HELPS YOU MAKE INSTANT DECISIONS AND CHANGES IN YOUR DELIVERY. ALSO, PUNCTUATION AND PARAGRAPH BREAKS ARE MORE OBVIOUS TO YOUR EYES IN UPPER- AND LOWERCASE TYPE. SCRIPTS IN ALL UPPERCASE LOOK MORE LIKE A SOLID BLOCK OF TEXT, WITH FEW VISUAL CLUES AS TO EMPHASIS AND PAUSES.

I find that scripts that are double-spaced are even easier to read and have the added advantage of leaving room to pencil in changes or aids to pronunciation, like phonetic spellings of unfamiliar words. Phonetics was another of those college courses that I managed to pass without ever really grasping. "When will I ever need this?" I convinced myself. When? Almost every day. Live and learn.

Speaking of living and learning, a speaking acquaintance with Latin would certainly help with medical scripts. Of course, that kind of farsightedness back in high school was far beyond me—but perhaps not for you.

If you really do grasp all the arcane details of phonetic Sanskrit, that's great—it'll come in handy with foreign, technical, and proper name pronunciation. If, like me, you're a "phoeneticphobe," do not despair—just invent your own. Hyperparathyroidism, simply becomes "hiper-pair-a-*thigh*-roid-ism."

I recently received a particularly nasty long-form script on Egyptology brimming with utterly unpronounceable names. To make matters worse, the copy was all uppercase and single-spaced. Since I was recording in my home studio, I scanned the script into my computer, opened it in my word processor, reformatted it in double-spaced lines, and then clicked on "change case" to upper and lower and, voilà, a script I could easily read and write notes on.

The second way to improve your cold reading (and you knew this was coming) is to *practice*. Voice-overs who have worked live on the air have had the advantage of forced practice. Of course they learned to cold read well with a very un-altruistic goal—staying employed. You can improve your rip-and-read skills immeasurably just by reading aloud every day. Start with something simple like a children's book, as your skill level goes up and the number of mistakes you make goes down, move on to more difficult books and newspapers.

Once you have your cold reading abilities in shape, keep them in shape by practicing every day. Many top VOs read a newspaper aloud every morning. It's a great idea. An even more productive and personally rewarding way of keeping your cold reading "chops" in shape is reading for the blind or for children as part of the "Book Pals" program of the Screen Actors Guild or on your own at a local school or library.

Also, practice—don't laugh—moving pages of script on the copy stand quietly. It's a minor art form as well. The performers I've been privileged to record with who worked in the Golden Age of Radio—like Harry Elders—simply held their script in one hand, and then silently dropped the pages to the floor as they finished them. When I try to do that, it always sounds like slabs of concrete hitting a bass drum. Instead, I've learned to work a page ahead, silently picking up the next page of script while I'm in the middle of the present page, and slipping it into my view when needed.

If you just can't seem to move the pages silently, relax. Just pause, move the page, and read on. Modern computer-based recording has made editing so much faster and easier than the razor blade and tape days that editing out pauses is now a quick and simple task. In fact, my recording software even has a handy "delete silence" command that instantly takes out the pauses.

Documentaries, narratives, and audio book scripts should be approached exactly the same way we did commercial broadcast copy, by asking the right questions to determine the right interpretation.

- ☉ Who—what individual living, breathing, human being—am I talking to?
- ☉ Who—what individual living, breathing, human being—am I?
- ☉ What—what am I trying to accomplish?

In a documentary I'm often portraying an expert—instructing and teaching—or a historical character giving a firsthand, first-person account. In an audio book I might be everybody—quite literally. Most audio books I've done have had a limited talent budget—limited, that is, to only me. So I'm often storyteller, husband, friend and enemy, young man, old man, mother, daughter, and even wife, all in the same script. Audio books stretch your storytelling skills, your acting ability, and your vocal range as much as animation voicework, with the added prerequisite that you have the concentration and physical ability to read for long stretches of time. The Audio Publishers Association is a great source of information on the audio book business; click on *www.audiopub.org*.

Generally speaking, long-form work pays far, far less than commercial voice-overs, especially if you compare the actual time required in a studio versus return. But most actors, especially voice actors, simply love to perform, and the hours spent creating different characters or learning bits of history you never knew is downright fun and addictive. Of course, there's fun and then there's free. Fun is good, free is not. A professional deserves to be paid for work, even if it's a pittance. If you are represented by an agent, he will usually handle the sometimes- uncomfortable details of negotiating your fee. Union performers have fairly strict rules to follow, and the producer or production company must be signatory to specific contracts. These agreements specify the minimum fees and working conditions. Even so, from time to time, I get a direct call from a long-form producer like this one, so be forewarned; you may, too.

YOUNG-SOUNDING FILMMAKER ON PHONE: We just finished this documentary on the history of Bratwurst, and we're looking for a voice-over.

ME: Great, I love Brats, especially Wisconsin Brats.

FILMMAKER: Me too! We filmed in Wisconsin at the Sheybogan Brat Fest. Got great scenes, man.

ME: Well, I'd love to be a part of it.

FILMMAKER: We're gonna pitch it to the Discovery Channel.

ME: Wonderful.

FILMMAKER: Have you got your own audio studio?

ME: Sure.

FILMMAKER: What kind of mikes?

ME: Sennheiser 416 and Neumann U-47.

FILMMAKER: You got a 47! That was Sinatra's favorite microphone, man—his, "Telly"—this is perfect. It'll save us a bundle.

ME: I understand, and I'll try to keep everything within your budget.

FILMMAKER: Budget?

ME: Your talent budget.

FILMMAKER: Were gonna pitch it the Discovery Channel and . . .

ME: And . . .

FILMMAKER: So, you know, if they buy it, then, you know . . .

Fortunately, I do know.
I know better.

7

THE TEAMSTERS MADE ME CHANGE MY NAME

"A self-made man may prefer a self-made name."—Judge Learned Hand, granting Samuel Goldfish permission to change his name to Goldwyn

The teamsters made me change my name—almost. I promised I'd explain the Bob-Harlan name thing, so here goes.

I always thought my dad had a really interesting name. He hated it. I suppose growing up in Cloquet, Minnesota, and later working in the steel mill, he'd have preferred a more "regular" name. A nice, easy-to-say, easy-to-spell, three-letter one like Jim, or Ted, or Dan. So my dad decided one day he'd no longer be Harlan. Instead, you could just call him Bill. I once pointed out to him that he'd set himself up to be called Junior since William was his father's name, but he failed to see the humor in that. His dad, Bill, was universally referred to as Happy Hogan anyway, so it was probably a moot point.

My older sister Marilan had already been given the "unusual" Hogan family name of *Marilan*, a combination of "Mar" from our mom, Marjorie, and "Lan" from our dad, Harlan. Of course, when I was born, there was no way he'd hang some weird moniker on me, so I was given the kind of All-American three-letter-name he'd longed for. His kid would be just plain "Bob." And Bob it was for almost thirty years, until I was ready to join the Teamsters, or actually, the two unions governing radio and TV commercials: the American Federation of Radio and TV Artists (AFTRA) and the Screen Actors Guild (SAG). Both unions are part of the AFL-CIO, though, so the Teamsters bit is almost true.

The woman in Los Angeles was as nice as a person can be. I'd called SAG after landing an on-camera part in a pulsating showerhead commercial. I was as excited and breathless as any actor who's finally eligible to get his "card."

There is this catch-22 situation in getting your SAG card. You can't be eligible for guild membership without getting a SAG job, but you can't get a union job if you're not in the union. Producers are fined a substantial penalty if they hire "off the card" in movies and TV shows, but not for commercials, so commercials have traditionally been the easiest way to earn your SAG card.

Now you *can* join AFTRA without ever having been hired for an AFTRA job. So, some actors think that if they join AFTRA, they'll automatically be welcomed into the SAG fold. Not so fast. AFTRA members are allowed to join SAG only if they can prove they've been employed as a principal performer in at least one AFTRA job. The "no free lunch" theory is alive and kicking at the Screen Actors Guild.

Meanwhile, the pleasant but somewhat world-weary voice on the phone ran through all the usual and customary preliminary information: address, social security number, and method of payment for the approximately $400 it cost to join SAG and AFTRA back then. Things were going smoothly, and I started to relax. Then she asked, "Name?"

"Bob Hogan."

"Hang on." I heard pages being turned rapidly. Computers hadn't invaded the SAG office yet.

"Nope." She said.

"Nope?" I asked.

"Already have a Bob, and that counts as Robert, but you can do a hyphen."

Since an actor's name is in many ways like a trademark, and confusion would reign supreme if there were twelve Robert Redfords and fifty-five Paul Newmans, SAG has strict rules regarding your performing name. First come, first served. Unbeknownst to me, "Bob" Hogan had already been claimed.

"What do you mean?" I stammered.

"Look, sweetie, you can't have the same name as any other working member of SAG, you know that, right?"

I did now.

"But," she went on, "You can do a Bob hyphen thingy like—what's your middle name?

"Charles," I said somewhat in a state of shock over this complication.

"So you could be 'Bob-Charles.' How's that?"

"Bob-Charles Hogan," I said aloud. "That's awful!"

"You can think about it, and call me back when you're ready, babe," she offered.

"OK, but my job is tomorrow. I'll call as soon as . . ."

Then it struck me. There was an unused first name floating around the Hogan family, a perfectly good name, a name I'd always liked. "How about Harlan?"

"Harlan Hogan? Good name for an actor, honey, hang on."

More page rattles, then she said, "Bingo! Wanna be Harlan?"

I did.

Later I changed my name legally to Harlan Robert Hogan and named my oldest son Jameson Charles, so my original middle name would have a proper home.

I hesitated telling my dad about the name change, unsure if he'd be flattered or upset that I'd thrown away my perfectly good All-American three-letter name. So when my folks came to see me at Chicago's Forum Theater in *The Gang's All Here* starring Dana Andrews, my secret was revealed right there on the playbill. As I met them in the lobby after the performance, my father smiled wryly, pointed to the program, and said, "Till I saw this I had no idea I was in this play."

Despite the fact that everybody, and I mean everybody, called my dad Bill, he signed his correspondence "H2." It's a habit I've adopted, and now that he's gone, I take a certain perverse delight in signing cards to my mom and sister as "H2-JR."

From the 1983 Harlan Hogan Production Calendar—John Sandford, Illustrator

Techniques of a Voice-Over: Corporate Voice-Overs —The Skills, the Opportunities

> "What do you call someone who doesn't know about operating systems and doesn't want to? Normal."—Scott Cook, Intuit Software Corporation

Corporate, or "industrial" voice-overs run the gamut, from long narrations explaining 401(k) benefit packages and step-by-step teaching programs to brief introductions of executives at the annual sales meeting:

> Vision 2006 is an action plan designed to help you, the HIM professional. . . .

One consequence of sustained cholestasis is hyperbilirubine-mia. . . .

Above us the very heavens were ablaze with thousands of flares. . . .

So welcome aboard, you'll find more than just a job here—you'll find a home. . . .

With his urging, Oregon adopted four election reforms, including the secret ballot and. . . .

If you have any doubts, read the M.S.D. sheet or contact your supervisor. . . .

These traditions have made Jim Beam the best selling bour-bon in the world. . . .

Begin polishing fiber optic material using six figure-eight lengthwise movements. . . .

Please welcome the heart and soul of Ronald McDonald House Children's charities, Joan Kroc. . . .

Almost always, you are speaking on behalf of the organization, often as an employee or as an expert in the field. It's critical that you can "talk the talk" of that particular business and sound believable. Asking the right questions is, as always, important to finding the right interpretation. In addition to "Who am I?" it's also helpful to ask, "Where is this being seen or heard? How big is the audience?"

Your approach will change dramatically based on these questions. A quiet, one-on-one reading, appropriate for an audio program listened to by company salespeople in their cars, isn't going to fly in a ballroom full of five thousand stockholders or at a bustling trade show kiosk.

Although corporate work doesn't usually provide any residual income like commercials do, corporate clients tend to be very loyal and use their favorite performers over and over, providing, in a sense, an informal residual structure. Over the years, I've become "the voice" of organizations like Signode, Mills Corporation, American College of Orthopedic Surgeons, and Panduit.

I may have been a slacker in school, but my corporate work has provided the most incredible postgraduate education in practically everything. Small talk at cocktail parties is never a problem. You say you're in HVAC? I can chat about air-change rates, and ASHRAE code specifications with the best of 'em, and sound sincerely interested in the heating, ventilation, and air conditioning business. Want to discuss moving sludges and slurries? I'll debate the advantages and disadvantages of macerator pumps with you all night.

It is vital to "get" and pronounce some pretty arcane words if you are going to be believed as a company spokesman. Hubometers and ferromanganese have to become as important to you as they are to the tractor-trailer builder and the steel maker.

It's surprising sometimes how difficult some words are to say out loud even though they look "easy" on paper. Quick, say "Healthsouth Corporation" three times in a row, or "North Dartmouth Massachusetts Mall" twice. Proper names and medical terms will probably need to be explained to you. I like to ask for a basic explanation of the meaning of a technical term because I think it helps me sound knowledgeable, even if I just barely comprehend what the heck it was I just said.

Here's a tip that works well for me. Cross out, or erase, any unfamiliar words in a script, and write in your version. This prevents that all-too-common visual "choke" that occurs between your eyes, brain, and mouth. It's only human that when your eyes see, "Cisatracurium Besylate" as the next word on a script, your brain thinks, "God! What-in-the-name-of-all-that's-holy is that word, and how do I say it?" while your mouth turns into flubber. See-sat-tra-curee-em Be-sigh-late, on the other hand, ain't so hard to say.

The real knack—the thing that separates the pros from the amateurs—is their ability to say words that may have little or no meaning to them and give the impression that they use those words constantly in daily conversation. After all, that's precisely what the audience does, and they must believe that you know exactly what you're talking about, or the illusion is shattered.

One parting thought: Do not—I repeat, do not—criticize or rewrite corporate copy or comment on the logic, grammar, or style of a script. Industrial/corporate copy is usually the stepchild of many, many rewrites. A lot of nonbroadcast scripts are not written by professional writers, and even when they are, constant changes often turn them into a hodgepodge despite the writers' best efforts. The last thing you want to do is suggest other changes that might result in a rerecording session. If your client makes changes later on and you have to redo the session, that's fine, and you'll get paid for your time. On the other hand, you don't want to be responsible for causing a redo. You might be paid, but my guess is it'll be the last session you'll do for that client.

Getting final script approval in the corporate world is so difficult that the creative director of Abbott Labs, Stacy Christie, told me, "I have this gigantic rubber stamp, Harlan. When a brand manager hands back my script and says, 'Okay,' I get their initials and then stamp it, 'Absolutely, Positively, Approved' in seventy-two point type."

So I have never, ever made any comment on the logic, structure, or intent of a corporate script.

Well, hardly ever.

Maybe once.

The last time I'd worked for Northrop Defense Systems, I somewhat naïvely asked just what it was they did out there in their Schaumburg, Illinois, facility. Oh, I knew that they were a government top-secret defense supplier. I'd narrated a video on security procedures for employees traveling abroad earlier in the year—very "Spy vs. Spy meets James Bond" stuff. But I wondered exactly what they did all day. The silence was deafening.

Finally, the project team leader, a man in his mid-forties with short-cropped salt-and-pepper hair and the unmistakable posture of an ex-military officer, said quietly, "You've no doubt heard of radar-seeking missiles being fired on American planes and then suddenly turning to destroy the enemy plane instead?"

I nodded assent. I'd heard of that during the many military crises in the Persian Gulf.

"Well, Harlan . . . that's what we do."

It was a scary thought, but even scarier was this line from page 1 of their script:

> **ANNOUNCER:** At Northrop Defense Systems we're rewriting the history of aviation.

That phrase seemed a bit much, and since I knew the producer, Chip Moore, well enough to venture a slightly barbed observation on the copy, I asked in mock-innocence:

"How do you do that?"

"Do what?" said Chip, with a wary half-smile.

"Rewrite history."

Chip turned to the ex–major general and said, "He's got a point."

"Nonsense!" He turned to me, and leaning close into the talkback mike, said in his best military stentorian voice, "History is dynamic and ongoing!"

"In Russia and China, perhaps, but not here," I quipped. I could see by his smile that he was enjoying the debate.

"What do you guys do," I continued, "slip into school rooms at night with bottles of white-out, changing history books?"

"Hey, there's a thought," Chip added.

"I've got it!" I said. "In 1903 Wilbur and Orville NORTHROP flew the first powered plane at Kitty Hawk. . . ."

"Or," Chip added, "Charles Lindbergh flew the *Sprit of Northrop* across the Atlantic, or. . . . "

"Guys!"

It was the voice of reason—the voice of our engineer.

In a recording studio, time really is money, and it was time to go back to work.

"Guess I should shut up and read this the way you wrote it," I ventured.

No one disagreed.

WCLR AND THE BIG BANG THEORY

"Illinois ranks second, behind California, in the number of bombings each year."—Jerry Singer, Special Agent, U.S. Bureau of Alcohol, Tobacco, and Firearms

I was ready for the plunge into a full-time acting career. Dick Rodnick and Advanced Systems had provided the impetus, and my wife was very supportive.

We even moved from the suburbs to a condo downtown, so I'd be closer to the auditions and (I hoped) sessions. Shirley Hamilton had started calling me fairly regularly for auditions, rather than just to troubleshoot her tape recorder.

We had saved some money, didn't yet have any children, and had realistic monetary goals—which is a nice way of saying, if I couldn't make a halfway livable wage after a few years, I'd be smart enough to move on. So, on the surface, I had nothing to worry about.

Except. . . Except that deep down inside, I was scared out of my wits. I needed a sedative. Not a drug, but something to calm the tidal wave developing in my stomach. I knew full well we'd have some rocky months ahead, and I thought some kind of part-time job might ease my angst and pocketbook.

Following the moving truck heading downtown, I switched on the car radio. It was tuned to WCLR, and Jack Kelly with his amazingly deep voice said, "It's 10:30 and 67 degrees." As the movers began unloading the truck, I called the station.

"Jack Kelly," he said over the phone, his voice sounding remarkably as smooth and rich as it did on the air.

"Hi Jack, my name's Harlan Hogan. You don't know me, but I was in radio for quite a while about ten years ago. Look, I know when I was a program director in Indiana, the one thing I could never find was a weekend and part-time announcer who was good, good enough to be full-time but who didn't want a full-time job. Is that true in Chicago, too?"

"Got an air check?" Jack asked.

"No, not any more, but I'll gladly come by and audition for you."

"How soon can you get here?"

My first day at WCLR was also my longest. I took the four-to-midnight shift on Sunday, and even though I'd been off the air for a long time, it all came back. At about 11:45 P.M. Bob Longbons came in.

We were both surprised. I'd met Bob at Advanced Systems one day when he was working as an on-camera talent, and I didn't know he did the all-night shift at 'CLR. He knew me as the ad manager at Advanced and was equally surprised to see me. One hour of conversation became two, and then three. Bob was remarkably helpful. He had advice on everything from the recommended length of my voice demo to what photographer took the best headshots.

He loaned me some demos to take home and listen to. He had a collection of all the "biggies" in Chicago at the time. Sophisticated Brad Bisk, soft-spoken Russ Reed, sexy-sounding Moana Abboud, quirky Joan Lazzerini, and of course the vocal chameleon Joel Cory, who could sound like anyone or anything. Three hours became four, and I was "going to school" for free.

Right after the 3:30 A.M. news, the phone rang. I heard Bob say how flattered he was, and, "Thanks, but it's not necessary."

"You get a lot of calls on the graveyard shift, Harlan. We've got everything from crazy Rae who describes weird sex acts she's having in my honor, to nice guys like that, who want to send over a bottle of booze."

The phone rang again, and it was obviously the liquor man. "No, but thanks . . . Well, Jack Daniels, but again, that's not necessary." Bob laughed, and we went back to my private lessons.

Forty-five minutes later a loud buzzer sounded. Bob looked surprised, "That's the main door downstairs. It might be our engineer."

I offered to take the elevator down the seven flights and check.

"Great," Bob said.

When I got to the lobby no one was there. Then I noticed a box just outside, in the hallway leading to the front door. Walking over, I could see that it was a case of Jack Daniels whiskey. Opening the locked inner door, I realized that I couldn't pick up the carton and get back to the door before it would slam shut, and since it was my first day I didn't have a key to open the door from outside in the hallway. So, holding the inner door open I tore the envelope off the carton and headed back upstairs.

I handed the envelope to Bob.

"How nice," he said reading his fan letter. "You know night workers really rely on us jocks to keep them company."

I told Bob how I couldn't wrestle the box upstairs, and was afraid I'd get locked out.

"No problem. I'll put it in the car when I leave."

Realizing how late it was I thanked Bob and left. Meanwhile, Bob began to ponder that carton downstairs. Reflecting on all the weird and strange calls he'd gotten late at night, Bob started to wonder. Was it really a case of Jack Daniels down there?

WCLR had a music automation system, so Bob quickly programmed three songs to play in a row, went downstairs, and saw the carton. It looked like a case of Jack Daniels, as I'd described. Laughing at himself, Bob quickly took the elevator back up to the studios, where for the next hour he tried to ignore the nagging doubts he entertained about that box.

"What if . . . ," he thought, "What if . . .What if . . . it's a bomb?" Of course it couldn't be. But "What if . . ." played over and over in his head like an album stuck on an old-fashioned record changer.

Thirty minutes later, he couldn't take it any more. He called the Skokie, Illinois, police. With the squad cars' screaming sirens piercing even the soundproof rooms of the radio station, Bob knew that they had arrived.

He watched from the studio window as the bomb squad cautiously entered through the unlocked outside hallway door. They were carrying a blast-proof steel container. A few moments later they gingerly carried it to the center of the empty parking lot. Soon, all the officers backed away from the box and a muffled bang reverberated through the plate glass window. Moments later, the downstairs door buzzer sounded and Bob again engaged the automation system, and went downstairs to unlock the inner door to the building and talk with the policemen.

Bob filled out the paperwork, and as he did he asked in a trembling voice, "So it was a bomb?"

"No, sir."

"But I heard the explosion."

"Sir," the officer said, "We do a controlled explosion inside our containment device of any suspicious package; it's only about the strength of a cherry bomb."

"Then it wasn't dangerous?" Bob asked, as he signed the report.

"Only if you drank enough of it sir. We've just successfully detonated a case of Jack Daniels."

"Thanks, we'll let you know..."

From the 1986 Harlan Hogan Production Calendar—John Hayes, Illustrator

Techniques of a Voice-Over: Character Voices and Your Multiple Personalities—The Skills, the Opportunities, the Misconceptions

"You know, that ain't them dogs' real voices . . ."—Jeff Foxworthy

Based on the e-mails I get, it seems as if everybody wants to do "character voices," and why not? For voice-overs, there isn't anything more fun than giving vocal life to, say, a goldfish or a wheel of cheese. Of these e-mails, though, only the woman telling stories with her "funny" voices is on the right track from a practical point of view. . . .

> You should hear my kid, he does the best Mickey Mouse I ever heard. . . .
>
> Please audition my John Wayne voice, it's like he's still alive. . . .
>
> My wife tells these hysterical stories in these funny little voices. . . .
>
> My Australian accent would fool a genuine Aussie. . . .

If an advertiser needed the voice of Mickey Mouse, they'd contact the Disney Company for an authorized voice-over actor or risk the wrath of a bevy of lawyers. The rights to the John Wayne "persona" are also owned and tightly controlled. In an age of high-speed Internet and ISDN, real Australian accents are a phone call away. But the story-telling wife—she has possibilities.

Character voices, whether for animation, radio, or interactive games, aren't just about sounding funny. They are mainly about—no surprise—the character. That goldfish or wheel of cheese, for example, has character the minute he or she speaks.

She might be a grandmotherly cheese, kind and gentle—or old, crusty, and crotchety. Undoubtedly, she has a name: Maria, or better yet, Esmeralda. Maybe Esmeralda is unhappy because she's Limburger cheese, scorned by all the other cheeses because of her—shall we say?—smell. So, over the years Esmeralda has built up a grumpy, tough-talking exterior, but deep down inside hides the soft gooey heart of warm Brie. On the other hand, our wheel of cheese could just as easily be a musty, dusty grandfatherly one, and have a musty, dusty-sounding voice. The goldfish? I'd probably call him Stan, and he has a whole life of his own, his "backstory."

All the basic voice-over questions we talked about previously need to be asked and answered for character voice work. Who is this goldfish named Stan? What's his relationship to his wife, Goldie? How old are they? Do they have any guppies? Maybe Goldie likes to boss Stan around, or is it the other way around? Maybe Stan has a crush on Angelfish in the next tank and maybe Goldie suspects. I have noticed that Goldie has put a few pounds on her formerly sleek body these last few years, so maybe the "angel affair" is true.

Only when you, with the help of the writer, producer, director, and, in the case of animation, the artist, have explored all these kinds of possibilities can you begin to develop the right "character" voice.

Okay, what does this goldfish couple sound like? It really doesn't matter whether Stan and Goldie are characters in a radio commercial, a computer game, or cartoons, the process is pretty much the same. How they sound is up to you—and that, of course, is the fun and the terror of character voice work, particularly when auditioning for it. Make the wrong choices and—"Next." But at the very least, make choices, even if "they" decide yours are wrong.

Understand what is going on between the characters, their relationship, and, perhaps, their ethnic background. What are they trying to accomplish? Physically, what are they like—and, physically, where will that voice come from in you? Goldie might have a high squeaky "top of the head" voice or a nasal-sounding one that emanates through her nose—if she had a nose. Stan might be a classic basso profundo with a "chest sound" coming from deep inside. I'll bet anything that their neighbor, Angel, has a soft, sexy "breathy" voice purring out of the back of her throat.

The more characters you can create, the more character voices you can do. Stop and reread that sentence. Create the character, and the voice will follow, not the other way around. If you have abilities in dialects and accents, the possibilities for creation become even more exciting. What if our pal Stan has a touch of Ireland in his speech, Angelfish is a Russian émigré, and Goldie's nasally voice has an unmistakable touch of the Bronx?

Soon you may discover hundreds and maybe thousands of voices within you. How do you keep them all straight? First, give each a unique name, something meaningful to you. Next, memorize the character by having them introduce themselves in their voice: "Hello dear, I'm Goldie. . . . This is Stan, and welcome to our bowl. . . ." This one-line shortcut to a character is a quick way to bring back to life those voices stored in your head. If you are serious about pursuing character work, particularly animation, you'll need that big repertoire of full-blown characters ready at a moment's notice in auditions and sessions.

Although the majority of animation work is done in Los Angeles, Orlando, and Toronto, opportunities do exist all across the country, and character work is not limited to cartoons only. Even television's venerable *Mr. Ed* show needed Allan "Rocky" Lane to voice Ed's lines 'cause (and I hope I'm not spoiling any illusions here) the real horse—Bamboo Harvester—couldn't actually talk.

Character voices are also needed in commercials, corporate programs, audio books, electronic games, and other things you probably never dreamed existed, like *The Stations of the Cross* record used in monasteries across the country. Years ago, yours truly was booked by an order of Catholic priests to play the part of—believe it or not—Jesus. I hope and pray I did him justice.

Whoops, I've got to go—Stan just called and said somebody had secretly put a stinky piece of Limburger cheese in Angel's bowl and she's accusing Goldie, but Esmeralda, the cheese, got into a big screaming match with Angel and . . . well, I'll get back to you in the next Techniques of a Voice-Over section.

9

NO LONGER A "WANNA-BE"—FAST-FORWARD ON THE RIGHT TRACK

"You know, I've never been able to understand why, when there's so much space in the world, people should deliberately choose to live in the Middle West."
—Lamar Trotti, *The Razor's Edge*, Twentieth Century Fox, 1946

There is no easy way to get to St. Charles, Illinois, from Chicago.

If I could show you a bird's-eye view of the Chicago metropolitan area, it's obvious that short of flying into the Pheasant Run Resort airstrip just outside of St. Charles, you just have to be content to follow a rat's maze of roads to get there. My first of five days appearing on-camera for the consulting firm of Arthur Andersen, located in St. Charles, I was determined to be on the set on time. I had packed my Honda Accord the night before with several requisite suits so I'd look like an auditor on-camera. Actually, I needed the suits even to eat at the Andersen offices. Back then, a suit and tie were required just to enter the cafeteria.

I set the alarm clock for 5:00 A.M. and spent a somewhat sleepless night, waking to a blanket of snow. Five inches had fallen with more on the way, but as I brushed off the car, I was confident I had plenty of time in reserve. It was now 6:00 A.M., which gave me a full three hours to drive the twenty-five miles to St. Charles.

I had only ten minutes to spare as the guard checked me in at the gates outside Andersen's mammoth training facility. The grounds had once housed a private college, and they could sleep and feed six hundred employees from around the world who attended the education center. At the time it was the only auditing firm in the world with its own golf course and liquor license.

With eight minutes left, I turned down the snaking road to the TV studios and spotted a car in the ditch. A young guy, a clean-cut Michael J. Fox–type dressed in a suit, was trying to push his car back on the road—impossible to do by himself.

"Must be an auditor," I thought, approaching him. I didn't want to be late, and yet he looked so desperate. I stopped, ran over, and shouted, "Get in and steer!"

As he drove, I used my adrenaline rush to push him out. I waved good-bye, and jumped back in my car. I made it to the set precisely at nine. Thirty seconds later, the young man in the now-wet suit burst through the doors.

"Hey, thanks!" he said. It was Jim Parks, my coactor on the job. Moments later, actress Shary Seltzer joined us. By the time she'd removed her oversized, dripping wet parka, and Jim and I had finished helping her tug off her black rubber boots, it seemed like we were already friends. Shary's bright blue eyes sparkled and her freckled face blossomed into a broad grin as she nibbled on a croissant, sipped coffee from a paper cup, and regaled us with her adventures that morning. She'd been stuck in the snow three times trying to get her two kids to her mother's and her husband Scott to the train station. It turned out that Shary's husband was an agent at A Plus Talent Agency, and during our shoot she arranged for me to meet him. Thanks to Shary, I now had a second agent in my corner.

Shary and I worked so well together, and so often, on radio commercials that a few years later we released a voice demo entitled "Shary and Harlan Together Forever." The word "forever" had a proofreader's delete mark through it and penciled below were the words, "for two minutes and ten seconds." To this day, some people think we were married; we had a vocal chemistry that sounded so much like a real couple.

Jim Parks returned the snow bank favor just a few days later.

"Harlan, it's Jim Parks," he said on the telephone. "Have you met Jim Dolan yet?"

"No."

"Well, he's a voice talent who owns Streeterville Recording Studios, and he also produces commercials. I've got a gig there tomorrow at one, and he asked me to recommend someone else in my age bracket for a couple of parts. Want to do some spots?" I did.

I instantly recognized Jim Dolan's rumbling bass voice from about a zillion commercials. There's something otherworldly about meeting someone and realizing this is the person who's been asking you for most of your life, "Aren't you glad you use Dial? Don't you wish everyone did?"

I also met some of the other top voice actors in town, like Ron McAdam. A master of impressions, Ron had not only voiced countless commercials but played a myriad of parts on radio shows from *Dragnet* with Jack Webb to the classic soap operas. Ron's celebrity impersonations entertained audiences in nightclubs around the country as well as on the *Ed Sullivan Show*. I was introduced to Magaret Travolta, too—John's sister, yes, and a major talent in her own right. I had an instant crush on Margaret, just like all the other guys. The minute Joan Lazzerini said, "Nice to meet you, Harlan," I chuckled. She has one of those "slightly-off-kilter" voices that always sounds funny, even when she's being perfectly serious.

It was heady company, especially meeting the almost legendary Joel Cory. To say I felt a little intimidated is a vast understatement. WCLR's Bob Longbons had given me a brief résumé of Joel's voice work. In addition to doing voice-overs for everything from Schlitz and Oldsmobile to Seven Up, Joel was also "The Helping Hand" for Hamburger Helper, "Pop" of "Snap, Crackle, Pop" for Rice Krispies— even the singing animated Cricket for Cricket Lighters—and, it seemed, just about every other commercial I'd ever heard. Joel looked so unremarkable, and was so down-to earth and self-deprecating, you'd never in a million years have picked him out on the street as a nationally successful voice-over.

The session itself was far more relaxed than I'd anticipated, and the nervous pressure I felt started to ease, as many of the actors frequently joked with Jim Dolan. Then Dolan asked Joel if he could "hit" the word "on" in the script a bit harder.

Joel grinned impishly and said, "Sure, and next thing you know you'll want me to emphasize 'in.'"

Dolan made an equally cryptic response, "Well, if you could just roll it around a bit more. . . . "

Ron McAdam murmured, "Whatever you want you know he just can't give it to you, because he just doesn't see it."

"You're such pests!" whispered Joan Lazzerini.

Jim Parks chimed in, "Yes, you and your friend."

"Well, I wouldn't direct any living actor in Shakespeare like this," added Joel.

"There's too much directing around here," purred Margaret Travolta.

And then our announcer Joe Slattery, the ultimate professional with impeccable diction and inflection, capped it off by adding in his deepest voice, "Get me a jury and show me how you can emphasize 'in' in 'in July,' and I'll go down on you!"

Everyone laughed heartily at the snappy repartee, including me, although I didn't have a clue as to what they were talking about, or why they found it all so funny.

Despite my confusion over the "in" jokes, every voice-over actor I met that day freely gave me good advice, from "Go see Louise Wilson at Leo Burnett; she'll like you," to "Be sure and drop your tape at 'TLK for Bob Carney."

"Start making the rounds," Joe Slattery said, "you'll work." Voice-overs made "rounds" back then, calling directly on writers and producers, sitting down, and playing their voice demos for them. Meanwhile, Jim Dolan jotted down a list of ad agencies that he knew were doing a lot of "scratch tracks," the kind of demo commercials I had done while I worked at J. Walter Thompson.

The voice-over talent pool was fairly small back then, and I was being welcomed in. Thanks to Jim Parks I was joining this exclusive club, or at least had begun my initiation.

What I didn't realize was how much luck, timing, and the economy of the late Seventies and early Eighties were stacking the Tarot deck in my favor. If there was a "Golden Age of Voice-overs," this was it. The big deep voices of traditional announcers were starting to fade in popularity, and a more conversational sound was coming into vogue. With an unremarkable voice like mine, I happened to be in the right place at the right time.

Some people say, "If the doorbell rings, answer the door. It might be Jesus."

I say, "If you see somebody stuck in the snow, stop and push him out. It just might be Jimmy Parks."

From the 1989 Harlan Hogan Production Calendar—John Hayes, Illustrator

Techniques of a Voice-Over: Other Voice Work—The Skills, the Opportunities, the Talking Beer Bottle Openers

"What other voices do I do? I do me, and me with a cold."
—Frank Babcock, Announcer, circa 1965

Remember the first cars that talked? You'd leave the door open accidentally, or sometimes on purpose just to impress your friends, and the soft-spoken female voice intoned, "The door is ajar." To which we—at least my band of like-thinking friends—would shout back, "No, the door is a door!" I'm not sure why we thought that was so funny.

Just a few years ago, my Triumph motorcycle came equipped with a voice as well. Anyone attempting to steal the bike would hear a John Cleese sound-alike loudly proclaiming, "Attention, Attention, this Triumph motorcycle is being stolen!" I particularly loved how John Bloor, the new owner of the venerable British motorcycle marquee, managed to work in a commercial for Triumph, even as bandits were spiriting the bike away. Perhaps, he thought, innocent onlookers, or even the police, would say to themselves, "Shame that Triumph bike's being stolen, but it sure must be some fine motorcycle, that Triumph. You know, if it's that desirable, maybe I should pop 'round the local dealer and take one for a spin."

Actually, all the bike needed was the slightest movement to set off the verbal assault. Big burly thugs shoving the motorcycle into a nondescript panel truck were not required. I learned this to my dismay one windy day in Richmond, Illinois. I returned to my motorcycle and found it surrounded by a crowd shaking their heads in laughter, as it loudly protested its imminent theft.

Today, damn near anything can and will talk, and that's where we voice-overs come in. From the ubiquitous "You've got mail," to "Please enter your sixty-five-digit pin number followed by the pound, slash tilde, slash ampersand, sign," there is a ton of work out there for voices of all kinds.

This work, like corporate and long-form, is often one-shot employment. You won't feel you've won the lottery, which can happen when you land a network TV commercial, but you'll have enough cash to buy a bunch of lottery tickets, and some groceries to boot.

Telephony, pronounced in Harlan-phonetics as "tel-*lef*-ah-knee" *not* "tel-e-fone-ey,"—is a growth market right now. Recorded voice-messages abound on wired and wireless phone systems. Organizations of all kinds need voices for phone-prompt work, as well as on-hold phone messages.

Those obnoxious prerecorded telemarketing messages? Well, personally, I can't abide that kind of invasion of my privacy, so I draw the line at performing those. On the other hand, a hot new telephone-based marketing approach is called "permission marketing." In permission marketing, consumers agree to listen to recorded messages in exchange for discounts or free merchandise. In that case, I'd be glad to voice it, since it's simply a commercial and actually less invasive, since the consumer has agreed to hear what I have to offer.

Talking yellow pages and movie information lines are other voice—venues that need voice-overs. Toys, pinball games, and even appliances are others.

My local True Value hardware store (shameless client plug) not only sells talking beer bottle openers, they have *brand-specific* talking beer bottle openers. Somebody, somewhere, recorded, "Hey! How about a Corona?" and "Hey! How about a Miller Lite?" so why not you?

But the biggest market for voice-work is without doubt the World Wide Web.

The Internet has been a fairly silent place for a while, but like those motion picture "talkies" of the 1920s, the Web is starting to make noise and sounds—and words. Audio on the Internet has been hamstrung to some degree by "bandwidth," the speed at which information, graphics, text, or audio can be transmitted at a reasonably acceptable speed to the consumer. Huge audio and graphic files are the reason so many people slowly doze off in front of their computers.

Compression algorithms (I used that word just to show off) allow video and, more importantly to us, audio to flow almost seamlessly over the Web. Audio compression, like MP3, has changed everything.

Even with relatively slow Internet connections, audio is accepted and welcomed by most consumers. *PC Magazine* predicts that consumers using high-speed connections such cable modems and DSL will reach approximately 27 million in the next four years. So the market for a talking Internet, one needing voice-over performers, couldn't look any brighter. A few weeks ago, I clicked on an e-mail from my ISP—Internet Service Provider—and heard a thirty-second talking commercial for DSL. Guess what? Not only did the message talk, it called me by name—twice!

"Hey, Harlan, how'd you like to win a new Toyota Camry? Well, Harlan, here's how. . . ." It was a little scary, but awfully encouraging too.

My friend Thom Huge was not only the voice of Garfield the cat's owner, Jon, but also the voice of the mammoth Navy Pier Ferris Wheel. Museums and public attractions regularly hire voices to explain displays or provide directions. It's my voice that helps German tourists find their way around O'Hare airport, that explains what black holes are at the Adler Planetarium, and that describes the proud history of the Jim Beam distillery. I'm even (and I feel pretty silly about this) the voice of a tour bus.

From live sports and concerts to talking elevators, the demand for voice-overs is everywhere. My fervent prayer is that even radio dramas might make a comeback, perhaps over the Internet; it'd be like performing back in junior high but with much better equipment.

If you are in an active film production area, "Walla" and "Looping" provide voice opportunities, too. When movies are filmed, only the principal performers are usually recorded; the background noises are added afterward during "postproduction," via ADR, or Automatic Dialogue Replacement. Voice performers are hired to do the background and supplemental voices needed to make a scene sound as real as it looks.

Educational programs are other sources of employment for voice-overs, as are computer-based games. CD-ROM games are a world—and a world of opportunity—unto themselves. Even though a majority of CD-ROM games are produced in Silicon Valley, there is work throughout the country. These games are not too far removed from performing in an old-time radio drama, with one major difference: CD-ROM games—unlike a normal drama—are not linear.

In a Sony Playstation game I did recently, my death scene was recorded in six different ways based on which character killed me. The weirdest for me was my "death by alien" in which, accompanied by appropriate agonized screams, my head was ripped off by an intergalactic monster. That took a while, and I had a sore throat for several hours. In another computer-based game, I recorded over thirty different answers to the question: "Do you know where Zara is?" Luckily, the producers had a huge flowchart on the studio wall, so we could all understand what character was asking me the question, our relationship, and what my attitude would be toward each questioner. Voicing games like these is great fun, and it gives a voice-actor the rare opportunity to improvise and get paid for it.

There's an ever-growing market for all those voices roiling around in your head.

Somewhere in the Cotswold Hills, nestled in a thatched roofed house, I imagine there's a gangly British voice-over proudly telling his children, "I'm the voice of the Triumph motorcycle alarm, you know. . . ," and proud he should be.

10

IN JULY—INSIDE JOKES OF THE VOICE-OVERS

"Every actor in his heart believes everything bad that's been printed about him."—Orson Welles

"We know a remote farm in Lincolnshire where Mrs. Buckley lives. . . ."

Thus begins, arguably, the most famous voice-over outtake of all time. Captured, and surreptitiously saved by an anonymous recording engineer in England, the infamous Orson Welles Findus Foods tracks are considered a classic. Quoting lines from the Welles outtake was the reason my fellow actors were cracking up on my inaugural session with Jim Dolan.

When I left Streeterville Studios after that first session with Joel Cory, he invited me to join several of the performers for coffee at the Cambridge House restaurant. When I got up enough courage, I asked, "Okay, what's with the 'in July' stuff?" Joel was kind enough to invite a total new-be to join the pros for coffee—he was also generous enough to send me a cassette of the Orson Welles Findus Foods outtakes. Next time, I got the joke.

Most voice-overs I know can practically quote the whole script by heart. It's amazing just how often one of us laughingly quips in a session, "There's no known way of saying an English sentence in which you begin a sentence with 'In' and emphasize it," or, "I wouldn't direct any living actor like this in Shakespeare," or "There's too much directing around here."

In 1994 *The Critic*, an animated TV show featuring the voice of Jon Lovitz, did a parody of the Orson Welles session, so you may already be familiar with what was once an inside joke in the recording industry. They rewrote it and, combining a bit of *Citizen Kane* trivia, called their parody "Rosebud Peas."

When the ego of an Orson Welles met the dual-edged opponent of a prissy producer and a horrible script, fireworks were bound to occur. Here's the transcript from this clandestine recording. As you read it, imagine the deep, unctuous voice of Orson Welles as he tries to read his copy and fit it to the film rolling past his monitor. Slowly, inexorably, he loses his temper and finally walks out of the session.

Better yet, listen to the actual recording by going to *www.HarlanHogan.com* and clicking on the "VO: Tales and Techniques of a Voice-Over Actor" button.

ORSON WELLES: We know a remote farm in Lincolnshire where Mrs. Buckley lives. Every July peas grow there. Do you really mean that?

PRODUCER: Yes. Well . . . in other words, I'd start a half-second later.

ORSON WELLES: Don't you really think you really want to say July over the snow? Isn't that the fun of it?

PRODUCER: It's . . . if you could make it almost when that shot disappears it would make my . . .

ORSON WELLES: I think it's so nice, that you see a snow-covered field and say, "Every July peas grow there."

ORSON WELLES: We know a remote farm in Lincolnshire where Mrs. Buckley lives. Every July peas grow there. We aren't even in the fields you see . . .

PRODUCER: Yeah, we aren't.

ORSON WELLES: We're talking about growing and she's picked them.

PRODUCER: Yeah.

ORSON WELLES: (cough) What?

PRODUCER: In July.

ORSON WELLES: I don't understand you then. What must be over for July?

PRODUCER: Ummmm, when we get out of that snowy field.

ORSON WELLES: But I was out. We were on to a big can of peas, a big dish of peas, when I said, "In July."

PRODUCER: Well, I'm sorry. In July . . .

ORSON WELLES: Yes. Always. I'm always past that. Yes that's about where I say, "In July."

PRODUCER: Can you emphasize a bit "in" in "In July"?

ORSON WELLES: Why? That doesn't make any sense. Sorry, there's no known way of saying an English sentence in which you begin a sentence with "In" and emphasize it. Get me a jury and show me how you can say "*In*" in "in July" and I'll go down on you! That's just idiotic, if you'll forgive me by saying so. That's just stupid! "*In*" July! I'd love to know how you emphasize "*In*" in "in July." Impossible, meaningless.

PRODUCER: I think all they were thinking about was that they didn't want to—

ORSON WELLES: He isn't thinking.
(Indicating the client)

PRODUCER: Orson, if we could just do one last—

ORSON WELLES: Yeah?

PRODUCER: It was my fault. I should, I said "In July," if you could leave every July.

ORSON WELLES: You didn't say it, HE said it. Your friend. . . . Every July? No, you don't really mean every July, but that's bad copy. It's *in* July, of course it's every July. There's too much directing around here.

TAPE EDIT

ORSON WELLES: Norway. . . . Fishfingers. . . . Findus Norway.

ORSON WELLES: We know a certain Fjord in Norway near where the cod gather in great shoals, there Jan Stan. . . . Stangolin. . . . shit!

PRODUCER: A fraction more on that shoals thing. You rolled it around very nicely.

ORSON WELLES: Yeah, roll it around and I have no more time. You don't know what I'm up against. Because it's full of things that are only correct because they're grammatical. But they're tough on the ear. You see, this is a very wearing one. It's unpleasant to read. Unrewarding. . . .

TAPE EDIT

ORSON WELLES: . . . Because Findus freezes the cod at sea, then add a crumb crisp. . . . Oh . . . crumb-crisp-coating. Ah, that's tough: crumb-crisp-coating. I think. . . . no, because of the way its written, you need to break it up. Because it's not as conversationally written. What?

PRODUCER: Take crumb out.

ORSON WELLES: Take crumb out. . . . good.

TAPE EDIT

ORSON WELLES: Here, under protest, is Beef Burgers.

We know a little place in the American far west where Charlie Briggs chops up the finest prairie-fed beef and tastes. . . . This is a lot of shit, you know that?

ORSON WELLES: You want one more?

PRODUCER: I do, actually. You missed the first beef actually, completely.

ORSON WELLES: What do you mean, "missed" it?

PRODUCER: You emphasized prairie fed.

ORSON WELLES: But you can't emphasize beef! That's like him wanting me to emphasize "IN" before July! C'mon fellas, you're losing your heads. I wouldn't direct any living actor like this in Shakespeare. Where you do this, it's impossible.

PRODUCER: Orson, you did six last year and by far the best, and I know the reason. . . .

ORSON WELLES: The right reading for this is the one I'm giving you. . . .

PRODUCER: For the moment.

ORSON WELLES: I spent twenty times more for you people than any other commercial I've ever made. You're such pests! Now what is it you want in your depths of your ignorance? What is it you want? Whatever it is you want I can't deliver, 'cause I just don't see it.

PRODUCER: That was absolutely fine. It really was. . . .

ORSON WELLES: No money is worth this. . . .

Orson storms out of the studio.

Breathes there a voice-over that hasn't at least once wanted to tell a recalcitrant producer:

This is a lot of shit! You know that.

Or . . .

You're such pests!

I think not.

In Chicago we had a character just about as colorful as Orson and damn near his size. Much more affable than Orson Welles, Gary Gears was nonetheless famous. He was famous for his heart-stopping, ear-numbing, deep bass voice, quite similar to Orson's. He was famous for his ever-enlarging and -shrinking, but mostly increasing, size. He was famous for his collection of fire trucks. He was famous for constantly rolling silver dollars across his right and left knuckles simultaneously in a lightning-fast streak of silver. At Gary's wake, someone placed silver dollars between each knuckle of his hands and a NO AUTOGRAPHS pin on his lapel.

He was also famous—most famous—for being late. He was such a good-natured character and so talented that no one ever seemed to mind. Everybody knew Gary would be late to a session and always, *always* have an imaginative, wonderful, unassailable excuse.

As Joel Cory, Shary Seltzer, Mona Abboud, and I sipped coffee in the control room at Studio One, the phone rang. It was ten minutes past ten and Gary, the fifth performer, was, of course, late. The producer picked up the phone, glanced up at us, and said simply, "Okay," and hung up the phone. No one spoke for a long moment.

"Let me guess," said Joel with a grin: "Gary's running—"

Mona, Shary, and I finished his sentence in unison, " . . . a little late."

Then the speculation began. Wagers were made as to just how late he'd be, with the winner getting the last poppy seed bagel left on the platter. Minutes ticked by. It was 10:30 A.M., but no one was too concerned.

Although studio time is far from inexpensive, everyone, and especially the producer, knew that this was a group of pros and no matter how late Gary might be, we'd wrap the spot in short order. By 10:40 talk had turned to just what creative and reasonable excuse Gary would have this time.

Guesses ranged from, "The Michigan Avenue bridge was up. . . ."

"Been done!" said Shary.

To the equally popular, "My agent told me the wrong time. . . ."

"Too easy to check!" said Joel.

All heads turned as we heard a muffled bang from the lobby. Knowing it must be Gary, the four of us rushed into the studio and stood at mock-attention behind our microphones.

The heavy studio door flew open from the force that only someone of Gary's size could muster. Gary, in a fleece warm-up suit, nodded to the producer and silently, swiftly, strode into the studio to the one microphone remaining. And still he offered no excuse; there was none of his famous wit—not even a feeble, "Sorry."

The silence was deafening as we put on our headphones. Then, Gary cleared his throat and uttered just one word. His excuse for being close to an hour late was distilled into only one word—and it was the perfect choice. Orson Welles couldn't have done better.

It was the kind of unarguable excuse Gary Gears was famous for.

"Diarrhea," he growled.

From the 1982 Harlan Hogan Production Calendar—John Sandford, Illustrator

Techniques of a Voice-Over: Flying Solo—Performing Alone

"They don't need to act, just be."— Stephen Katz, *Shadow of the Vampire*, Lions Gate Films, 2001

Belief.

That's all I have to say.

Belief.

Either listeners hear your voice and believe what it is you are saying to them, or they don't.

If they don't, I need say nothing.

If they do, then you've already got it made.

When you are flying solo, talking one-on-one, with no dynamic dialogue, or even necessarily catchy copy, it's just you and the listener establishing belief, or disbelief.

As always, you have to ask yourself the requisite questions—who are you talking to? You'll glance at the script and find out what you are trying to convince the listener to do or believe, and where you are physically. Your approach and voice level will certainly be different if your character is in a noisy restaurant, a car, or a quiet living room. It's smart to spend some moments figuring out, or making up, a backstory. What were you doing just prior to speaking? Blowing your nose, or being handed these new, lower prices?

Now, figure out how you are going to have a conversation with one, individual listener for the next fifteen seconds or fifteen minutes. You won't be "reading" or "announcing." You'll be telling them some kind of story, even if it's as simple as the fact that there's a sale going on, and they'd be smart to hurry on in.

It always helps to visualize a specific person's face right where the microphone is. I'm often imagining that I'm talking to my wife or one of my kids. Talking to a very *specific*—albeit imaginary—listener also serves as a great "bullshit meter" for me. Would the person I've conjured up actually believe me, or laugh at my egocentric nonsense? If they wouldn't believe, then I better stop and reapproach this script and my character.

We all have friends who are born storytellers. We hang on their every word, even though they might just be describing the most mundane tale of trying to find a decent parking spot at the mall since "all the spaces in the same zip code were taken by these acne-ridden valet car hikers, stuffed in little red Santa helper vests." Then, there are those folks who'd read the *Story of* O with all the excitement of a bored substitute teacher drilling first-graders on the alphabet. Strive to be the storyteller.

Performing alone can be, well, lonely. You are isolated in the sound booth while people discuss your performance, eat lunch, or make phone calls. It's hard not to imagine that they are calling your agent to complain about your total and complete lack of talent. On the other hand, you are the center of attention, the star of the studio, if only for a short time—so enjoy it.

Working alone can be fatiguing, and doing take after take tiresome. Regardless, it's your job to make take 25 sound as fresh as take 1, complete with all the direction and nuances you've been directed to add to your reading. Besides, we voice-overs spend so much time, energy, and money for the opportunity to perform in a studio, why be in such a hurry to get out?

Flying solo is all about belief. Hard sell, soft sell, narrations, audio books, comedic copy, or serious—it's all the same. You must establish a one-to-one rapport with listeners so they feel comfortable believing you. We all know that sometimes the copy sucks, the product may suck, the whole concept may suck—but *you can't*. If you can bring order from the chaos, believe in what you've been given to say, and get your listener to believe in you as well, then you've got it, and they'll pay you well for it.

Believe me.

SMACK DAB IN THE GOLDEN AGE OF VOICE-OVER

"Doing commercials is like having a money truck show up at your house each week."—Danny Dark, Announcer, circa 1980

Who knew?

I'm pretty sure that the great stars of vaudeville had no idea at the height of their careers that they were in the "Golden Age" of vaudeville. In 1906, vaudeville was grossing $30 million a year (that's roughly the equivalent of over $520 million today). As many as 25,000 people each week went to see Houdini, Buster Keaton, Burns and Allen, Will Rogers, and Eddie Cantor.

But the Depression, talking pictures, and radio, as exciting then as the Internet is today, ended the era. Vaudeville didn't die overnight, of course. Some performers were able to make the transition to movies and radio, but others, like the knife-throwers and plate-spinners, couldn't. Meanwhile, the all-powerful Keith-Orpheum vaudeville circuit quickly became RKO—Radio Keith-Orpheum—producing movies and radio programs in addition to live variety shows. Still, the gold rush was over, and those acts that couldn't, or wouldn't, change with the times were left behind.

I know that those of us lucky enough to be doing voice-overs and singing jingles in the late Seventies and early Eighties had no idea that this, too, was the "Golden Age."

Advertising is often counter-cyclical to the economy; the worse the economic conditions, the more many companies are forced to advertise just to maintain market share. One hundred and thirty-eight banks failed during this period. Average wages declined anywhere from 14 to 26 percent, and the U.S. trade imbalance continued to grow out of control. In the late Eighties, as many as 30 million people lost their jobs because of company restructuring. But even as the economy worsened and advertising budgets got tighter and tighter, the need to advertise actually increased.

Chicago advertising agencies were forced to produce and finish more and more of their commercials locally to save costs. In tough economic times, clients were not willing to foot the bill for creatives to fly to the West Coast and other locations just to shoot and edit their commercials.

During the same period, the "industrial/corporate" market for slide films, meetings, and videos was blossoming. For a minuscule cost, video was, and is, a great way to inform, motivate, and train workers throughout a company. It's precisely why global companies were so busy creating in-house training videos with actors like me, rather than continuing the expensive practice of flying employees to centralized training centers. On-camera and off, Chicago actors were booked solid performing for corporate America.

Best of all, in this Golden Age, there were only three TV networks.

Cable TV as we know it didn't exist. TV was free; just stick an antenna on the roof or fiddle with the rabbit ears.

Major advertisers who wanted to reach consumers in the late Seventies and early Eighties simply put all their commercial dollar "eggs" in the networks' baskets.

Since commercials that played on the networks paid performers every time the commercial ran—a throwback to the days when actors performed those commercials live—the opportunity to earn large residuals was enormous.

This combination of limited production budgets, limited media choices, and a burgeoning industrial and corporate market opened a vein of gold for many voice-overs. Money trucks weren't quite pulling up to everybody's door, but occasionally a small station wagon drove in. Despite a six-week SAG-AFTRA strike, our voices blared from radios and TVs everywhere.

Personally, I was having a ball as the new kid on the block. My wife and I launched a thirty-five-foot sailboat and two sons. I was able to quit my part-time gig at WCLR, and I grew a beard.

Growing a beard may sound unimportant, but it was a calculated business decision based on a sound strategy—grow facial hair, and fast.

I'd been so blessed to find a niche starting out in my career, working for companies who needed on-camera presenters that understood computers. The problem was that my voice work was reaching a point where I was losing money every time I worked on-camera. Although I could only do one job per day on-camera, I could, potentially, do several voice sessions in a day. I felt like I'd be turning my back on the people who believed in me and gave me a start, and yet I had to stop working on-camera.

How could I say "no thanks" to clients who had become family? Explaining the situation openly and honestly was one option, and a mature one at that—which explains why I didn't choose it. Instead I went on a European vacation and came back with a beard.

Finis. The End. Corporate America certainly didn't want any video hosts with—God forbid—facial hair.

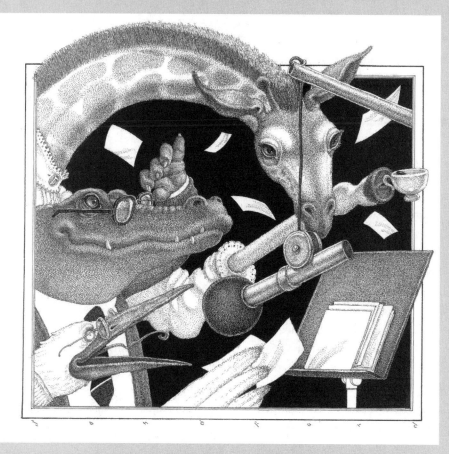

From the 1983 Harlan Hogan Production Calendar—John Sandford, Illustrator

Techniques of a Voice-Over: Playing Well with Others—The Art of Dialogue

"Keep your mouth shut when she's speaking. She Talks. You answer. You talk. She answers. It's what they call conversation."— Carl Reiner, *Enter Laughing*, Columbia Pictures, 1967

You may not be aware of a little-publicized fact of corporate life. Companies, large and small, spend tons of time and money on something they call "Team Building."

"Heidi, do you trust Wally, Mel, and Sharon?"

———————————— 101 ————————————

"Uh . . . . Yes!"

"Okay, then, you jump from this cliff at the count of three, do two double back flips cutting loose your bungee cords, and free fall eighty feet into the waiting arms of your team members, okay?"

"Heidi?"

"Heidi?"

"Heidi?"

"It's critical that you be a team player here at Ally Mikey and Schwartz, Heidi! Ready?"

Heidi, always a team player—and fearful of losing her position as assistant to the assistant executive in charge of assistants at AM & S—leaps and back-flips with abandon, into the arms of her compatriots. Suffering only minor scrapes and contusions, largely due to Wally's preoccupation with the wind mussing his carefully coifed comb-over, she is triumphant, courageous, and employed—at least until the next round of corporate downsizing.

We actors leap into an abyss far greater than Heidi's every time we're booked for dialogue voice-overs. We build a team—a team of trust—in nanoseconds, putting our faith in actors we met just moments before. And it's the best!

If solo performing is all about believability, dialogue is all about believability *and* trust. Other voices, other performers, invade the fortress of solitude of your solo work, and you must *trust* them, as well as yourself, to create dialogue that's *believable*.

Dialogue voice work, sometimes called doubles, is often exhilarating because it gives you a chance to play, experiment, and create three-dimensional characters interacting with each other. Dialogue is also more demanding because now, not only do you have to examine a script, ask all the usual questions of yourself, and make decisions, but all of your decisions must meld with the decisions of your fellow actors. Companies call it team building; we call it an ensemble.

At least we don't have to invent some invisible person to talk and react to. We've got company, and, almost always, good company.

Acting, at its best, is simply natural conversation. Conversation is what humans do—every day—in real life. We listen and then react to another person. Acting, though, demands a bit more, because real-life conversation has a high probability of being boring. And real-life conversation might also not mention the client's name, address, and telephone number, and that's not going to fly. So we actors have to create believable conversations, *but* in an imaginative and theatrical way.

Conversations—dialogues—have a rhythm and pace, both in real life and in the studio. The dialogue may demand a fast-paced line-on-top-of-line approach, or a slow, quiet conversation punctuated with dramatic pauses. Comedy demands both rhythm and timing, and the interplay between two or more characters is what makes the dialogue work or not. A very wise producer once told me as I was "milking" a line for a laugh—and she was right—"The key to being funny is to be absolutely, positively serious." It's true; the laugh will come from the surprise or twist in the script itself, coupled with the fact that you took everything so seriously and at face value.

Most producers, at least the wise ones, will let you run through dialogues several times to warm up before they begin to direct. If you haven't performed with the other actors on the session, you will all need to quickly get to know each other's rhythms and approach. The script will no doubt provide some clues about your character, but you'll need to delve deeper, developing a backstory, ferreting out who you are, what you want, and what your relationship is to the other characters.

The director, producer, or writer will now usually have suggestions, and before long, you'll start recording. It never hurts to ask, "Can we improvise a bit?" or, "Okay if we step on each other's lines?" or "Could I throw in a 'hmm' . . . or 'um' . . . or 'uhh' . . . ?"

If you and your playmates can work well off each other, relax, and be creative within the confines of the script, you can make even the strangest, most unlikely-to-have-been-spoken-by-anyone-other-than-an-advertising-person lines sound believable. Confines of the script? Yep, there's no getting around that one; clients have this weird predilection for hearing their product names in scripts—frequently. It'll take all of your acting and reacting ability to say, with a straight face, "Who's ready for my Betty Crocker American-as-the-Fourth-of-July Pie?" Make it sound real and actually believable, and you'll work all the time.

On only a handful of occasions have I seen a performer not "play well with others." A good producer will sense that, and more than likely say the things you'd never, ever say, although you'd like to. One actor, obviously enamoured with his comedic talent, steadfastly refused to speed up his lines, as had the other five actors, to get a commercial in on time. The producer, God love her, said over the talkback microphone, "Look I know you think you're really funny, but your stubbornness isn't, and if you don't pick up your pace no one will ever hear this spot, 'cause I can't sell a sixty-two-second commercial." Yes!

Courtesy to and cooperation with your fellow performers is important when doing dialogue. You might be arch competitors on auditions, but right now you are the closest of friends, helping each other to perform at your mutual best. In some studios you may even be sharing a microphone. So play nice, get out of the other actor's way, and be real quiet when they're talking. Oh, and don't run with scissors, either.

Performing dialogue voice-overs is just about as much fun as you can have in a studio and not get arrested.

Trust me.

12

SAY THE SECRET WORD—"BLOOPER'S SOAP"

**"If we can just get rid of these actors and directors,
maybe we've got something here."
—Michael Tolkin, *The Player*, Fine Line Features, 1992**

One afternoon, sometime in the early Eighties, I was waiting my turn to audition at the Foote, Cone, and Belding advertising agency when Russ Reed walked over and introduced himself, having just finished his audition. I was thrilled to be included on an audition with voice-overs of his caliber, but even more thrilled that Russ had taken the time to speak to me. I knew his reputation well, as a skilled voice-actor and genuinely warm person. As he was leaving he looked over his shoulder to be sure the producer wasn't there and whispered, "Blooper's Soap!" I nodded, smiled, and called Joel Cory as soon as I got home to find out what Blooper's Soap meant. Joel clued me in on the secret.

A secret I'm about to tell you. A secret as closely guarded as the wartime code written with the Nazi Enigma machine. A secret code far more obscure than the "Red head and the blue-tail fly" tape-header system I learned in my radio days. It consists of only those two words, but there isn't a voice-over performer in the United States who doesn't instantly recognize those words and their implicit meaning. Like a storm warning, those two words explain what thousands of words cannot: "Warning—you are about to enter a disaster zone, a swirling out-of-control hurricane known as a Blooper's Soap session."

When John Harmon and Shepard Menken joined Herschel Bernardi and Daws Butler at Hollywood's Quartet Films in the late 1950s to record a promotional record Daws had written, they couldn't have guessed that "All that Jazz" would become legendary as "Blooper's Soap." All four did know firsthand, however, just how complex producing even the simplest commercial could become and were anxious to perform in Daws's comedy sketch of a recording session gone wrong.

Daws Butler was often called the voice magician and created the voices of hundreds of characters from Huckleberry Hound to Captain Crunch. He read the part of the neurotic, anxiety-ridden advertising agency creative director, Miltown Jag. His character's name was actually a topical joke. At the time, Miltown, a supposedly safe and nonaddictive tranquilizer, had taken the country by storm. By 1956, just a year after its debut, 5 percent of the American public was popping Miltowns to ease their stress, but those who took too many capsules soon found themselves even more anxious and nervous and on a . . ."Miltown Jag."

Morrie Siduals, the announcer's name, was a play on words as well—"more residuals." Morrie was played by veteran voice actor Shepard Menken. Many years ago, I had the privilege of seeing him perform at a *Plastic Man* cartoon recording session in Hollywood. Shep was one of those rare artists who could create an infinite number of different voices on demand. No wonder he was constantly employed on shows like *Alvin and the Chipmunks, The Jetsons*, and *Mr. Magoo*.

The unflappable engineer, George, was voiced by John Harmon. Harmon, a bald, hook-nosed character actor, had a career that spanned the decades from 1939 on, and was featured in dozens of movies and TV shows, from *Funny Girl* to *Star Trek.*

Chuck, the "Been there, done that . . ." producer, was acted by Herschel Bernardi. Bernardi was an amazingly versatile performer, on-camera, off-camera, and on the stage. He created the voice of Starkist's Charlie the Tuna, won an Emmy for his role as Lieutenant Jacoby on the TV series *Peter Gunn*, starred on Broadway in over seven hundred performances of *Fiddler on the Roof*, and appeared in such classic films as *Irma La Douce* and *The Front.*

"All that Jazz—Blooper's Soap" was never intended for the general public. It was a record designed to showcase the abilities of the production house and the voice talents to the advertising community, although in 1979, Dr. Demento did air it on his popular radio show. Within the industry though, Daws Butler's wonderful parody has lived on, mostly through word of mouth. Copies have been passed on from one generation of voice-overs and recording engineers to the next. Blooper's Soap stands the test of time because nothing changes. Back then, as now, the writer has his spin on how a spot should sound and the actor another, the producer has her two cents' worth, as does the account executive. At the top or bottom, depending on how you choose to look at this pyramid, is the client. And most of the time, it's their direction that counts in real life, or in the made-up world of "Blooper's Soap." You can listen to the actual recording by visiting *www.HarlanHogan.com* and clicking on the "VO: Tales and Techniques of a Voice-Over Actor" button.

ENGINEER: Hi, Chuck.

PRODUCER: Hi, George.

ENGINEER: Well, what'cha got?

PRODUCER: A real quickie, George. Five words. Morrie's coming in to read one line. We'll be out of here in a few minutes.

ENGINEER: Yea, I'll bet. When's Morrie due?

PRODUCER: Hmm? Sorry, George, what?

ENGINEER: Morrie Siduals, the actor, when's he getting here?

PRODUCER: Oh, he oughta be here any minute.

MORRIE: Hi, Chuck, Hi, George.

PRODUCER: Hi, Morrie.

ENGINEER: Hi, Morrie, we were just talking about you.

MORRIE: Why does everybody hate actors?

PRODUCER: Not everybody, Morrie, Just me. Now, we want sort of a simple, straight, sincere, throwaway kind of reading.

MORRIE: Blooper's Soap is real good.

PRODUCER: Perfect. I mean, what the hell can you do with a simple, sincere line? Just say it. You ought to be out of here in a few minutes.

CREATIVE DIRECTOR: Uh, hello, Chuck.

PRODUCER: Oh, hi, Miltown, glad you came down. Meet Morrie Siduals.

CREATIVE DIRECTOR: Hello, Morrie.

PRODUCER: Morrie, this is Miltown Jag from the agency.

CREATIVE DIRECTOR: You fellows, uh, just kinda pretend I'm not here. I just want to, you know, watch from the sidelines. Morrie see the storyboard?

PRODUCER: Yeah, yeah.

CREATIVE DIRECTOR: He know what we want, what kind of a reading we want?

PRODUCER: Yeah, he understands.

CREATIVE DIRECTOR: Just a simple, sort of sincere, throwaway-type reading.

PRODUCER: Yeah, he's got the picture.

CREATIVE DIRECTOR: We don't want any big sell on this.

PRODUCER: I know, I know. Well, Morrie, you want to get out to the mike? We'll do her, huh.

MORRIE: Okay.

ENGINEER: You want to give us a level, Morrie?

MORRIE: Blooper's Soap is real good.

ENGINEER: Okay. You want to slate it, Chuck.

PRODUCER: This is production 24 eggs dash 16 dash 33 dash 12, 18th revision, revised, take 1.

MORRIE: Blooper's Soap is real good.

CREATIVE DIRECTOR: Cut. That sounds fine in here, nice easy reading. We, uh, we, uh, better take another one for our protection, though. And, as long as you're doing it again, Morrie, I was just thinking the account executive is a real stickler for client name identification, so maybe you could goose "Bloopers" a little, okay?

MORRIE: Okay.

ENGINEER: Take 2.

MORRIE: Blooper's Soap is real good.

CREATIVE DIRECTOR: Cut. I think we got it, don't you, Chuck?

PRODUCER: Sounds right on the nose to me.

CREATIVE DIRECTOR: Fine, fine, fine. Wait a minute, the only thing is, our copy chief is pretty adamant about product mention.

MORRIE: You mean soap? I mentioned it.

CREATIVE DIRECTOR: But not with great pride, mention it with great pride, Morrie. Put a frame around "Soap" and I think we've got it made.

MORRIE: Okay, Miltown.

ENGINEER: Take 3.

CREATIVE DIRECTOR: With great pride, Morrie.

MORRIE: Blooper's *pride* is real good.

CREATIVE DIRECTOR: Perfect. Oh, that was it, cut, cut, cut it, George. Perfect Morrie!

PRODUCER: But he said Blooper's "pride."

CREATIVE DIRECTOR: Oh, I know, and it was splendid the way he . . . what did he say?

PRODUCER: He said Blooper's *pride* is real good.

CREATIVE DIRECTOR: Oh no, no. It should be Blooper's *Soap* is real good. You got a script there, Morrie?

MORRIE: Yes, Miltown, I was thinking about pride, and I . . .

CREATIVE DIRECTOR: All right, but it's soap, Morrie, remember that.

MORRIE: Okay.

ENGINEER: Take 4.

MORRIE: Blooper's Soap is real good.

CREATIVE DIRECTOR: Getting there, Morrie. Don't lose that nice, easy sell. Chuck? Could I make one suggestion?

PRODUCER: Feel free.

CREATIVE DIRECTOR: Well, look, the agency head is very particular about qualifications. Morrie should hit "real'" a bit, don't you think. It's real good. Hit "real," Morrie.

MORRIE: I got ya.

ENGINEER: Take 5.

MORRIE: Blooper's Soap is reeeeal good.

CREATIVE DIRECTOR: Well, I think that just about wraps it up. I mean I'm satisfied if you are, Chuck.

PRODUCER: Sounds fine.

CREATIVE DIRECTOR: Splendid, splendid. I uh, ah, now wait a minute, wait a minute here. I do have a slight worry, Chuck. The client loves the word "good." He's used it in his copy for years, he tried to copyright it several times, spent a fortune, but "no soap," you know. Morrie, make more out of "good," will ya.

ENGINEER: Rolling, take 6.

MORRIE: Blooper's Soap's reeeeal gooood.

CREATIVE DIRECTOR: Only terrific, Morrie! But there is one little thing that worries me. It sounds like you're making a contraction out of "is"—sounds like you're saying "Blooper's Soap's real good." Will you give that "is" great conviction Morrie?"

ENGINEER: Take 7.

MORRIE: Blooper's Soap IS reeeeal gooood!

CREATIVE DIRECTOR: That's it, we got it Chuck! That's just the amount of undersell I wanted.

PRODUCER: Yeah . . .

I've never been in any studio—anywhere—where anyone didn't know what a Blooper's Soap session was. Often, in the middle of a recording that's bouncing off the studio walls, I've had an engineer smile at me through the glass and mouth, "Blooper's Soap."

Blooper's Soap is more than just funny, it's our secret word, our shorthand, and it's as calming as a quick dose of Prozac when you feel the rumblings of an oncoming panic attack. Those awful moments in the studio when you just can't seem to understand what it is they want you to do.

"Of course," you think to yourself: "It's not me. This is Blooper's Soap!" Then, with a silent, private chuckle, you can get out of your own way, and enjoy the roller coaster ride of direction and misdirection—all the while silently repeating to yourself: "Blooper's Soap IS reeeeal gooood!"

My own Blooper's Soap session happened a few years later. It was the simplest of scripts—no more than five minutes long—for Wurlitzer Corporation's annual meeting. Our audio engineer Bill Kovacs unintentionally delivered the kiss of death. "Well, this won't take long," he said to me over the studio talkback microphone, adding, "We're rolling on take 1, Harlan."

"At Wurlitzer Corpora . . . ," I began.

"Question of interpretation!" The producer shouted in my head-phones. "Whirl lit zurrrrrr!"

"At Whirl lit zurrrrrr Corporation, we're dedicated . . ."

"Question of interpretation!" She shouted, "*dedicated!*"

"At Wurlitzer corporation, we're *dedicated!* To . . ."

"Question of interpretation! Whirl lit zurrrrrr!"

And so it went, line by line, word by word, for the next two hours.

"Question of interpretation!"

"Question of interpretation!"

"Question of interpretation!"

"Question of interpretation!"

"Question of interpretation!"

I thought I'd go insane, or at the very least, deaf.

As take after take and reel after reel of audiotape piled up, we even-tually approached the final paragraph.

In a vain attempt to fend off any more "Questions of Interpretation!" I stopped, and strolled into the control room to ask her face-to-face and rather facetiously, "I'm just wondering, before we do the wrap-up, is there anything in this last paragraph you don't want emphasized?

"Not really!" She smiled.

I glanced at Bill who, seated behind her, had his head in his hands, I wasn't sure if he was laughing or crying. I dutifully underlined every sin-gle word in the last paragraph, and as I headed back toward the announce booth I noticed that Bill had written two words in the margin of his session log sheet:

Blooper's Soap

**Secretly, Roger looked forward to the agents'
annual hayride and voice demo bonfire.**

From the 1989 Harlan Hogan Voice Demo—Kurt Mitchell, Illustrator

Techniques of a Voice-Over: Making the First or Fiftieth Voice Demo—A Never-Ending Project

"When you write a story, you're telling yourself the story. When you rewrite, your main job is taking out all the things that are not the story."—John Gould, editor, *Lisbon Weekly Enterprise*

To paraphrase the quote above, when you make a voice demo—tell the story of what you sound like, and what you can do, then edit out all the things that get in the way of that story.

The perfect voice demo has become the Holy Grail of voice-over actors. "You've got to have a 'killer' demo or you're dust . . . " is the current mantra, helped along in no small measure by some voice demo producers anxious to charge thousands of dollars for that killer demo. Nonsense.

You, with the help of a good engineer, can produce a terrific voice demo without breaking the bank. If you've got the bucks to farm out your demo to someone you believe has the magic formula, that's fine, and more power to you. Personally, I'd rather take that same money and invest it in promotion and distribution of my demo. I've known several voice-overs who spent so much money producing their demos that they had practically nothing left to spend on packaging and postage.

Voice demos—the good ones—all have the same basic structure, no matter who creates them. They are simple stories with an "arc"—a beginning, middle, and end. They always begin with the "money voice." If it isn't obvious, your money voice is the sound you are hired for (or hope to be hired for) 99 percent of the time. Many people call this your "signature voice." Call it anything you like, but your basic, most employable sound and interpretative style always starts your demo—to lead off with anything else might be creative but pretty stupid. Next comes the other voices and approaches you are known, or not known, for—"the variety" section, which may include some snappy dialogue or character voices. And we end up with—the money voice. We want to leave them with another version of your most popular—and profitable—signature sound.

I'm never quite sure what people mean when they talk about "killer voice demos," anyway. If "killer" means they'll get you actually *hired*, count me in. But if "killer" means—and this is my suspicion—that it's a triumph of production over substance, a demonstration more of the art of audio engineering than of the art of voice-over, forget it.

As an occasional producer, I've found the current crop of "MTV–VH1–Quick-Cut" type voice demos I've listened to useless as serious casting tools.

Many voice-overs decry the fact that producers don't seem to be able to just cast from our voice demos anymore—a complaint I'm guilty of as well. It seems as if they want to audition every part. But when I put my producer hat on, I don't feel comfortable casting from talent demos either, unless I already know the performer's work. Listening to a voice-over perform only four to five seconds of copy, and then switch to a different approach for three or four seconds, followed by a flurry of accents and a moment of frenetic dialogue, just doesn't help me to cast. I simply don't have the confidence I need to believe that this voice-over actor can sustain a reading and interpret my copy from such short snippets. Nope, even I feel obligated to hold auditions for even the smallest of roles.

When I'm casting, it's my dime, and if I miscast a role and the client is unhappy, I pay for the redo. So most of the time I don't even bother listening to demos. I call the agents or casting directors I trust instead.

So can we create voice demos that are viable casting tools?

Absolutely, thanks to CDs and DVDs.

We have been freed from the linear limitations of tape but sometimes don't even realize it. Voice demos duplicated on reel-to-reel and, more recently, cassette tape had to be listened to in a linear manner. Most voice actors felt obligated to cram everything they could into the shortest amount of time, hoping their work would at least be listened to before the auditioner moved on to the next demo. But digital media like CDs and DVDs allow our listeners the option of random access. We no longer need to fight for their attention second by second.

One approach that I like, both as a performer and producer, is to provide two "cuts" or versions of each of your demos. The first is the very short overview of, let's say, your commercial work, followed by the same spots in longer versions at a slower pace. Plus, with so much available time on digital media, you can include all your various demo types—animation voices, dialogue, long-form, documentaries, corporate, and so forth. You can even cross-index your demo so a producer looking for a particular sound or style can zip to it immediately—for example, "perky southern girl—cut 19," and "soft sexy siren—cut 22."

It's easy to overanalyze your voice demos. Like it or not, they are always moving targets and often out of date the day they're done. You do need a really good demo to get started and to sustain voice work; it's your calling card, and you won't get an agent or very many auditions without it. But keep everything in perspective. Whether you're working on your first or your fiftieth demo, the real goal is to get *cast*, and your demo is only *one* of the tools of the trade.

Here are a few tips if you're preparing your first voice demo. You probably don't have many—or any—actual radio or TV commercials to include or even scripts to read. But you can easily create your own copy by "borrowing" from magazine ads. Like radio commercials, where a writer must communicate only with sound, magazine copywriters have only the written word to express their sales message. That limitation often leads to great creativity. You'll need to rewrite a bit, probably converting the language to the first person and making it more conversational, but in general, magazine copy can often be made into great voice demo copy.

It's often advisable not to mention the names of products specifically, for two reasons. First, a listener in an ad agency may think you have a "conflict." If you have a "fake" insurance commercial on your demo that mentions a real insurance company, the producer or writer listening might not cast you for his or her insurance client. It's usually easy to cut to another sample spot before even mentioning a particular brand name.

Secondly, this is your first demo, not a résumé. Your goal is to provide an honest representation of your voice and interpretive skills. If you give the impression that you have actually performed the commercials on your first demo by including brand names, you are being far from honest. Exaggerating will invariably get you into trouble. It's hardly worth the downside risk of starting out on the wrong foot in the voice-over business by having a dishonest demo. Soon enough, you'll have some real spots to use.

I often hear demos with "stolen" spots on them. Commercials voiced by other performers redone by a wanna-be. Bad idea. Everyone in this tight-knit community of actors and agents knows who actually did the real work. I once had a newcomer not only rerecord my Amana and Raid spots for his demo—he copied the entire back of my label word for word. Although it was hardly great prose, it had taken several hours of planning, writing, and rewriting. To see my own words on someone else's demo did not, as I'm sure you'll understand, please me.

Voice-over pros see hundreds of scripts a year at auditions and may be tempted to record one of those really good pieces of copy for their demo—another bad idea. You really have no right to use that material, and hundreds of other actors have seen the same script and just might have the same idea. Recently, while listening to the "house" voice demo of a New York talent agency, I heard the same promo spot four times. Three men and one woman all liked the audition copy so much, they put it on their demos, but in the process they sounded like rank amateurs with no real tracks to include. Worse yet, I heard the same promo copy on a Los Angeles agent's house demo. I guess it shows just how little good copy there is out there.

Once you have a "rough cut" of your demo, play it for your agent, engineers you trust and admire, and other voice talents or producers you may know. Skip the friends and relatives—they'll love everything you do, but they aren't your target market. Whether you're an old pro or a newcomer, you'll inevitably be back at the studio removing, rerecording, or reordering the elements. When you are creating the first draft, you're too close to the project to be objective; it takes a few third parties to listen with fresh ears. Welcome their help, but when it's all said and done, you'll have to make the final production decisions, get the packaging and artwork prepared, and get the damn thing out there.

Irving Thalberg, regarded as the best film producer who ever lived, followed these three rules of production:

1. "Never take any one man's opinion as final."
2. "Never take your own opinion as final."
3. "Never expect anyone to help you but yourself."

Nothing's changed.

THE VOICE TALENT'S CONNECTION—GO AHEAD,
MAKE MY DAY . . . BEEP ME!

"One ringy dingy, two ringy dingys . . ."—Lily Tomlin as Earnestine,
Laugh In, NBC

It was originally named Marietta's Answering Service and later the Talent Connection, but to Chicago voice-overs and actors it was simply called "Service." Everybody was on Service. Service could find you even when you didn't want to be found. From wake-up calls to anniversary reminders, the women at Service made sure you didn't screw up. Although always circumspect, Service somehow always knew who was sleeping with whom, even when husbands and wives were blissfully unaware of a tryst.

Service ran interference for you by screening incoming calls much better than any answering machine or voicemail ever could. I remember getting this call one day: "Harlan, it's Service. A woman just called wanting your home number. We refused, but she claimed she's your mother." It was my mother, of course, who had somehow misplaced my new Chicago telephone number, but I appreciated their efforts to protect me. When a "groupie" listener of WCLR radio started calling over and over at all times of the day and night, everybody at Service instantly knew to disregard any messages from a lady who called herself "Murph." In fact, Service became so much a part of our lives that most of us hung out at an actor-owned bar called the Boul-Mich, just because the owners, Jerry and Ron, had a free, direct phone line to Service. At least that was the excuse we'd tell ourselves.

In an era when we voice performers were mavericks, not exclusively represented by any one agent, and frequently handling all our bookings ourselves, Service was our lifeline. Service was also our actors' "Communication Command Central."

When Tom and Jane Alderman announced another of their annual "Actors' Tacky Picnics" on the shoreline of Lake Michigan, it was Service who told you where and when to show up. Service informed you, "No excuse was acceptable, and prizes would be awarded for the tackiest outfit, tackiest lunch, and tackiest mode of transportation." I still remember one actress arriving in a bright red Radio Flyer wagon, dressed in gold lamé pedal pushers, munching on a roasted turkey leg.

Service also let us know whose home would be hosting that month's "Picture Palace." A rotating, casual get-together to watch a classic movie (this was before home videos, so you rented a 16mm projector) and feast on Raisinettes, Goobers, and buttered popcorn.

Service made sure you knew when the next SAG-AFTRA meeting was, and whether you'd been invited to participate in that year's "Argyle Street Film Festival"—a party, complete with plastic "Oscars," where we'd exhibit our homemade Super 8 movies.

Service was the glue that held us all together, giving us the news:

The good: "You're booked."

The bad: "You're released."

The sad: "Bill Guthrie passed away last night."

The unthinkable: "There's been a suicide."

Three times I have heard those horrible words about fellow actors for whom the pressures of performance and life became too much to bear.

But technology was changing. Motorola introduced small, inexpensive beepers. For a voice-actor it meant far fewer lost last-minute sessions, no more carrying rolls of quarters for pay phones, and not having to call Service every hour on the hour to see if you had "anything." I wanted a beeper just to keep from feeling so depressed when Marietta or Pat would say, as kindly as possible, "Nothing right now, Harlan, call back later."

Eventually, voice-over actors almost rivaled doctors as the primary wearers of the ubiquitous beeper.

Right after getting my first beeper—it was as large, I just realized, as today's tiny cellular phones—it went off in traffic court.

The judge was outraged, demanding I come forward.

"Next time you come in my court you turn that thing off!"

"Yes, your honor," I said sheepishly.

"Does that mean you're needed in surgery or something?"

"Yes, your honor," I said sheepishly.

"What are you here for?" he said, warming up.

"Parking ticket," I said sheepishly.

"Dismissed. Give your ticket to the clerk and get out of here!"

I didn't feel I was lying exactly, only acting.

It had always been easy to pick out the photo models on the street because of their big portfolios full of glossy photos. On-camera actors were forever lugging garment bags full of wardrobe, so they too, were recognizable. But voice-overs had been tougher to identify. Now, however, the beeper was a dead giveaway.

Lounging outside Chicago Recording Company one day, my thunder-throated voice buddy Brad Bisk commented on how a beeper had become as much a part of being a voice-over as a demo tape. Having a beeper told the acting world you were busy. At least it gave the illusion that you were.

Watching five or six voice-overs scurry by, beepers strapped to their waists, Brad remarked:

"It's like that old song, Harlan."

"Which old song?" I asked, warily, well aware of Brad's acerbic but sometimes obscure sense of humor.

"That Smothers Brothers' parody of 'The Streets of Laredo.'"

It took me several moments, running the original song through my mind, and then I remembered the comedy version, with Dick and Tom singing,

I see by your outfit that you are a cowboy.

I see by your outfit that you're a cowboy, too.

We see by our outfits that we are both cowboys.

Get yourself an outfit, and be a cowboy, too!

"Got it, got it, got it. . . ." I said and laughed.

A week later I spied Brad at a huge casting "cattle call." My sons Jamie and Graham were about seven and ten years old at the time and were tagging along with me on their spring break. We entered the huge lunchroom at Universal Studios on Randolph Street that was jammed with voice-over actors and, of course, beepers.

Suddenly, I heard Brad sing out in his magnificent baritone voice, from the other side of the room, his parody of the parody:

"I can see by your beeper that you are a voice guy. . . ."

He nodded at me to continue, and realizing where he was going with this, I managed to sing back in my tone-deaf monotone:

"I see by your beeper that you're a voice guy, too."

The room was stone silent now, all eyes on us, as together we sang out,

"We can see by our beepers that we both are voice guys. . . ."

I glanced at my sons. They were saucer-eyed in disbelief as we belted out our unplanned, unrehearsed, big finish,

"If you buy a beeper you can be a voice guy, too!"

A smattering of applause, and a lot of head shaking—Brad and I loved every note of it.

My sons have finally forgiven me, just this year.

In time, sophisticated answering machines, voicemail, and cell phones eliminated the need for an answering service. The days of a real, live person on the other end of the line handling your schedule, reminding you of appointments, or waking you up were over. It was the end of our beeper song, too, and the end of Marietta's and the Talent Connection, our beloved, reliable, and very personal "Service."

Somehow, Rodger knew this was one voice demo he had to listen to...

From the 1988 Harlan Hogan Voice Demo—Kurt Mitchell, Illustrator

Techniques of a Voice-Over: All about Agents—Hearts of Gold

"They said he had a heart of gold—only harder."—William Wellman, Dorothy Parker, Alan Campbell, and Robert Carson, *A Star Is Born*, United Artists, 1937

In my experience, the movies got it all wrong. Agents are seldom steel-hearted wheeler-dealers, slamming down phones, tearing-up contracts, indulging in three-martini lunches. They are, instead, businesspeople, something most actors aren't. We love them for that and hate them for that. With a few exceptions, we actors are pretty lousy businesspeople, so while we grudgingly admire an agent's businesslike approach to our "art," we also long for an agent who'll coddle us, root for us, and attend every play we're in. We want a tough business partner and a best friend.

We want agents who'll hold out to the last minute to get every red cent that we know we're worth, but we'll be outraged if the agent holds out for every last red cent and the client casts someone else—someone less demanding.

So what can an agent do for you? Do you really need one?

A lot, and probably.

If you are carving out a voice-over career in a larger market, it's awfully hard to get by without an agent. Employers, like advertising agencies or corporate producers, often rely on agents as a sort of filter. They know that agents—like themselves—are inundated by people trying to break into voice-over, some of whom simply aren't ready or talented enough to do the job. Producers feel more comfortable booking talent through an agent they trust, since they know the agent wouldn't represent performers who weren't good enough to do the job.

Agents also provide—usually at no cost—auditions for producers, a great convenience for them. It's possible for a producer to call a talent directly to come and audition, but fairly unlikely, and increasingly unusual.

Agents offer not only a kind of one-stop shopping for voice-talent, they also do the grunt work—scheduling voice-overs once they're cast, making sure the contracts and paperwork are correct, and ensuring that the performers get paid on time. Speaking of payment, agents really come into their own when they negotiate talent payment. Your agent can certainly negotiate better terms and rates for you than you could possibly do for yourself. How awkward would it be to do that? Let's see, "Well, you know, Joe, I'm really damn good and a whole lot of other people probably want me for a similar spot, so I'd like you to pony up with some more bread . . . okay?" *Right.*

Can you afford an agent?

I don't know how you can't afford one.

Let's see, you get an auditioning service, promotion of you and the agency, your demo on the house voice demo, and maybe the agency's Web site. In addition, you've now got an expert on the often-confusing union contracts, and help with your marketing—sometimes including a mailing list of prospects.

But that's not all! Your agent will no doubt give you educated and objective guidance on your voice demos, provide a full-service accounting department, plus be a top-notch negotiator, all for a low, low 10 percent!

Union, "franchised" agents are the bargain of the century, even if you are asked to contribute to the cost of the house voice demo or to a special promotion from time to time. Go shop around and see how much you'd spend in the real world for all these services. Crazy part is that on AFTRA jobs (unless they are booked at overscale rates) you don't even pay the 10 percent commission—the client does! Nonunion agents often charge more, 20 percent and up, and like modeling agencies they "double-dip," charging a commission to the talent *and* the client. But, fact is, they too are still a bargain in real-world terms.

The question is probably not, *Can I afford an agent?* or, *Do I need an agent?* but, *How can I get one?*

Even if you've been a working (read: money-making) voice-over professional, it can be difficult to sign with an agent. Why? Because agents have to keep their stable of performers down to a size they can realistically manage. Good agents also want variety among the talent they represent, so they're not anxious to handle too many performers who are similar in sound and vocal style. And, sadly, a number of talent agencies had to downsize, or even close their doors, during the SAG-AFTRA commercials contract strike in 2000 and the following years' threat of a theatrical contract strike, so there are also simply fewer agents around.

Some, though not all, agents will represent voice-overs on a "nonexclusive" basis. They naturally will put most of their efforts into promoting their exclusively signed clients, but even being a nonexclusive client beats being unrepresented entirely. Often, it's a way for an agent to try out the relationship.

Union talent agents are franchised, which means that they are state licensed where required, bonded, and in compliance with the unions' rules governing agents and agencies. Both AFTRA and SAG maintain lists of these agents on their Web sites, which you can view at *www.aftra.org* and *www.sag.org*. SAG members are represented only by franchised agents, and the same is true for AFTRA members in most cities.

Talent agents can also be found in the phone book and in entertainment directories. The *Ross Reports*, published monthly, lists agents and casting directors in New York and Los Angeles, as does the *Back Stage Handbook for Performing Artists*. Be careful and do some homework before signing with any prospective agent, particularly nonunion ones. Ask the same kinds of questions you did when looking for a voice coach. If at all possible, talk to other actors represented by the agent and maybe even a few of the agencies' clients. There are still a few scam-artists out there.

You can get a top-notch talent agent, assuming you have all the right stuff, but as we've discussed, it isn't easy, even for the pros. You may have to get started without an agent's help at all, although that might be a blessing in disguise. Working your first jobs, and having an opportunity to "fail" (we ALL do . . .) and learn from your mistakes, will be far less devastating than if you have an agent to answer to. When you are ready and have a client or two, getting an agent will be much easier.

Almost every day when I'm at my agent's, I pass by a cardboard box about the size of a large kitchen wastebasket. That box is jammed with scads of unopened voice-over demos. The vast majority of the demos are from new-comers. Almost universally, they are in padded manila envelopes. Most are neatly addressed, and others, unfortunately, in handwriting as atrocious as mine. Many of these tapes aren't even addressed to one of my agents by name.

That's stupid.

If you are seeking a personal representation from an agent, a quick phone call to the receptionist would at least get you the various voice-over agents' names. But even with that information, your expensive voice demo that you agonized over, bored your friends with, cut and recut, is most likely languishing in a cardboard box, along with fifty to a hundred identical packages. Depressing, isn't it?

I'm not saying agents will never get around to listening to your demo—they will, when they have time, which is rare.

Sending out an unsolicited voice demo is tantamount to my sending this entire manuscript to a publisher, expecting them to say, "Wow, a book about voice-overs by someone I never heard of. I think I'll stop everything and read it!" Not even remotely likely.

So you need to call before just sending your demo, but remember that agents are busy. They're busy auditioning performers, negotiating with producers, and booking sessions. In other words, they're busy doing all the things that bring money into the agency. So unless you are a known commodity, a money-making professional they know of, expect them to say, "Send over your demo." Fair enough, but will it get listened to?

First, if you do send your demo, address it personally, and at least package it just a bit differently than the standard manila envelope.

White, pink, or blue makes it stand out from the other mailers. It doesn't matter how clever your graphics are on your actual demo; if it doesn't get opened, it's never seen. You might want to put an intriguing headline on the outside like "Surprise, the demo inside is actually worth a listen." Or "Give me two minutes and I'll make you a believer." Or, "Sure, here's another voice demo . . . BUT . . . this one is certainly not *just* another demo!"

Caution, *do not even dream* of wrapping your voice demo up as a gift. An agent I know had this happen to her. When she opened her "Christmas gift" and discovered a voice-over demo, she threw it across the room, where it shattered into a holiday tinsel of plastic and paper.

Worst of all, she made a mental note to never represent a performer that insensitive and dumb.

So don't get too cute with the outside package. But it's an advantage to be able to say to your prospective agent, after he or she calls you (that's right, they are going to call *you*), "My demo is the one in the paisley envelope." If you have arresting graphics on your demo, consider putting it in a transparent envelope, or shrink wrapping it, then dropping it off personally at the agent's.

Okay, how are we going to get this agent to call you? Two words: Bring work. That's right—bring them a booking.

I've used this technique, and it works every time.

If you were an agent, which would you rather have? Another call from an unknown talent seeking representation, or a talent who calls and says, "Hi, I'm Harlan Hogan. We haven't met, but I'm a voice-over in Chicago. I sent you my demo last week. It's the one with the obnoxiously bright yellow question mark on it. Listen, I don't have representation in New York yet, but I just got a call about a Purina Dog Chow spot, and I'm wondering if you could handle it for me?"

Of course, it's much easier to bring booked sessions to an agent if you are already working and established. Regardless, I've known a number of new talents who have used this little trick as well, when they managed to bag a local spot, or a corporate voice session. Of course, it will cost you the agent's fee of 10 percent of the gig, but that's peanuts. Now you have a good chance of signing on with that agent—an agent who can help you obtain more and more work in the future.

So, instead of putting all your energy into trying to get an agent, put all your energy into trying to get those first jobs, then *give* them to the agent you want to represent you.

How do you do it if you're unknown? For starters, call everybody and anybody you know who might help. Maybe you've got a cousin who works at an ad agency, or a family friend who's the director of advertising for the Lahlahleelu Company. This is no time for shyness or pride; call in the markers, get those first jobs, and *give them to an agent*.

Most ad agencies still do a lot of "scratch tracks"—demos of potential commercials. These "spec" commercials won't ever air on radio or TV, so the stakes are low, and creatives are more likely to try someone new. The pay is lower too, but who cares? This is a chance to get started.

Send postcards, pound the pavement, and call those school friends who work in an ad agency. Do whatever it takes. And by the way, many ad agencies have their own in-house audio studios, and getting to know the audio engineers there is a very good idea, too.

If your first employers are "signatories" to the SAG or AFTRA contracts, and you are not yet a member, there are certain rules that apply. Here's briefly how it works, but for specifics, please call the closest SAG or AFTRA office.

Under the provisions of the federal government's Taft-Hartley labor laws, in "non-right-to-work" states such as New York, Illinois, and California, you can work as many jobs under a specific union's jurisdiction for a period of thirty days from your first employment date, without having to pay dues and initiation fees to that union. After those thirty days, however, you become a "must-pay" for that union, if and when you book your next job under its jurisdiction.

For you pros reading this section, hopefully you're very happy with your present agent. But if you are changing agents, or seeking representation outside your market, my advice still stands. Consider bringing your prospective new agent your best new voice-over demo, as well as a booking.

If you want to get work, bring work.

Getting an agent, like everything about the voice-over business is a numbers game, so whether you are a newcomer or an old pro, don't sit back and wait for the phone to ring. You can, and should, talk with lots of agents and follow up with a *reasonable* number of phone calls. I asked my Chicago agent, Joan Sparks, how she felt about receiving calls from talent seeking representation. Joan said she didn't mind voice-overs calling her—she expects it: "If they aren't aggressive enough to call me, I don't see how they could ever make it in this business anyway." Don't be suicidal or depressed if an agent turns you down, though. Go on to the next, and the next, and the next, if that's what it takes.

Even if he or she is "taking a pass" on representing you, many agents will offer constructive criticism, perhaps about your demo, or they might suggest additional training they feel you need. This is good, because it leaves the door open for you to contact them again in the future. Thank them for their help, and ask if you can call back when you've redone the demo or gotten that recommended training. You are halfway home. Follow their suggestions, then go see them again. When you do, I'm betting you'll get signed and enjoy a profitable business and personal relationship—one that's hopefully a bit more successful than this one from Neil Simon's 1975 movie version of *The Sunshine Boys*:

> **BEN:** You know, this is the first time you've treated me like a nephew instead of an agent. It's a whole new relationship.
>
> **WILLIE:** I hope this one works out better than the other one.

Remember that your agent is not a free voice coach, psychiatrist, or parent. Your agent is a business partner and an integral part of the tools of the trade. There's always that fine line between business and friendship, which you and your agent need to preserve. We actors are—by nature—consummate dreamers, and we like to believe that we have a "special relationship" with our agent *du jour*, a relationship that's a little warmer, a little friendlier, and just a smidgen more personal than that of any of our fellow Thespians.

Which reminds me of an old Hollywood story about a fading actor who's summoned off the set of a "B" movie by a police detective. The detective tells the actor to sit down and take a deep breath, because he won't believe what just happened. Panicky, the actor does as he's told and the officer relates a sordid tale.

It seems the actor's agent drove out to the actor's Beverly Hills home, broke in, and shot the actor's wife, maid, and gardener dead. The actor is stunned—speechless—finally he manages to mumble, "I can't believe it."

The detective, placing a comforting hand on his shoulder says, "I know, it is unbelievable."

"You bet it's unbelievable," the actor replies, breaking into a broad grin, jumping to his feet, and shouting at the top of his lungs to the cast and crew, "Hey everybody, guess what? *My* agent went to *my* house!"

Actually, my agent did come to my house, or more correctly our house, because on July 29, 1989, I married my second wife, voice-over agent Lesley Schwartz. Hell, how else could I get her to come over?

WHAT PLANET ARE YOU FROM? BRAND MANAGERS— BE AFRAID. BE VERY AFRAID

"You know those ponds out in front of most corporate offices? Well, I'm convinced they contain an inexhaustible supply of alien pods, waiting to hatch—like the ones in *Invasion of the Body Snatchers*. Inside each pod is a being clad in a suit and tie that looks perfectly human. But these beings have no knowledge of reality, no human history, or future. They're called Brand Managers."—Anonymous.

Pam Thompson was a receptionist at a small Midwest ad agency. Her bosses were in big trouble. Their biggest account, Jeno's Pizza Rolls, was about to go south. Nothing the agency had created had pleased Jeno's. So Pam, strikingly blonde and beautiful, knocked on the conference room door interrupting a desperate creative meeting.

"I have an idea," she said simply. Most creatives are pretty protective of their turf, but these guys were at their wits' ends, so the executive creative director sighed and invited her in.

Pam quietly walked to the front of the room and—sang. She sang her version of a song originally recorded by Marv Johnson in 1960 and redone by The Dave Clark Five in 1968: "You Got What It Takes." Pam had written original lyrics, turning it into: "Jeno's, you got what it takes."

The creatives were stunned, but they liked it. So did Jeno's. A receptionist no more, Pam produced her first of probably thousands of commercials. I was lucky enough to be cast as the Jeno's Pizza Roll announcer and to meet Pam. Foote, Cone, and Belding advertising soon heard of Pam's talent and hired her to work on their S. C. Johnson accounts.

A few years later, Pam's unmistakable voice resonated through my telephone on a fall Sunday morning. "Hey, Har . . . got any plans today?"

I did, but was happy to postpone them—first, because I admired Pam's talent and unbridled enthusiasm so much, and second, Sundays pay double scale (twice the weekday session fee), so I was doubly pleased to drive on down to Universal Recording Studios.

"It's a redo on the stupid toilet paper roller spot, and you are never gonna believe this one, kiddo. See you at eleven o'clock."

We had recorded tracks on Tuesday the prior week for Glade Spin Fresh, an air freshener concealed in a toilet paper roller. Despite the dumbness of the product, I thought the spot was cute with an adorable kid spinning the roll over and over, which supposedly activated the fragrance beads. The final few seconds were an ECU (extreme close-up) shot of the kid and the roll.

Pam looked a little haggard that morning.

"The redeye from L.A.," she said, brushing her hair back. "We had to fly out, rebuild the set, and reshoot the last scene overnight, and it cost us a fortune."

"What was wrong with the original?" I asked.

"Take a look," Pam said, nodding to our engineer, Bill Reiss, to roll picture.

The spot ran, and for the life of me I didn't see any major change. My original voice-over wasn't lining up with the picture, so some footage had obviously been lengthened, or shortened, but I couldn't quite put my finger on it.

"Final shot, Harlan," Pam smiled, noting my obvious confusion. "Remember that tight shot of the kid, with the toilet paper roll?"

"Sure," I said.

"Well, our beloved client said it was too tight, and the audience couldn't see enough of the room, *the bathroom*. And that they "'won't know what room the kid is in!'" Har, you got toilet paper rollers in any rooms other than the bathroom in your house?"

"Not that I've noticed," I said, shaking my head.

"Me neither," Pam sighed. "But I guess the Glade brand manager does. Told you, you wouldn't believe it."

She was right.

The next day, ninety miles north of Universal Recording Studios, another Foote, Cone, and Belding creative was doing battle with his own little band of S. C. Johnson brand manglers—oops, sorry—brand managers.

Racine, Wisconsin, is home of the Johnson Wax office building designed by Frank Lloyd Wright. The world-famous building is unique for, among other features, its twin circular towers and the fact that instead of transparent glass windows to admit light into the building, Mr. Wright used translucent glass tubes so you can't see out. When asked why he designed the offices that way, Wright quipped, "Because Racine is ugly."

Whether that's true or not, it was getting ugly inside the S. C. Johnson headquarters building as Rick Steinman showed his latest Raid commercial for the assembled brand managers and executives. Some bright soul thought the announcer (me) wasn't mean enough on the word "dead." Another wondered what the tag line really meant: "Kills bugs fast, kills bugs dead."

"If you kill bugs fast," she pondered, "then of course they'd be dead." I have to admit I agreed, but this was, after all, advertising copy, and the line did have a nice ring to it.

A vice president of sales interrupted the meeting just as the spot was ending. With chairs sliding on the poured concrete floors, he thought he'd heard the voice-over say, "Messy Johnson Wax."

Rick assured the latecomer that I'd said, "S. C. Johnson Wax," but it was very fast since we had just tenths of a second to say it in. The agency had fought long and hard to avoid having to tack on this meaningless extra tag line and clutter up the spot, but to no avail.

The commercial featured a delightful animated Nero fiddling while Rome was burning, as the famous Raid Bugs were happily chomping on a bright red apple, until they shouted "Raid!" and croaked.

Then a portly man from legal stood up. "I feel compelled to point out in the interest of historical accuracy that during ancient Roman times apples were not red! They were buff or golden in color."

"Wow," Rick stage-whispered from the back of the room. "If he finds out bugs can't talk, we're really in trouble."

"He's much too jolly"   "Too ethnic"   "Too old"

From the 1981 Harlan Hogan Production Calendar—John Sandford, Illustrator

Techniques of a Voice-Over: All about Auditions—The Art of One-Upmanship

"Will the dancing Hitlers please wait in the wings! We are only seeing singing Hitlers."— Mel Brooks, *The Producers*, Embassy Films, 1968

It's a fact of life, maybe even death, for performers if we can believe playwright Rupert Holmes. In his *Say Goodnight, Gracie*, George Burns—one hundred years old—has to audition for God so he can to get into heaven and see his wife. As farfetched as the premise may seem, remember that the late George Burns actually had to audition for the movie *The Sunshine Boys* when he was seventy-nine. Burns, who hadn't made a movie in thirty-seven years at that time, won an Oscar for his performance as vaudevillian Al Lewis. Must have been a hell of an audition.

While waiting for my turn at a recent Thursday audition, I thought about George Burns and the fact that I, too, was getting older.

Thursday auditions are different at my agent's because Thursdays are "runway" days.

Stewart Talent Agency also owns Elite Modeling Agency, and on Thursdays all the wanna-be runway models troop in, walk a bit for Eva the runway agent, and, for the most part, troop on out. Runway models *must* fit the following description: *very young, very tall, very pretty*, and *very thin.*

There were eight or nine of us old farts, sitting in our rumpled suits, desperately trying to memorize some corporate mishmash about Motorola and its latest wireless wonder, when Eva and the wanna-bes paraded down the stairs into the waiting room.

The girls were as advertised: young, pretty, tall, and thin—too thin, for my taste, and I guess for the actor sitting next to me, too.

"You know, Harlan, I must be getting old," he whispered.

"Why's that?"

"Well, I look at these young girls now . . . and all I want to do is buy 'em a sandwich."

Young or old, your audition skills are critical to being cast, whether it's on or off camera. First, be on time, and early if possible. Once you've signed in and been given a script, take the time to really study it. Begin by asking all the pertinent questions we've talked about earlier:

- ☺ Who—what individual living, breathing, human being—am I talking to?
- ☺ Who—what individual living, breathing, human being—am I?
- ☺ What—what am I trying to accomplish?
- ☺ What—what has happened previously, the backstory?
- ☺ Where—where am I and how does that affect me?

Actors are, in general, social beings, but they are so often deprived of regular contact with other actors that it's very tempting for them to mingle in the waiting room, instead of concentrating on the job of auditioning. Don't. You can always go out for coffee later. Right now, read the copy, ask your basic questions, and look at the end of the script to see the payoff.

Don't be thrown by rather obtuse or shorthand script directions. When the script asks for Donald Sutherland or Linda Hunt or Gene Hackman, it does not mean they want an impersonation of those actors. They are giving a broad stroke idea of the quality and tone of voice they are (or think they are) seeking. *Think* Sutherland's slow, rather flat cadence, but *speak* in your own, unique voice.

I prefer not to read the copy out loud or mark it up a lot, because sometimes just reading it the first time in the audition sparks an unplanned surprise in my performance. But if you want to verbalize the script, go ahead. The wonderful thing about being an actor waiting to audition is that it's one of the few places on earth—outside a psychiatric hospital—where you can talk out loud to yourself and nobody notices or cares.

If you're auditioning a dialogue script, by all means rehearse with your assigned partner, if possible. Together, work out a mutually acceptable opening approach to the script.

Solo or double, don't overrehearse. You can get stale, and worse yet, run the risk of "locking in" a reading. You may then find it difficult, or impossible, to change your approach at the suggestion of the casting person. Take chances, make decisions. Don't be afraid to ask for direction from the casting agent, producer, or writer if they're present. More often than not, you'll be auditioning at your agent's, so take what direction you get, even though it's at least third-hand.

Once you are in the recording booth, the engineer will probably ask for a level to set the volume controls prior to recording. Usually a few lines of the script will suffice. Then you'll be asked to "slate"—usually your name, the part you're auditioning for, and sometimes your agent's name. Then, it's game time.

Here are two facts about auditions that might help calm your nerves—facts I certainly didn't know when I started:

1) **An audition is not a test of your acting ability.**

2) **Everybody—everybody—from your agent to the casting director, to the producer and the client, wants you to get the part.**

I've been on both sides of the studio glass, and no one discusses your acting skill or whether you were sufficiently "in the moment." They do discuss whether you had the right sound, the right approach, and the right twist to the copy. Everyone wants you to be "the one." Life's hard enough without casting becoming a production nightmare; they want you to get the job just as much as you do.

Most of the time, you won't get the job. Another fact. Get used to it. That doesn't mean you weren't a good enough actor; it just means that someone else seemed, somehow, more right for the part than you.

If you're given the chance to do more than one take on an audition, don't just repeat your first with a minor adjustment. A second or third take is like being "comped" in Vegas. You have nothing to lose in doing a reading that's

180 degrees different from your first take. Take a fling, 'cause you never know. A good friend and producer at J. Walter Thompson advertising candidly told me how often they have cast a voice-over who did the "wrong" reading. He said that after listening to actor after actor audition a script *exactly* the way they asked for it, sometimes someone reads the script in a way they *hadn't* asked for, or even imagined, and ends up getting the job! So taking a flyer *after* you've done the requested approach can pay off.

Auditioning and doing the actual session are two different things, although they require the same skills. Pros in particular often forget that the audition is not the job. Years of experience cloud their judgment, and they start to worry about bringing an overwritten script in on time, or scoff at the script and how "it's never going to work." Never, never forget, this is the audition, and the job—as always—is getting the job. They'll cut down the copy when the session occurs, maybe even rework its logic. Hopefully, you'll be the one at the actual session to see those changes. But you won't be if you don't concentrate on getting the job now.

Don't spend the hours after an audition second-guessing your read; move on to the next audition, and the next. Remember that your performance, and you, will be remembered even if you don't get that particular job. Many, many times I've had a writer or producer tell me things like, "You came in on that blah blah spot, but I needed a real dark, sinister sound—but I knew you'd be right for this." In other words, you might not get this particular job, but if you are professional and pleasant and do your very best, they will remember you. You don't win or lose an audition. You build a career.

I'd like to tell you that in the audition room we professional actors are always models of camaraderie. After all, so much of casting is chance. You have the right sound, the right look, or even the right friend in the upper echelons of the ad agency. I'd like to tell you that we root for one another all the time, but then again, I'd like to be able to levitate, too.

Truth is, we are pretty supportive of each other, but sometimes, just as in real life, personal feelings overcome our professional veneer. So it's not too unusual to hear a snide comment behind someone's back. "Nice to see Joe's off the sauce." Or, "Did you see 'Mount' Mary? She's so big she's getting her own zip code." But probably the all-time best putdown from the audition waiting room I've ever heard was this. A young up-and-comer spied an ascot-wrapped, old-time, full-of-himself, pontificating actor and inquired, "So, how are things in the shallow end of the talent pool?"

15

A REMARKABLE WAY TO MAKE A BUCK—PLATES, STATUES, AND THE PEOPLE WHO COLLECT THEM

"We pull advertising executives in and work them to death. And then they begin moving in sushi circles and lose touch with Velveeta and the people who eat it."—Gordon Bowen, Ogilvy & Mather Advertising

We voice-overs hope to get every job we audition for. Well, usually.

There were two scripts to record at my agents that day, and glancing over them, I couldn't help feeling I'd just sat in traffic for an hour and spent a fortune to park, all for spots I wasn't sure I'd even want to do. The first script I glanced at set my teeth on edge. It was a commemorative plate featuring the miracles of "Our Lady of Lourdes." I wasn't thrown off by the subject matter, being a very fallen-away Catholic, as much as what seemed to me the crass commercialization of the events that occurred in 1858.

The second script wasn't nearly as onerous, but still pretty corny. It introduced "The first-ever musical movie themed collectors' plate!"

"Tara, Scarlett's True Love" commemorated the fiftieth anniversary of the movie version of *Gone with the Wind* by playing the "immortal" Tara's theme. "Geesh," I thought, but I'd driven all the way down, so what the heck.

The next morning, my agent called. "Harlan, You're booked for Bradford Exchange—one spot at Swell at ten tomorrow morning."

"Great. Uhhhh, which spot?" I held my breath.

"Gone with the Wind."

I gave a silent prayer of thanks to Our Lady of Lourdes.

The agency writer and his client from the Bradford Exchange met me at Swell Pictures the next morning. Swell is, in fact, a swell postproduction facility located high in the NBC Towers building, commanding a magnificent 360-degree view of Chicago and the lake. Swell has a grand piano, pool table, a coffee and espresso bar that puts Starbucks to shame, three great audio studios, and God knows how many gorgeous film and video editing suites.

Once in Steve Wilke's studio, I ran through the spot for time and level, and we began to record. They say that a salesman is the easiest person in the world to sell, and I'm certainly proof of that. The more I read the copy, the more I became convinced that this commemorative plate was actually pretty neat, and had great potential to increase in value over the years.

I might not buy one for myself, but it did sound like these plates were top quality and, for those interested in this sort of thing, very collectible. My sister Marilan's birthday was coming up. She collects those little "Precious Moments" statues and was always telling me how much they had increased in value. What the heck, I could buy her one of these plates and start her on a new collection. After all, it was a measly $29.95.

At least, I justified to myself, a plate has some intrinsic use, and though these were almost certainly not dishwasher safe, and the music box on the back would play havoc with a microwave oven, if push came to shove, you could eat off the damn thing. My sister's Precious Moments, on the other hand, would only be useful as a doorstop in a pinch.

In fact, the script *guaranteed* that the musical *Gone with the Wind* plate was strictly limited to only 150 firing days. It all sounded so legitimate that I felt a little guilty about my snobby attitude of the day before. Imagine, thinking I didn't want to get this job.

Leaving the studio after the final take, my client reverently unwrapped one of the plates to show me. It was nicely done, despite the hokey music box.

"So these plates really are limited editions, huh?"

"Absolutely," said the man from Bradford.

"Limited to 150 . . ."

". . . to 150 firing days, Harlan," he concluded.

"And—I'm just curious—how many plates can you make in a firing day?" The client grinned, paused, and said, "Harlan, more than you could ever imagine."

A few months after the great plate collection revelation, I was booked at Streeterville Studios, just a block west of Swell Pictures, for another lesson in the power of collectibles.

My producer that day was a charming young man with long hair named Jon. Surrounded by stacks and stacks of CDs, he was just finishing choosing the music for the narration I was about to record.

"Harlan, do you know what 'Precious Moments' are?" Jon asked.

Any number of smart-aleck responses to that question leapt to mind, but I said only, "Yeah, my sister collects them."

I almost confided that I thought the whole idea seemed silly to me. Maybe not as silly as collecting plates, but I kept my opinion to myself.

The script was for the annual Precious Moments collectors' meeting, and Jon said, "These things are the number one collectible in the world." I shook my head, in disbelief.

"Man," I thought, "this is even weirder than the plate people."

Jon looked much too hip to own any Precious Moments himself, but he obviously knew all about his client and their success.

"So, here's the deal: Your voice will be used at the convention, and then they'll probably use parts of the narration at the exhibits in the chapel," he said, handing me the script.

"Chapel?"

"The Precious Moments Chapel. Just opened in Carthage, Missouri."

"There's a chapel?" I asked, wondering how come my sister hadn't made a pilgrimage yet, and imagining giant Precious Moment statues replacing the sculptures of the saints I'd grown up with.

I resisted an urge to say "Gimme a break!"

"See," Jon explained, "most people don't know that Precious Moments began as religious-themed greeting cards. Then the Enesco Corporation decided they'd make great little collectible statues."

I hadn't realized that, and felt slightly guilty for my snide thoughts about the Chapel.

"You'll learn all about it in the narration . . . Ready?"

I was, and as I read the script, I did learn a lot. Nonbeliever though I am, I was still dutifully impressed with the story of Sam Butcher, the creator of Precious Moments. He appeared to have a genuine desire to create art that combined warm human emotions with his sense of faith. I was impressed—despite myself—even though I now realized, after almost buying a collectible plate, just how easy it was to sell me.

After I finished the script and strolled back into the control room, Jon asked if my sister had any of the twenty-one original statutes from 1979.

"I think she's got six or seven of them."

"Hang on to them. They'll be worth a fortune." Shaking hands, he asked me to hang on a second as he dialed the phone.

"Hi," Jon said. "Harlan's all done. Listen, his sister's a collector, so can we? . . . How does she spell her name, Harlan?"

"It's M-a-r-i-l-a-n." I replied.

"Okay, talk to you later," Jon said, hanging up the phone.

"Sam's going to autograph his latest statue for your sister, and you can pick it up later this afternoon."

"You have just made me the hero of the Western world! I can't thank you enough."

"It's no problem, Harlan. Dad's always happy to do it."

"Dad?"

"My dad is Sam Butcher," he said, with just the slightest trace of pride.

Whew! All the disparaging remarks I almost said about Precious Moments, and the Chapel, rolled through my mind. Another quick "thank you" to the Lady of Lourdes for helping me to keep my big mouth shut.

Jon went on to become the President of Precious Moments figurines and CEO of three other companies, as well as an artist and media producer. His latest multimedia production was featured on *Oprah* recently: his completely automated and computer-controlled home.

Oh, that "collectible" *Gone with the Wind* plate has, in fact, increased in value: from $29.95 to $37.00. In comparison, if you'd "collected" one share of IBM stock for about the same price back then, its value today has increased fourfold.

On the other hand, prices for the original Precious Moments statues have considerably escalated in price. Costing $7 to $15 originally, today they fetch from $120 to as much as $1,050. So, my older sister Marilan was right. Right, maybe, but *still* older.

From the 1980 Harlan Hogan Production Calendar-John Sandford, Illustrator

Techniques of a Voice-Over: Terms of Employment—Talking the Talk

"I guess I should warn you, if I turn out to be particularly clear, you've probably misunderstood what I've said."—Alan Greenspan, Chairman, the Federal Reserve

Every business has its set of code words and phrases—like radio's "Red-*head* and the blue-*tail* fly" and voice-over's "Blooper's Soap." I've got several friends in information technology who speak a language so full of techno-jargon that I feel I'm eavesdropping on Martians.

The acting business is no different. Whether you're performing on stage, on camera, or voice-over, you've got to know the language—it's a necessary part of your training. For example, do you know the difference between *camera* left and right and *stage* left and right? What do you do when an engineer says, "How are your cans?" Do you know whether a "Class A" commercial is likely to earn enough to pay off your MasterCard—or your mortgage? You may eat doughnuts in a recording studio, but did you know you'd be reading some too, along with "tags" and "pick-ups"? Like other professions, if you don't know the "terms of employment," you're immediately labeled an amateur. Let's talk some VO: speak so you can "talk the talk." This isn't meant to be an all-inclusive glossary of recording and film terms, just some of the stranger-sounding phrases you'll hear most often.

THEY SAY:	THEY MEAN:
You're *booked* tomorrow for two *anamatics*—probably *stealomatics*—Studio 300.	You're *hired* to do two demo TV commercials that are for testing purposes. An *animatic* is a videotaped version of a storyboard, using illustrations to demonstrate how a finished commercial might look and sound. A *stealomatic* is the same, only pictures from movies and directors' demo reels are "stolen" to create the presentation.
You're *on hold* for an *ADR* session at two; they're *checking avail* and want *right of first refusal.*	You are being asked (as a courtesy) to keep time open for a *possible booking* at 2:00. They are checking your *availability* and want to be notified first if someone else tries to book you at that time. The hold is for an *Automatic Dialogue Replacement* session—also known as *looping*—replacing on-camera lines with your voice.
Bonnie called and you'll be doing one *Class A*, a *dealer spot*, and three *wild spots*—no *majors*.	The *Class A TV* commercial is going to run on the major *networks*, paying a residual every time it plays. You'll also be doing a *dealer commercial* paying

a flat fee for six months for use anywhere in the United States. A "spot" means a *spot announcement* and could run on many different programs. *Program announcements* usually air on client-sponsored television shows. The *wild* spots will run on various programs across the country. In this scenario they will not air in the *major markets* of New York, Chicago, and Los Angeles. If the wild spot did include these markets, you'd be paid more.

They might also have a *PSA* for you.

A PSA is a *Public Service Announcement* and—if it meets the strict guidelines set by the unions—it would pay a fixed fee for a set time period, usually one year.

The best they offered was a *buy-out*.

Union actors cannot, under any circumstances, accept a *buy-out*, a one-time fee *"forever" payment*.

You don't have a *conflict*, do you?

You don't have a commercial running anywhere for a *competing service* or *product*, do you? This is where the "buy-out" will do you in—forever.

They'll only pay *scale*.

The producer is unwilling to pay more than union *minimum*.

I've got a *callback* for you tomorrow at Sound Impressions.

A second *audition*, but for usually only a handful of competitors.

You've been *upgraded*.

A demo or audition you recorded is going to go directly on *the air*, and you'll be paid additional fees.

THEY SAY:	THEY MEAN:
You've been *outgraded*.	You are being *removed* from the finished commercial and will not receive any additional payments.
They're going to *lift* your tracks for the new spots.	Instead of rerecording, the producers are going to reuse your prior performance on new commercials. You'll be paid the same as if you had actually rerecorded them.
We've got an *industrial* for you tomorrow for Cineco Centrill at Studiomedia. It's a *category one*.	Your *category one corporate* (a.k.a.: *industrial*) recording will probably be used to train, inform, or promote a product or perform a public relations function and may be exhibited in a library or museum or other place where no admission fees are charged. On the other hand, a *category two* industrial program is intended for unrestricted exhibition to the general public and pays an additional fee. Corporate, nonbroadcast voice-overs do not air on broadcast TV or radio.
Thanks for coming in. Why don't you head for the *booth*, and we'll get a *level*.	The engineer wants you to go from his or her *control room* and enter the soundproof *announce booth*. You'll read a few sentences of the script so they can adjust the volume they'll be recording you at—your *level*.
How are your *cans*?	Are your *headphones* too loud—too *hot* —or too quiet?
Could you *back off* the mike a bit?	*Move* a little further away from the microphone, usually only a few inches.
You're *off mike*.	You are either too far right or left of the microphone.

Let's try a *full-read* for time and *level*.	Read the *whole script* while the engineer fine-tunes the recording *levels* and the producer sees if the recording is going to be too long or short.
Hang on while I *slate*.	The engineer will record pertinent information about the session, including code numbers and agency names via the *talkback* microphone in the control room at the start of the session. Often, the engineer will verbally number each reading or *take* just before you begin to perform. On auditions, you'll usually *slate* yourself, saying your name, the part you are playing, and sometimes your agent or contact information.
We're going to *patch in* the client.	Either via regular telephone or ISDN lines, you'll be able to hear, on your headphones, the client who is not present at the session. He or she will hear you as well, and may provide additional direction and comments.
Let's do a *pick-up*, *wild* on the last line, *a-b-c*, please.	You'll read only the last line of the script, but *three times* in a row—often called *triples*, *triplets*, *three-in-a row* or simply *a-b-c*. The producer may also direct you to *start* or *pick up* your performance from a specific point in the script, rather than reading the whole thing.
Let's do the *bookends* first.	You'll record the stock *opening* and *closing* of the commercial first.
We've got a couple of *doughnuts* for you.	Not the gooey kind, these doughnuts are blocks of script—advertising copy- that fill the center of a commercial, between the *bookends*.

THEY SAY:	THEY MEAN:
WFAA TV just called; Wally needs a bunch of *bumpers* recorded when you get home.	When you get back to your ISDN-equipped home studio, you are going to record some short announcements that *bump* up against a show and lead the viewer into, or out of, a commercial break. For example, "We will return to *A Christmas Carol* after this word from Hallmark," or, "Now back to *A Christmas Carol*, on the Hallmark network."
Got a couple of *tags* to *lay down*, and it's a *wrap*.	*Short bits of information*, like price or availability of a product, are *recorded* and *tagged* onto the commercial, usually at the end. When those are done, the session will be *wrapped* and over.

Talking the talk in any field also means understanding the culture, beliefs, and even superstitions of that business. Acting is no different. Actors—voice, stage, on-camera, and off, have plenty of longstanding superstitions and beliefs, which you need to know. As a group we're probably the most paranoid people on earth. We actors embrace our good luck charms and good luck sayings, and steadfastly believe every old wives' tale there is.

I was nine years old and about to perform my first magic act at Saint Anne's church when someone whispered to me, "Break a leg!" Back home, my mom, an ex-vaudeville dancer, explained that it was considered bad luck to wish performers good luck, so instead you say, "Break a leg!"—wishing them bad luck to ensure good luck.

"Oh, and by the way," she added, "never whistle backstage! It'll bring bad luck."

A few years later in high school, as a group of us were about to start rehearsing scenes from *Macbeth*, I was roundly "shushed" by the director, a student teacher.

"What did I say?" I asked.

"You said the name of the play," she hissed.

"Macbeth?" I said again.

"Shush!" she commanded.

Dumbfounded, I sarcastically asked, "That is the name of the play, isn't it?"

"Yes, but you never ever speak that name in a theater," she said emphatically. "It's very, very, very bad luck, so actors always refer to it as the 'Scottish Play.'"

Years later, I encountered another bit of theatrical paranoia. My agent laughingly told me she'd gotten a call that day for a "Harlan Hogan type."

"It's the five stages, pal," she said.

"I'll bite," I responded. "What five stages?"

"You've never heard of Herschel Bernardi's five stages of an actor's career?"

I shook my head

"It's an old wives' tale, Harlan."

"One," she announced, holding up her index finger, 'Who is Harlan Hogan?'"

"Two, 'Get me Harlan Hogan.'"

"Three, 'Get me a Harlan Hogan type.'"

"So I'm in stage three now?" I asked.

"Looks like it," she chuckled.

"Do I want to hear the rest of the stages?" I asked warily.

"Probably not," she responded with a broad smile, as she raised another finger.

"Four, 'Get me a young Harlan Hogan.'"

I winced but kept silent.

"Five, 'Who is Harlan Hogan?'"

I laughed back then, and I laugh today. But lately, just between you and me, the thought of stage five doesn't seem nearly as funny.

THE NINETIES' CELEBRITY VOICE-OVER INVASION—STARS, SATELLITES, AND CABLE TV SLITHER ONTO OUR TURF

"Anyone who tells you a star's voice increases sales is just blowing a lot of smoke."—Larry Postear, Writer of Honda commercials featuring Jack Lemmon's voice

By the end of the Eighties, change was really in the air, personally and professionally: a divorce, changes in technology, an improving general economy, and the "Celebrity Voice-Over Invasion," when the money trucks U-turned and headed westward.

The 1990s became a time of unprecedented growth for the U.S. economy, but a difficult decade for most journeyman actors. Celebrities, and cable TV, invaded our world.

The rallying cry at major ad agencies seemed to be "Budgets are big, so let's go produce our commercials on the coast or maybe the south of France!" Who could blame them?

"Let's see," the creative director would ponder, "I could go to L.A., stay at the Four Seasons for a month, cast, post, and finish the spot in eighty-five degrees of sun and sand, or I could stay home and hike up and down Michigan Avenue freezing my ass off."

Tough decision. The same scenario was playing out in Minneapolis, Detroit, and even New York.

Los Angeles was largely the source of another phenomenon that proved hazardous to the career health of journeyman voice-overs, even those working regularly in L.A.—celebrities. Seemingly overnight, hordes of celebrities became anxious to do voice-overs.

Of course, some celebrities had performed in commercials in the past, but usually for huge sums of money, and almost always on-camera. Performing commercials only as a voice-over was a whole different phenomenon for celebrities.

The ad agency creatives seemed to be thinking, "Wow, I can get so-and-so for my spot, at a fraction of what it would cost on-camera, but even if you can't see her—the public will know it's her!"

Meanwhile the stars seemed to be thinking, "Wow, I can make some quick money doing commercials for products I wouldn't be caught dead being associated with on-camera and—the public won't even know it's me!"

Soon celebrity voices were not only touting products and services, they even became the norm on cartoons, once the almost exclusive purview of anonymous journeymen voice-actors. Luke Perry, Elizabeth Taylor, and even Michael Jackson's voices were showing up on *The Simpsons*. Before long, celebrities were voicing the telephone callers on *Frasier*.

Did celebrity voices increase sales in commercials? That's hard to say. Certainly, unique and easily recognizable voices, like Donald Sutherland, Gene Hackman, and Robert Mitchum brought a lot to the party. Most likely, the images of the products they advertised were enhanced by their voice-overs, even if they didn't directly affect sales. Other unseen celebrity voices were so unrecognizable, though, that it's awfully hard to imagine they justified the additional expense.

Guessing the celebrity voice-over became a national pastime for a while, with newspaper articles clarifying which star voiced which product. In more demanding economic times, advertisers would have been unhappy that consumers were spending more time identifying disembodied voices than paying attention to their commercials, but the economy was great, sales were swift, so who cared?

Rick Elliott, another Chicago-based voice-over, and I were on a plane flying to an AFTRA meeting in Hollywood in the mid-Nineties. We began chatting with two young guys across the aisle. It turned out they were producers going to L.A. to record some voice-overs with Richard Dreyfuss's brother.

"It's a great deal," the one enthused. "He sounds exactly like Richard, but we only have to pay him scale!"

"Do you think people recognize Richard Dreyfuss's voice, anyway?" I asked.

"Who knows," the other replied.

"If they do recognize him, or think his brother is him," Rick added, "do you think that helps sell your product?"

"Who knows," they said together.

Rick and I just let it go at that.

The economic impact of the celebrity invasion and big production budgets was worsened by the increasing popularity of cable and satellite TV. In 1976 the average home had seven channels to choose from; by 1991 that number had jumped to thirty-three.

We performers and our unions and had vastly misjudged the impact and importance of cable TV, accepting a fixed payment for our commercials that ran on the then-fledging media in the 1980s. Seemingly overnight, cable TV was booming, our commercials were running continuously, and we were being paid next to nothing for this tremendous and often devastating overexposure.

Commercials running on the major TV networks pay a residual payment each time they run—it's usually referred to as "pay for play." Here's why. Actors are paid for their *exposure* and *affiliation* with a product. If you are, for the sake of argument, the spokesperson for Ford Trucks, you contractually cannot do commercials for Dodge or Mitsubishi or any other competing truck manufacturer. In addition, your association with Ford will almost certainly affect your ability to be cast for other, noncompetitive products. The conversation goes something like this at the casting office as you leave the audition room:

"He's good."

"Yeah, but I see him on the those God-awful Ford Truck spots constantly."

"Next!"

Think, for example, that veteran actor Dick Wilson would be cast for this same commercial? Probably not, despite his thirty-six years of experience in commercials. Why? Because Dick has had thirty-six years of *exposure* and *affiliation* with Charmin tissue, as the venerable "Mr. Whipple."

So "pay for play" on the networks protected and compensated actors for their exposure and affiliation. Cable TV commercials did just the opposite. Cable spot prices and actors' fees were so cheap that our commercials ran ad infinitum.

This disparity was the crux of the SAG-AFTRA 2000 commercials strike. The ad industry wanted to eliminate residuals on network TV while we actors wanted residuals to be paid on cable, too. It was a standoff and resulted in the longest strike in entertainment history. In the end, after over six months, residuals were retained on network TV, and cable rates increased by as much as 130 percent, but *still* without "pay for play."

As the millennium approached and one after another of the dot.com businesses fizzled, fewer celebrity voices were being heard. The booming economy started falter, and the hopes of the journeyman voice-actor and local production facilities rose.

From the 1983 Harlan Hogan Production Calendar—John Sandford, Illustrator

Techniques of a Voice-Over: Studio Smarts—Twenty Studio Commandments for VOs

"Marlon Brando slurred his words, you know. Montgomery Clift slurred his words. James Dean slurred his words. They were the greatest actors in the world, and nobody could understand a word they said."—Christopher Gore, *Fame*, MGM–United Artists, 1980.

1

𝔗hou shalt not slur thy words, nor spitteth on the microphone.

2

𝔗hou shalt not sticketh thy gum on the studio easel.

3

Thou shalt not touch the microphone—ever.

4

Thou shalt not demand unto thy producer playback of takes they did not like.

5

Thou shalt not blasphemeth thy copy.

6

Thou shalt not direct thy fellow actors.

7

Thou shalt not bear false witness that thou hast other sessions today.

8

Thou shalt not covet thy partners' parts or sayeth their lines.

9

Thou shalt not talk in the tongues of actors—speaketh not of "shaping the read" or of being "in the moment."

10

Thou shalt not make of thyself a graven fool—demonstrating all thy clever voices . . . unasked.

Furthermore . . .

11

Thou shalt arriveth on time.

12

Thou shalt honor thy producer and writer and be thee a pleasure to work with.

13

Thou shalt gird thy loins with clean clothes that maketh not noise.

14

Thou shalt remember thy beeper and thy cell phone belong outside the booth.

15

Thou shalt stayeth on mike.

16

Thou shalt committeth to silence when others are performing.

17

𝕿hou shalt understandeth thy script and accepteth direction.

18

𝕿hou shalt cast asunder thy jangling jewelry.

19

𝕿hou shalt quiet thy stomach, filling it with food, and partake of
God's little green apples if dry be thy mouth.

20

𝕿hou shalt perform thy part, signeth thy contract, and be thee gone.

The actor at the easel next to me was unquestionably talented. Despite the fact
that he was tall and skinny and about forty years old, he sounded exactly like
Santa Claus.

I'd flown to Ohio to record a series of Christmas auto parts commercials.
I know that dipsticks and lug wrenches might not be your favorite stocking
stuffers, but it takes all kinds. I was doing "announcer 101" and had just
met Jolly Old Saint Nick, who'd come in from California rather than the
North Pole.

The engineer asked him for a level, and Kris Kringle proceeded to read the
entire script, including my part, switching in and out of his Santa voice to his
announcer voice. It was a perfectly fine reading, but obviously rude, disre-
spectful to me, and in very bad form. I was half-tempted to do my best Santa
when I gave my level. But I knew nothing good would come from a "Battle of
the Clauses."

It soon became apparent that this man worked only because he was talented. Take my slightly tongue-in-cheek commandments above, and other than
jangling jewelry, Mr. Kringle did 'em all. He refused direction and made so
much noise when he wasn't speaking that most of my takes were ruined. Santa
insisted on listening to a playback of each and every take, despite the protests
of both the engineer and the producer, so the session took twice as long as it
should have. During a short break, he gleefully handed the writer new scripts,
which he had rewritten, and with a wink said, "I'd suggest you try these."

We muddled through. I've never seen so much eye-rolling and head-
shaking from the other side of the glass. As the engineer was telling us we were
wrapping, Jolly Saint Nick said, "Hang on, I've got an idea." Thoughts of missing the last plane to Chicago began to flood my brain. "I was thinking," he went
on, "that Santa ought to have some elves."

Stunned silence filled the booth as the engineer, writer, and producer tried to ferret out what he meant. Santa quickly elaborated.

"See, I could say things like, 'Right, Santa!' or maybe, 'Great gift, Santa!' or, 'I want one!' in different little elf voices." He proceeded to demonstrate his mastery of elf voices for us.

Following another prolonged silence, the producer said with a slightly sly smile, "I'll tell you what, that would be just fine." Santa beamed. "Of course we don't have any budget for additional voices, but if you want to do them as a little Christmas present to us, why then, sure."

Santa turned beet-red; he'd been caught flat-footed with his hand in the till. Had the producer not been savvy to the AFTRA radio contract, Santa could have padded his part and his paycheck big-time, since he'd be paid for each additional voice he recorded.

On the plane going home as I stuffed my sack full of frozen Skyline chili into the overhead compartment, I couldn't stop thinking about the audacity of "Mr. Claus" and his too-big-for-the-room approach to voice work. Perhaps because he was working in a smaller market, he thought he had nothing to lose by pushing the envelope, but word still gets around fast in the relatively tiny production community. It doesn't pay to not be studio smart, courteous, and honest.

Studio smarts are really just common sense. Be pleasant to work with, on time, and grateful for the job. Welcome direction, make a friend of the engineer, and when you're done, say thanks. Realize that your job may be finished, but your clients' work of mixing and finishing the tracks is just beginning, so get out of their way.

Oh, in Southern California Santa's' honor, I'm adding a twenty-first commandment: *Thou shalt not* ask thy client, "Want any elves with that?"

TALKING IN CORPORATE TONGUES—THIS MAY NOT SOUND LIKE ENGLISH

"I find it rather easy to portray a businessman. Being bland, rather cruel, and incompetent comes naturally to me."—John Cleese

Many of my corporate clients are located outside of the immediate Chicago area, and we work via phone patch, Internet, or ISDN. But when I'm booked in neighboring Milwaukee, I'm always happy to physically make the trip. I'm an avid motorcycle rider, and Wisconsin, only an hour from my home, offers so much. When the weather cooperates, riding to Wisconsin gives me a rare opportunity to combine business with pleasure. Wisconsin has scenic twisty roads, inexpensive food and lodging, a scenic river road along the Mississippi, and the north woods. Wisconsin also seems populated with friendly, unprepossessing people—with possibly one exception.

Eric was an executive with a large company based in Milwaukee. He's the kind of corporate mogul with whom I, thankfully, have very little contact. Once in a while however, someone invites his type into a recording session, and it's then that I'm grateful to be protected behind two plates of thick studio glass.

It was about 9:30 that morning. I had done the first take on a "Welcome to Our Wonderful Company" video for this organization's new employees.

The producer, writer, and project manager all seemed very pleased. I had dreams of a leisurely journey home on the back roads, after a stop in Milwaukee's third ward for a cup of Alterra coffee. Maybe, if I were really lucky, there'd be time for a quick trip down the block from Fifth Floor Recording Studios to a secret treasure trove—Select Sound. It's an unimposing blue metal warehouse that, just between us, houses one of the finest private collections of well over a thousand—mostly antique—microphones in the world. You'd never know that unless someone in the business told you, and I just did. Bob Paquette, Sr., will welcome your visit; just call first.

My dreams started to fade when the producer said, "That sounds just great, Harlan. Relax a minute—we just want to run it by Eric."

Five minutes later, a hyperactive vision of corporate America appeared, clad in those formerly trendy red suspenders (I refuse to call them braces) and a custom made, vertical-pin-striped, one-trillion-thread-count Egyptian cotton shirt with contrasting collar. The shirt was replete with a very prominent *E M* embroidered on the cuff.

I've never understood why people feel compelled to put their initials on their clothes. Is it to reaffirm to yourself that yes, indeed, *this is my shirt*, or to let others know that yes, indeed, *I'm wearing my own shirt today*.

Eric surveyed the room, nodded in my direction through the studio glass, placed his right hand on his hip, left hand to his temple, looking for all the world like a Shakespearean actor. He nodded low and deep to the engineer. About a paragraph of the track played when Eric raised his hands to the heavens and theatrically drew his index finger across his throat in an overblown imitation of the signal to "cut" from the old radio days.

I watched as all eyes focused intently on him. It seemed that they were on pins and needles waiting for his pronouncement. From the sanctity of my glassed-in fortress of solitude, I saw him reach for the talkback microphone so that I, too, could hear his verdict.

Smiling and in the most condescending tone of voice I've ever experienced, he said, "People, people go with me on this, it seems that . . . that . . ."—he looked at me blankly as someone whispered my name to him— "Yes! It seems that . . . 'Harlan,' is it?"

"Yes, sir," I mouthed restraining my natural urge to retch.

"Well, people, it seems to me that 'Harlan' is emphasizing the nouns and verbs in the sentences, and I wonder, I wonder, just what it would be like if he didn't do that!"

Silence.

More silence.

A very long silence.

While his "people" tried to find a way to respond to this nonsense, my mind raced ahead to the obvious problems with his pithy direction.

For openers, it wouldn't be English. After all what would I emphasize? Conjunctions? AND! THE! English, unlike many Asian languages, is all about nouns and verbs, and this was a video welcoming new hires to this supposedly wonderful, friendly, homespun company on the plains of Wisconsin. I could almost hear what the ghost of Orson Welles would have said. "Why? That doesn't make any sense," the great voice would bellow. "Sorry, there's no known way of saying English sentences in which you don't emphasize nouns and verbs. That's just idiotic, if you'll forgive me by saying so. That's just stupid! 'Don't emphasize the nouns and verbs.' Impossible, meaningless. I wouldn't direct any living actor like this in Shakespeare!"

I, of course, kept that daydream to myself, and I did what any self-respecting actor would do. I smiled, nodded, and said, "Sure, let's try it!"

Eric beamed. His "people" looked very relieved, and I read a few paragraphs of the script as flat as a pancake, with no emphasis or interest at all.

Eric beamed even more. He pushed the talkback button again, "Yes, Yes! Very interesting!" And with that he was gone, a corporate apparition dissolving in a blur of cotton and gabardine.

The engineer, with a wink, repeated Eric's "cut" sign. As I left the booth, I said, "Sure you don't want to do one his way?"

"Oh, no," the producer laughed, "no, no, we're happy with what you did on the first take. We just go through this every time. Last week he tried to fire a producer for the mortal sin of wearing tennis shoes to a videotaping of our CEO."

"Jeez, what happened?" I asked.

"Oh, we fired her," the producer said without emotion.

I cringed.

"Oh, only in spirit, mind you," she added. "You see, Eric didn't know she was freelance, anyway. Plus, we all know that the next time he sees her, he'll just walk up and . . ."

"Introduce himself?" I interjected.

"You got it! Welcome to our laugh-behind-the-boss's-back corporate culture, Harlan."

Donning my helmet, sunglasses, and gloves, I mounted my Beemer (BMW *motorcycles* are called "Beemers," while BMW automobiles are properly referred to as "Bimmers") and, since Eric had eaten up most of my spare time, I bit the bullet and headed south on the expressway. I was still shaking my head at his audacity, and counting my blessings that the only weird, goofy, and out-of-control boss I had to answer to was me.

Riding a motorcycle requires concentration, far more than driving in a cage. To complete your motorcycle vocabulary lesson for today, motorcyclists refer to a car as a "cage" and to automobile drivers as "cagers." There is no place for zoning out and driving along on autopilot when eighteen wheelers and cagers are mere inches from your legs, zooming along at seventy-five miles an hour.

On the other hand, driving my car on autopilot is something that happens a little too often to me. Perhaps you've had the same experience. I'm not talking cruise control, here. I'm talking autopilot. You find yourself at the exit for home, *but* you don't remember getting there. It's a little scary.

It's also a little scary that the same thing happens to me in long narration sessions.

My friend and client Gaylord Viller's sales training audio programs took eight to ten hours to read. Knowing how long the finished programs would be, Gaylord rightly insisted the scripts be read as rapidly as possible. But the faster you read something, the more likely it is you'll screw up, and since this is all rip and read work, total concentration is crucial. It's not that the scripts were necessarily dull or boring, just long—long on facts, long on detail.

> **VO:** . . . The formal sales message provides key product information for the customer. But depending on where you are in the sales process, you may decide that a formal sales message isn't necessary. Every call, however, should include a dialogue, because that is your best opportunity to discuss your products in terms of customer needs and interests. Of course, you'll need to use the skill of probing to determine which product or service might best fulfill the client's needs, and don't forget to. . . .

Inevitably, somewhere in the sixth or seventh hour of recording, my conscious mind started to shut down, and I'd slip into verbal autopilot.

One minute, I'd be reading page 133, and the next thing I'd know, I'd be breezing along on page 148. I'd glance up, expecting to see Gaylord and his client laughing at me for dozing off—or talking in tongues—but no. They would be happily reading along, making notes, and sipping Diet Cokes and coffee. Realizing what just happened, I'd keep droning on and on for another couple of hours. Meanwhile, I'd have several more Twilight Zone autopilot experiences until the blessed sound of "That's a wrap."

Autopilot is the all-time best way to narrate a script. Instead of slaving over piles of copy, I can mentally lounge on the Beach at Maui, sipping a piña colada, with autopilot-directed words pouring forth automatically.

I spoke to several top narrators and, after a little coaxing, every one admitted that they, too, had experienced an "auto-reading" ability at least once during their career. And every narrator also agreed that life would be so sweet if we could only figure out how to do it on demand.

Scientists have actually studied this phenomenon. Author and professor of psychology at the University of Chicago Mihaly Csikszentmihalyi calls it "flow" in his book of the same name. It's full of case studies, controlled experiments, and references to famous figures, philosophers, and scientists, all of whom believe humans can re-create this "in the zone" autopilot state at will.

Personally, I think it's just an occasional fortuitous accident, aided by just a touch of magic.

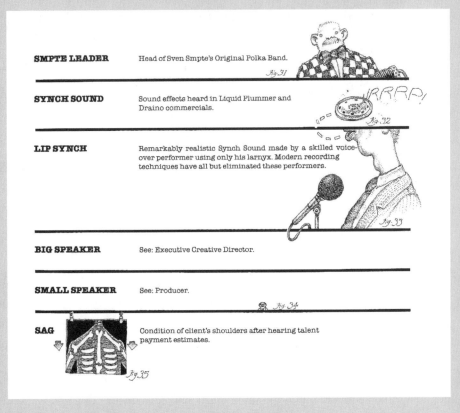

SMPTE LEADER	Head of Sven Smpte's Original Polka Band.
	fig. 31
SYNCH SOUND	Sound effects heard in Liquid Plummer and Draino commercials.
	fig. 32
LIP SYNCH	Remarkably realistic Synch Sound made by a skilled voice-over performer using only his larynx. Modern recording techniques have all but eliminated these performers.
	fig. 33
BIG SPEAKER	See: Executive Creative Director.
SMALL SPEAKER	See: Producer.
	fig. 34
SAG	Condition of client's shoulders after hearing talent payment estimates.
	fig. 35

From the 1984 Harlan Hogan Production Calendar—John Sandford, Illustrator

Techniques of a Voice-Over: All about Unions—To Join or Not to Join? That Is the Question

"Informed, passionate members and their solidarity is our biggest asset. The union cannot run itself. It is you. It is me. It is a theater student in Idaho who someday will be a member."—William Daniels, Former President, Screen Actors Guild

"Preunion." It's an interesting word born of interesting times, and interestingly, it changed almost everything I thought about union performers versus nonunion performers. That one word—"preunion"—removed "versus" from my vocabulary.

I don't know who coined the term "preunion," but I know it came to be during the commercials contract strike of 2000, and it speaks volumes about the history and tradition of the labor movement and how it has changed, adapted, and sometimes failed to adapt in the twenty-first century. In prior strikes "we" the union members regarded nonunion performers as our enemies, rather than seeing them as ourselves not very many years before—a time when we, too, weren't members of SAG or AFTRA.

As the strike stretched on and on, the Screen Actors Guild offered an unprecedented opportunity to nonunion—whoops—preunion performers. In return for eighty hours of service to the unions' strike effort they could become eligible to join SAG, without the normal requirement of being booked for a part under its jurisdiction. In Chicago alone, more than one hundred performers accepted and completed the challenge. As of this date, practically all have gone on to work under union contracts.

The offer marked a turning point and a change in attitude within the performing unions that can only be good for all its members and soon-to-be members.

So, should you join SAG and AFTRA?

There are a number of factors to consider, and no one, certainly not I, can decide for you.

No one should be in a hurry to join. You need to take some time, get some experience, and talk to other voice-overs and your agent. Honestly evaluate your progress so far, and whether you see acting as your long-term career. Geography will also play a part in your decision. Larger cities have more of a union presence, while in smaller markets and in some so-called right-to-work states, there are fewer union jobs. And joining SAG or AFTRA isn't without considerable cost.

First, you'll be paying an initiation fee and initial dues. Each union will require an investment of well over a thousand dollars. More often than not, the cost of joining one of the unions exceeds what you'll earn on your first union job. From then on, twice a year, you'll pay dues, based on your earnings. You'll also be agreeing not to accept any more nonunion jobs. If you've developed some nonunion clients, it won't be easy to turn down work and money.

But joining SAG and AFTRA isn't without considerable benefits. In addition to guaranteed minimum fees and residuals—and standard contracts limiting your exposure—the unions make sure you get paid, and paid promptly, for your work. They also provide medical, dental, and life insurance, as well as pension benefits for members who earn certain minimum amounts each year. By the way, those benefits are paid for by your employers, and they are exceptional. My son Graham needed life-saving heart surgery when he was three months old. Just last year, my wife Lesley needed a total hip replacement. In both cases we paid next to nothing, with SAG and AFTRA picking up the tab. For me, joining SAG and AFTRA has always been a win-win proposition.

Both unions also invest time and money in furthering your career with regular workshops, seminars, and often a place to hang your hat between sessions. For example, Chicago's Kaufherr Center is all that and much more. The center is available to any member, every business day, and has it's own recording studio, video equipment, and computer with Internet connection, plus a meeting room and lounge.

Union members are also eligible to join the AFTRA-SAG Federal Credit Union, one of those oh-so-rare financial institutions that likes to see on loan applications under Occupation: Actor. The credit union offers lower interest rates and even a credit card. There is also the psychological boost of declaring yourself a professional and joining a large group of peers.

When you're ready to make the decision, visit *www.sag.org* and *www.aftra.org*, and read everything. You'll learn a lot, including the location of the nearest office. Don't hesitate to call and ask all the questions you're bound to have. Some locals even offer regular seminars for preunion actors. They'll tell you "everything you ever wanted to know about the unions but were afraid to ask."

Still, by joining together, we've managed to ensure ourselves not only a decent living wage and health care coverage, but retirement benefits as well, in preparation for when that fifth stage in an actor's career—that "Who is Harlan Hogan?" stage—inevitably sets in.

ADVERTISING IN THE TWENTY-FIRST CENTURY—TOO HIP FOR THE ROOM

"The first rule of modern advertising is: Never reveal what it is you are advertising."—Dave Barry

Although motorcycles can't carry a lot of cargo, my BMW R1100 RT has more storage than most and can, if pushed, hold almost a dozen six packs of Schlitz beer. Actually, I could cram all but two of those cans of Schlitz aboard, and though I like an occasional beer, I found myself leaving the spare cans on the doorstep of the discount liquor store in New Buffalo, Michigan. I chuckled at the sign in the store's window that said they sold "Strong Beer." I assumed the sign referred to regular beer, compared to that wimpy 3.5 percent alcohol beer we teenagers were often "forced" to drink twice as much of back in the 1960s.

I'd love to tell you that I abandoned the spare cans of Schlitz because I'd never, ever dream of drinking a beer and then operating a motorcycle. But the truth is, I loathe the taste of Schlitz. It once ranked as one of America's favorite brews, but the formula changed, and now it's almost unobtainable, with good reason. On the other hand, I loved my father, and he loved Schlitz—to literally his last dying day.

At eighty-nine my dad knew as much about advertising as anyone in the world. Forget that he worked in the steel mills, drove a Chevy, and still drank Schlitz. No, my dad knew more about the sorry state of advertising in the late 1990s than anyone.

I'd spent the weekend sailing in Michigan, had scored the Schlitz, and stopped in Lansing, Illinois, on my way home to drop it off and visit. Dad was, as usual, ensconced in his brown Naugahyde chair watching the Cubs lose.

I've always counted myself lucky that he was a Cubs man. I never had to check the paper for stats regarding a game I find tiresome. Instead, I could safely hug my dad and just say with feigned sincerity, "How 'bout those Cubs," shaking my head sympathetically.

This visit, however, he was giving me a sympathetic headshake.

"I think I see what you've been talking about, son. Advertising really stinks!"

He was referring to my most recent rant on the necessity of having what's called a "loose brick" in your TV ads. Simply put, although copywriters have only 29.5 seconds in which to sell a client's product, many—assuming they are hip and cool—must also eat up some of that valuable time making a hip and cool statement with a so-called loose brick. Loose bricks are elements in a commercial that are total non sequiturs: words, music, or visuals that are unexpected, unexplained, and unexplainable. It's "unadvertising": advertising designed not to sell products, but to impress your coworkers and the creative award juries who hand out the advertising equivalents of Academy Awards. Jim Morris, in Chicago's *Screen Magazine* aptly dubbed it, "Huh? advertising."

Rick Fizdale, former chairman of the huge Leo Burnett Company advertising agency, agreed with my dad. A memo of his quoted in a Chicago newspaper article said, "I believe in taking creative risks . . . but I detest, as you should, advertising designed to impress juries and make us appear cool and above it all." He goes on to wonder if "our creative department is populated by artless seventeen-year-olds playing at advertising."

My father instinctively knew how ridiculous this unadvertising was. In his innocence, he said, gesturing to his omnipresent TV, "Look, I'm eighty-nine years old, and I know these ads aren't aimed at me. Heck, I still drink this stuff," he toasted me with his can of Schlitz. "But you know, I watch these ads and . . . and . . . I don't know what it is I'm supposed to do." Six months later he was dead, but his salient comments on modern advertising lived on.

In *Charlotte's Web*, E. B. White spins his wondrous tale of life after death, postulating that a piece of us continues to live on and on through others. Well, I think my dad would get a big bang out of knowing that not long ago, my friend Jim Stephen, President of Weber Stephen Products, quoted him.

When Jim's advertising agency presented storyboards chock full of loose bricks and practically no mention of the qualities and features that have made Weber grills the undisputed finest in the world, he repeated my dad's words.

"These ads remind me of a comment made by a very wise expert on advertising," Jim said. "When I see these commercials—I don't know what it is I'm supposed to do."

Needless to say, he sent the agency scurrying back to produce commercials that sell his family's grills, ads that tell consumers precisely what it is they are supposed to do—buy. Dad, your voice lives on.

The time has come, the producer said, to talk of many things: of soaps and oils and deodorants... and dirty bathtub rings.

From the 1985 Harlan Hogan Production Calendar—John Sandford, Illustrator

Techniques of a Voice-Over: Persistent Self-Promotion—From PR to the Post Office

"In a post office . . . wear a bulletproof vest, and don't make fun of the guy who talks to himself."—Craig Hartglas, *501 Survival Tips* (Citadel Press, 1994)

I'm in the Northbrook, Illinois, post office today buying stamps. Sometimes it seems that whenever I'm not in a studio, I'm buying stamps for one promotion or another. I know I could get a postage meter or buy stamps online, but where's the challenge, excitement, and danger in that?

This is a pretty sophisticated suburban post office. They even have one of those bright red "Take-a-Number" ticket dispensers. I guess it brings a note of civility to the waiting crowds, and no doubt cuts down on fistfights as customers while away the hours, reading and rereading the FBI's most wanted list.

As I'm killing time, I'm reminded of a very clever trick I saw a senior citizen pull in a southside suburban bakery. He shuffled in, took a look at the crowd, and then surreptitiously picked up a discarded number from the floor. The counter girls were up to number ninety-seven at that point.

"Number ninety-seven?" one barked, "ninety-seven, ninety-eight?"

"I have number sixty," the old man creaked.

Even the hardened heart of a teen-aged-after-school counter girl was melted. "Oh my God," I could almost hear her thinking, "Pop's been standing there clutching number sixty in his hand for the last half hour!" Everyone turned to the old man in silence, nodding to him, relinquishing their place in line to this stalwart, this septuagenarian, this prince among men.

"That deceitful old bastard," I thought, but admiring his nerve, I too remained silent. Secretly, I promised myself to one day try the old man's scam, but instead, today, I've resigned myself to waiting with the other lemmings till my number was finally called. I elbowed my way to the counter and asked for six thousand twenty-four-cent stamps.

"Six thousand?" The government-pensioned counter woman asked.

"Self-stick," I added. "They have to be self-stick." (I talk for a living, after all, and the very thought of licking that many stamps was enough to give me dreaded "dry mouth" for a month.)

"What are you going to do with six thousand stamps?" the clerk said incredulously.

"Look for voice work," I *thought*, as I surreptitiously patted my chest to make sure my bulletproof vest was still in place.

"Send postcards to my . . . my policyholders," I *said*.

I swear I heard a muffled "insurance man" as she turned, shook her head, and ever-so-slowly shuffled the ten feet to the oh-so-distant stamp vault.

If you want to do voice work, the *work* is *getting the work*.

Sticking stamps on promotional postcards and demos in hopes of getting booked isn't very exciting, but I'm confident it beats selling insurance or working at the post office. Promotion is the price of admission to a successful long-term career, and there are three musts:

1. Persistent self-promotion
2. Relentless self-promotion
3. Continuous self-promotion

There, I've said what most voice-overs don't want to hear. We may communicate for a living, but most of us don't want to accept the fact we've got to communicate—and communicate constantly—with our prospects to get hired.

"I'm an artist—I shouldn't have to promote."

"I'm an established pro—I shouldn't have to promote."

"I'm so busy—I don't have to promote."

"Business is so slow—there's no point in promoting."

Denial.

Denial.

Denial.

Denial.

Every voice-over from the bottom to the top and back down again has to promote. The streets are littered with terribly talented voice-overs that made a terrible mistake—they stopped self-promotion. Careers, like scripts, have an arc—a beginning, middle, and end. Remember the old wives tale—the five stages of an actor's career? Well, we want to prolong the "Get me Harlan Hogan" middle stage as long as possible. The only way to do that is to constantly, consistently, and persistently promote. Don't become the voice-over actor that says, "All of a sudden the bottom dropped out, and now I can't afford to promote."

There are hundreds, if not thousands, of books for small businesses (that's us) on promotion, and I'll recommend several. Bottom line (see, we're already talking like corporate moguls) is that most of our promotion will fall under five general categories:

1. Face-to-face contact—known in the real world as sales calls.

2. Public relations—usually articles or mentions in industry and general-interest publications.

3. Direct response—targeted marketing sent to prospects like postcards and voice demos.

4. Advertising specialties—"giveaways" like stopwatches, mouse pads, coffee cups, and the like.

5. Advertising—buying space in periodicals or establishing a Web presence.

When I started as a voice-over, "rounds," or direct face-to-face visits with potential employers, were common. Today, at least in major markets, it's almost unheard of. Producers and writers use agents as a filter before they even consider including a performer on an audition, let alone actually sitting down with a talent and listening to his demo. But sometimes—if you handle it right—and particularly in smaller markets, a direct sales call is still possible.

You've got your demo ready, and you've scoured the yellow pages for advertising agencies, film or video production companies, or organizations who just might need a voice for their phone system, trade show, or training video. So pick up the phone and call. Yeah, I know, easier said than done. Remember, you do have something of value to offer and if you get to the right prospects, they will be interested, assuming they need your services. So, go ahead and pick up the phone.

My pal Steve King had success using this self-effacing approach. "Hi, I'm a voice-over talent, and I'd love to stop by and drop off my demo, but I promise, actually insist, that we don't listen to it together. I'll just say hello, and if I'm in your office more than two minutes, it'll be because you made me stay." Thanks, Steve, that's a great way to put it.

You'd be smart to use some basic sales skills when you've finally gotten through to your prospect as well, like "yes-yes" questions. "Would it be better if I came by Monday or Thursday?" "Would afternoon or morning be better?" Corporate marketing programs have been using simple techniques like these for years, and they work. I know, because I've voiced hundreds of them.

PR, or public relations, is often a cost-effective way to build your name—or "brand"—recognition. Well-placed articles about you create an image of success and desirability that often translates into bookings and money in your pocket. Public relations also has the appearance of being third party. It's not you bragging about your phenomenal rise to the top, it's the newspaper. You can do a lot of your own PR, writing press releases and so on, but you may find you need a professional to get them placed in important periodicals. That will require an investment on your part and a certain willingness to take a chance. Unlike buying an ad or mailing a postcard, there are no guarantees those articles and mentions about you will ever appear in print or be seen by a prospect. Even if they are, there is no guarantee that the exposure will result in more work for you. All your friends and relations will see the article and be dutifully impressed, but who cares if nobody calls. That's an inherent risk of public relations, but the largest, most successful corporations in the world have huge staffs dedicated just to PR, so you be the judge. As for me, public relations has always paid off, way beyond the admission fee.

Direct-response advertising often means mailing postcards, letters, calendars, reprints of PR articles, and voice demos directly to likely prospects. Direct-response advertising targets the specific potential employers out there—the writers, producers, and marketing communications managers—who have a high probability of hiring you. The stumbling block, for most of us, is developing the mailing list necessary to reach these potential employers, but it's not as difficult as you might think. Standard Rate and Data (SRDS), for example, publishes books that list advertising agencies and broadcast stations. Both NAPTE and Promax have lists of radio and TV stations, and don't discount the yellow pages, traditional and online, as a source for prospects to add to your database. Your agent, if you have one, may also have a list available to you.

You'll need to build a database of prospects and clients as time goes on, so you can contact and mail to these likely prospects regularly. There are lots of computer database programs out there; I've had good luck with Approach— and, more recently, Act. Both help you to assemble, manage, contact, and mail to your prospects on a regular basis—and regular, persistent contact is what it's all about.

Advertising specialties—"giveaways" like stopwatches, mouse pads, coffee cups, and the like—are usually a reminder of you and of how well the session went. Giveaways are a wonderful promotion and a small present to your present clients, but they don't reach the *potential* clients who haven't yet heard or hired you. To reach these clients, you'll still need good, old-fashioned advertising.

Advertising—buying space in periodicals or establishing a Web presence— is tried and true but can be expensive. By nature, advertising is "scattershot." Although your ad will be seen by many potential employers, all too often the bulk of the people exposed to your ads will not be potential employers. Indeed, it sometimes seems that in actor-oriented periodicals we spend our money promoting ourselves to—ourselves! Pretty silly, but gratifying to your ego.

Each of these five promotional techniques—or weapons—are at your disposal within the limits of budget and desire, and it's up to you to decide (or guess) what the right approach is for you.

Most professional marketers would advise you that *all* these and other techniques need to be used by you—over the long run—to promote your business, the business of you. What promotional tool you choose will be based on your "sales strategy" and whether you are a wanna-be, a newcomer, or an experienced professional.

Sales strategy is one of those terms—like database—that sound complex and sophisticated but really aren't. Your sales strategy in voice-overs is exactly the same as it is in any small, medium, or large corporation. Sales strategy consists of just three goals:

1. Get new clients.
2. Do more business with your existing clients.
3. Keep your existing clients.

That's it. Your self-promotional efforts are the *tactics* you choose based on one or more of these basic sales strategy *goals*. The next time you cop an excuse like, "There's no new work right now, why spend money on promotion?" Realize that the point of your promotion in slow times may only be to expand and keep the clients you already have, not necessarily to find new ones.

All your promotional materials, from voice demo cover art to ads in trade periodicals, must look professional. Remember that we're advertising and promoting to advertising and promotion pros. Amateur artwork will brand you as an amateur. It's not necessary to spend a fortune on four-color graphics—simple, professional-looking black-and-white artwork is fine. Skimp on dinner, change your own oil, skip a few first-run movies, but don't shortchange yourself on the appearance of your promotional pieces; they are a direct reflection on you as a professional voice-over actor.

I'm a big believer in the power of "positioning." Actors might think of positioning as a kind of typecasting, and typecasting is a very bad thing. Or is it?

When I was starting out and facing tough competition from established voice-overs—as do you—I figured I'd be typecast anyway as a young, conversational-sounding voice. It seemed reasonable to me that if producers wanted a voice-over who sounded older, deeper, or more unusual, they'd cast someone older, deeper, or more unusual than me anyway. So, I chose the unique selling proposition that I was "the voice of the baby boom," positioning myself as the voice of the (then!) young baby-boom consumers. It worked—I positioned myself as *the* conversational-sounding young voice.

Al Ries and Jack Trout are business authors who first championed the concept of positioning. They believe your mind contains a limited number of "slots" that a product or service attempts to fill. If your potential client already has six or so voice-overs in his head under the label "young female," then your challenge will be to either "dislodge" one of those names with yours, or create a *new* category with available slots, like "quirky young female" or "raspy young female." The theories behind positioning are fascinating, so do yourself a favor and read *Positioning: The Battle for Your Mind*.

While you're at the bookstore pick up any—or all—of the *Guerrilla Marketing* books. These are the best-selling series of books on marketing, and with good reason. *The Guerrilla Marketing Handbook*, for example, is practical, thought-provoking, and aimed at individuals who sell to other individuals—like us.

Don't forget that self-promotion continues even after you've done a session. A nice thank-you card or a giveaway promotional item like notepads or pens is always appreciated. Don't go crazy, though. You're thanking a client, not bribing one. A producer at a large ad agency once told me how embarrassed she was to receive a dozen long-stem red roses on her desk from a young new voice talent she'd used the day before. "I knew the roses cost half what we paid him, and I spent all day being teased about 'my new boyfriend.'"

So use a bit of discretion and never get too important or too humble to promote. I said it before, and I'm about to say it again: Long-term success requires three thing—persistent self-promotion, relentless self-promotion, and continuous self-promotion.

19

PRESCRIPTION DRUGS AND THOSE PESKY CONTRAINDICATIONS—SIDE EFFECTS WORSE THAN YOUR DISEASE

"The indiscriminate use of such words as 'safe,' 'without risk,' 'harmless,' or terms of similar meaning should not be accepted in the advertising of medical products on television stations."—National Association of Broadcasters Television Code, 1969

I love mandatories.

A mandatory is a short voice-over "tag" at the end of a commercial. It's required information, like: "an equal opportunity employer"; "member FSLIC"; "prices may vary in Alaska and Hawaii"; "parental supervision required"; "read label and follow directions"; "void where prohibited"; and the granddaddy of them all, "batteries not included."

Often, we voice-overs serve as audible disclaimers, the spoken equivalent of the "fine print"—like "substantial penalty for early withdrawal"—that, come to think of it, works well for banks and certain pharmaceuticals. Naturally, sponsors don't want to spend any more of their precious and expensive airtime on trivial details than they have to, so most mandatories and disclaimers are delivered at lighting speed.

Lately, voice-overs have had even more mandatories to record. As Richard H. Kolbe, marketing professor at Kent State University, points out in the January 2001 *Consumer Reports*, two out of three primetime TV commercials contain some fine print, often accompanied by a voice-over explanation. On the radio, of course, there's no choice but to have a voice read the mandatories. With the current glut of prescription drug advertising, reading the contraindications—the possible harmful side effects for pharmaceuticals—has brought voice-overs some new mandatory work.

With my macabre sense of humor, I find it funny that after fifty-five seconds of stunning commercial footage touting the incredible benefits of drug X, someone like me then has to point out that all those benefits are not without risks. Saying, "Side effects include nausea, constipation, dizziness, inability to urinate, black or bloody stools, and risk of addiction . . ." just as fast, and in as serious a tone as possible, is darkly humorous.

Before those commercials are produced to foster consumer demand for the latest prescription wonder drug, though, the drug manufacturer must train a small army of salesmen and -women called "detailers." Their job is to make face-to-face sales calls on doctors. The detailer's goal is always the same; get those physicians to write "scripts"—prescriptions—for the company's new product.

Many pharmaceutical companies produce sales training audio programs for their detailers. That way they can listen and learn in their cars, while driving from appointment to appointment.

It was delightful to be working with Steve King on one of those programs a few years back. It's always more fun to work with a close friend, and as an added benefit we were able to take one car to the studio, which was inconveniently located in the far western suburbs of Chicago. I was cast to play a doctor in dialogues with an actress we both knew well, while he would provide the "glue"—the continuing narration—that explains and summarizes the results of each dramatized sales call.

The three of us were seated at a card table in the studio, and as the engineer adjusted the microphones, Steve and I both started scanning the several hundred pages of script. Meanwhile, the actress got up, tripped, regained her feet, and then asked where she could get some water. Returning, she sat down, glanced at the scripts, and then managed to spill her glass of water all over the pages. We helped her blot them off, and we all laughed, grateful it hadn't been coffee.

For the actress, and myself, this was an easy gig. Steve had all the work, cold reading four or five paragraphs of technical information, while we had the luxury of reading ahead and studying our next piece of dialogue.

On our very first interchange, there was a problem. The actress stumbled over several lines. I figured she must just be a little nervous and would do better as she warmed up. But take after take went by and she was having problems stringing the words together.

Soon, the engineer stopped the session and came into the studio to ostensibly "adjust her microphone." Knowing that the clients couldn't hear us back in the control room, he confidentially said to the actress, "I'm hearing a lot of lip-smacking sounds, can I get you an apple or fruit juice?"

"That would be lovely," she said. Then, to us, she confided, "I don't know what it is, but I've got such a case of dry mouth lately."

We were, of course, sympathetic to her plight. By sipping some fruit juice between dialogues she managed to continue without too much "mouth noise." But still, she screwed up line after line, botching almost every take.

Glancing up during one of Steve's narratives, I saw that she wasn't even reading ahead in the script. In fact, she looked as though she was about to doze off. On the next take, her speech sounded slightly slurred. I suggested we take a bathroom break.

Sitting back down at the table and seconds before Steve started to speak, the actress reached into her purse and got out her knitting needles and yarn. While Steve was slogging his way through the chemical makeup of Tricycyclic Anti-Depressants, our actress friend was clicking away with her needles. Finally my friend Steve, as even-tempered as they come in a session, just couldn't take it any more.

"Cut," he said, and glancing through the studio glass he swiped his index finger across his throat in the traditional, "turn off my microphone" gesture.

In a steely tone he informed the actress that:

"A: Your constant fidgeting with the knitting needles is distracting me. B: Please just sit still. C: It wouldn't be a bad idea to study the script while I'm talking, so we can get out of here sometime during our limited lifetimes."

More takes, more stumbles, more dry mouth, more slurring of words, and now she was actually twiddling her thumbs during our dialogue.

We were, however, almost finished, and Steve began his wrap-up.

"Today, we've reviewed the mechanism of action of Tricyclic Anti-Depressants, and their efficacy. Now let's examine the contraindications for Tricyclic Anti-Depressants. "The most common side effects include: unsteadiness, dry mouth, drowsiness, inability to concentrate, dysphonia—slurring of words—and undirected, rapid small motor activities."

I just stared at my script. It was obvious she was taking this drug! I knew that if I looked up at Steve we would both dissolve in a gale of laughter. There would be plenty of time to giggle all the way home in the car.

That ill-fated session was fairly early in my career as a TV doctor, and I've had lots of opportunity since to brush up on my diagnostic skills. Even my beard, which made me pretty much "uncastable" in corporate videos, recently turned into an advantage when Advocate Hospitals chose me to play an on-camera physician for their TV campaign. The producers and their clients loved the beard and raved on and on about how much I looked like a real M.D.

Of course, looking like a doctor and thinking like one are two entirely different things. Steve pointed this out to me recently as he and I were once again grousing, kvetching, and complaining about business—and that week's lack of it—at the Cherry Pit, an ill-named restaurant in Deerfield, Illinois, halfway between our homes. He was quite concerned about his wife Connie's health. As he described the symptoms, I found myself almost shouting, "I've got it!"

"Got what?"

"Helicobactor Pylori!"

"Is that on the menu?"

"Steve, I just did this whole audio program on H. Pylori. It causes 80 percent of stomach ulcers and 90 percent of duodenal ulcers. They only discovered it in 1982, so a lot of doctors still don't know about it. Has Connie been tested?"

He didn't doubt me and called home on his cell phone.

"Connie? Harlan wants to know if you've been tested for . . . for . . . ."

"Helicobachter Pylori, H. Pylori," I prompted.

"H. Pylori . . . Really?"

Hanging up, Steve shook his head, laughed, and said, "Alright, I guess lunch is on me. Her doctor called an hour ago—to schedule her for an H. Pylori test!"

Happily, it turned out Connie didn't have an H. Pylori infection, and from now on, I vow to only play doctor. I've shelved my plans to turn our rarely used breakfast nook into my examining room.

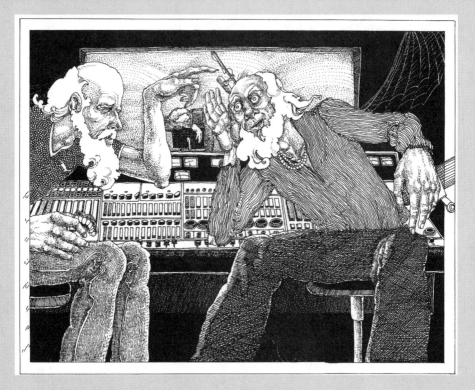

From the 1980 Harlan Hogan Production Calendar—John Sandford, Illustrator

Techniques of a Voice-Over: Preserving the Tools of the Trade—Although I'm Not a Doctor, I've Played One on TV

"Once you taste this coffee of mine, you'll know nothing worse can happen."—Philip Yordan, *The Day of the Triffids*, United Artists, 1963

Although it's true that more than forty of the wildly popular 1960s *Flintstones* cartoons were recorded at the irreplaceable Mel Blanc's bedside after his almost fatal car crash, it's unlikely any producer would do the same for you or me. Nobody did "Barney Rubble," "Dino," and "Bamm Bamm" like Mel, and the seven months he was confined to bed were too long for producer Joe Barbera to wait.

But the late Mel Blanc was *the* Mel Blanc—the voice of Bugs Bunny, Daffy Duck, Woody Woodpecker, and Porky Pig. You and I are for the most part journeymen voice workers and—like it or not—pretty easily replaced if we become sick or injured.

If you regularly go to sporting events and join in screaming "Give me an *I*, give me a *D*, give me an *I-O-T!*" Well, you deserve the sore throat in the morning. Your clients—however—deserve you, without the raspy hoarse sound, so use some common sense.

Headaches, broken bones, stomachaches, and hangovers don't qualify as being sick—not to a voice-over actor. Laryngitis, or the loss of hearing or sight—now that's being sick and too sick to perform. God willing, none of those things will ever happen to you.

If you should develop a severe sore throat, bad enough that you'd consider going to an emergency room, there is some new medical help. Mayo Clinic researchers have discovered that the steroid dexamethasone dramatically eases the pain. Obviously, you'd need a prescription and wouldn't want to take any steroidal medication unless it were absolutely necessary, but it's nice to know there is some relief available. This was a recent discovery, so your physician may not even be aware of it, but now you are.

Every so often, no matter how careful you are, you are going to wake up with a big, fat, sneezey, runny-nose, sandpaper-throat cold. What will you do?

First, be considerate of everyone else around you, from fellow performers and engineers to your agent. No kissing, hugging, or coughing, and please stash those tissues in your own pocket or the trash. Try not to touch anything. You can work through almost any cold, so don't panic. But if you really sound bad, so bad that you are afraid you'll show up and they'll have to cancel the session, then by all means call the producer or your agent and cancel.

If you're confident you can fake it, then first and foremost, tell your engineer privately. Generally, don't tell the producer—they are usually paranoid enough. The engineer can do wonders with electronic settings like "EQ" and make you actually sound pretty damn good.

I've found taking echinacea at the first sign of a cold or flu works wonders and often stops the onset of a cold *cold*, if you'll pardon the pun. It may be psychosomatic, but if it works, who cares. You can't take echinacea all the time, though, or you'll build up an immunity to it, so stop when the symptoms disappear. Many people—my wife Lesley among them—swear by the Neti Pot. It's a little "tea" pot that you can pick up in most health food stores. The Neti Pot lets you rinse your sinuses out with a water, salt, and baking soda mixture. Many voice-overs swear by a gargle of warm salt water, and others brew up some hot tea with lemon. I've gotten through many a session by spraying my mouth with Chloraseptic between takes. Right after Thanksgiving, I began to feel a cold coming on and tried Zicam homeopathic Nasal Gel. It's claimed to reduce the longevity of a cold and less than two weeks later I'm a believer. Getting a flu shot should naturally be on your must-do list, but be careful of over-the-counter cold remedies. Some can make you drowsy, and often the decongestants in them will dry out your mouth.

There's also a serious health danger lurking in every recording studio. Despite the best of intentions, once in a while, you'll get "zapped" by an ear-piercing shot of feedback through your headphones. This is no laughing matter, because temporary or even permanent hearing loss can result. Please don't ever put headphones on until the engineer tells you to, *then always wear only one*. Personally, I think your performance with only one headphone will be better and less self-aware, but from a safety standpoint, if an accident were to occur, at least you haven't blown out both ears. If the cans are too loud, perhaps because the prior performer liked them hot, don't hesitate to ask for them to be turned down. If you play in a band, shoot handguns, or ride motorcycles, you must wear hearing protection. A great site to visit for more information about protecting your hearing is *www.hearnet.com* run by the Hearing Awareness for Rockers, a nonprofit organization started by a musician and a motorcyclist.

We all know smoking, listening to loud music without earplugs, and screaming at rude cab drivers is pretty silly, especially for people who make their living talking. On the other hand, although some caution with your voice, hearing, and general well-being is important, don't become overly fixated. There is more to life than work.

Back in her vaudeville days my mom came pretty close to hooking up with this bass player named Skippy. But there was one problem: Skip was so worried all the time about his precious hands that he just wasn't any fun. He wouldn't go roller-skating, wouldn't go bowling, wouldn't even finger-paint. So my mom dumped him like a worn-out bag of rosin. Skippy—like us voice-overs—needed to keep work and life in perspective. I'm grateful for his phobia, though. Lord knows, if they'd gotten married, I could have been ended up being named little Leapy or Hoppy or Stumbly.

THE FINE ART OF DIRECTING VOICE-OVERS—REAL VOICE MEN DON'T ASK . . .

"When I use a word it means just what I choose it to mean—neither more nor less."—Lewis Carroll, *Alice in Wonderland*

"And we're on take 62, rolling on 62."

I could see small beads of perspiration break out on Jerry Betram's face as we tried to make sense out of this dialogue radio commercial for a local telephone directory.

Take after take, as we tried harder and harder to please the producer, we got farther and farther from what he had in mind. It seemed so simple, so easy. Jerry was playing a salesman. My part was a guy looking for a computer. Jerry kept explaining that all I really needed was the directory. But take after take, our producer asked for "more character, more character!"

"Character voice" to a voice actor means: French chefs, Bronx cabbies, leprechauns, German psychiatrists, and creatures of all sorts, from squeaky chipmunks to rumbling elephants.

Try as we might, none of the characters Jerry and I dredged from our vocal bag of tricks worked. We broke for coffee, and I smiled weakly at the producer.

"Actually," he said, "you guys were closer on take 1. I just need a little more character."

"Got ya," I said, which is actor response number 174 to anything we don't comprehend.

"You know," he went on, "more character, like a couple of real guys just talking."

"OH MY GOD!" He wanted real people—a slice of life—just two plain Joes talking. We were giving him thugs, trolls, and parakeets. Back in the studio I winked at Jerry and mouthed "Real People." He nodded, and we were finished in two takes.

Directing voice actors is far from easy. Unlike music, there are no notes and scales to indicate precise pitch and tempo. One misconstrued, misperceived bit of direction can send you swirling close to the event horizon, to be sucked into the black hole's abyss.

Almost all of the great, funny, outrageous, and sometimes sad war stories in the voice-over business are the result of "errors" in direction. Having sat on the opposite side of the glass, recently, producing spots and interactive games I've written, I have to admit I have a new appreciation for the fine art of directing—without suppressing—talent.

Don't get me wrong. The obvious flip side of *misdirection* from a writer or producer is *misinterpretation* by us actors, but that's still another book—one I'll let someone else write.

Some people just seem to have a gift for direction, like writer-producer Jack Badofsky. Jack directs with phrases like, "Harlan, think of that 'now' as a finger raise, a caution," instead of giving obvious direction like: "Hit that *now*!" or, "Be sure to raise your voice on *now*!"

Other producers and writers are, unfortunately, masters of *another* kind of direction: the kind magicians are famous for—misdirection. David Bamberg was the most celebrated magician in South America. He, like his father Theo, masqueraded as a Chinese court magician. Many people never realized that Okito and Fu Manchu were descendants of seven generations of court magicians, but to the kings and queens of Holland, not China! Go figure.

The Thief of Baghdad was one of David's (Fu Manchu's) most popular tricks. Standing surrounded in the audience, he would carefully thread a long ribbon through a hole in a solid plate of glass, while weaving a delightful story of a pickpocket so skilled that he could never, ever be caught. Two audience members held the ends of the ribbon, and as he reached the point in his story when the glass was to be magically "stolen" and released from the ribbon, Bamberg would manage to distract the audience. A cymbal crash, or a flickering stage light at just the critical moment was enough. As he told—and retold—the story of the famous thief, performing the trick over and over, the distractions became bigger and bigger and bigger. Finally, a shot would ring out from the stage-left balcony, a woman's scream would echo through the theater, a body would fall from the balcony to the floor, and . . . and . . . and . . . when the audience finally turned back to Fu Manchu, he was standing with the plate of glass free once more. Fu Manchu smiled in triumph, and bowed to the applause and laughter. It was a masterpiece of humor and—misdirection.

Misdirection is by definition at once subtle and wildly off base. It's the producer who says, "Now as you read this, remember you are a sweater—*but* not just any sweater—a WOOL sweater!" Or consider the well-meaning client who spent thirty minutes of $600 per hour studio time explaining my inner motivations and my career path from fledgling accountant to CFO before a narration:

"Harlan, I want you to imagine that you are the chairman of our company. You probably attended Princeton, or maybe Harvard (fat chance). Later, you worked the client side, but still you always felt that you could someday migrate into management if given the. . . ."

Perhaps she watched *Inside the Actor's Studio* one too many times. The truth is, if you ask most voice-overs their motivation in reading a script, nine out of ten would say, "My paycheck." It's not that we're jaded, just practical.

During a recent audition for an insurance company gig, voice-overs were asked to be "young and hip, with medium energy, sincere and slightly innocent, with wry humor that gives it an edge without being sarcastic." An audition this week for the voice of a weathercaster asked for "your average weather woman, with a wet voice."

But even once voice-over actors get cast, thoughts of future residual checks won't help focus their performance if the producer is leading them down a garden path from which there is no escape:

Yes, Jay, but I need a little more warmth to the reading—without losing your aggression.

I'll need much more of that approachable authority, Bob.

You're selling it too much. Back off, Joel . . . but be sure to hit that "'sale ends soon'" line a lot harder.

You don't get it, Anne. You have to sound as if you would never, ever buy this stuff.

Put more puke in it, Tom.

We need 10 percent less sex, 20 percent more intimacy, and 90 percent more energy. Oh, and we're three seconds long, Al.

Chris, give me a lot more whimsy, but with an ironic touch.

Much more conversational please, Kathy, especially on the "'Members FSLIC'" line. Think of yourself as just one of the tellers telling a friend about the bank, and this, this great club you all belong to.

C'mon, c'mon, you know what to do . . . just double throat it.

The winner in the misguided misdirection contest has to be Brad Bisk's Zenith TV session. The copywriter had painstakingly marked each word in his script with a different colored highlighter. The writer had included a color legend in the margin of the script:

Blue = A cool, relaxed phrasing.

Red = Hot, now, really hit the words!

Yellow = Slow down here.

Orange = Keep the pace halfway between Red and Yellow.

And so on. You gotta give the guy credit for trying to avoid misdirection, but he'd also handcuffed Brad into a stiff, mechanical reading.

Occasionally, a less-than-candid performer takes advantage of the inherent difficulties in directing actors. One nonunion narrator had developed a remarkable "misdirection" scheme. He charged only about two-thirds of the going rate for top union narrators, so on the surface he seemed to be a real bargain.

A warm, congenial fellow, he'd immediately sit down with the producer in the control room instead of heading for the booth and getting to work. Pulling an orange highlighter and a black felt-tipped pen from his pocket, he'd spend the next hour or so going over each and every word in the script.

"Shall I go up on 'excellence,' or down?" "Get real dramatic on 'new challenges' or soft?" He dissected each line, ad infinitum. By the time "Mr. Let's-Go-Over-the-Script-First" was finished marking, and finally reading, the script, he'd often doubled and sometimes tripled his fee.

The scam was short-lived. Soon, all the recording engineers in town knew what to expect and found subtle, and sometimes not-so-subtle, ways to get him into the booth. Richard Hawksworth of Broadview Media had the best solution. " I just removed any 'spare' chairs from the control room."

I thought it was brilliant; that way, the "talent" (and I'm using the term loosely) would have no choice but to head for the mike.

From the 1989 Harlan Hogan Production Calendar—John Hayes, Illustrator

Techniques of a Voice-Over: You, Yourself, and the IRS—The Business of Show Business

"An 'entrepreneur.' That's what you're called when you don't have a job."—Ted Turner

Get out one of those yellow legal-size pads, we are about to make some lists. Let's title this, for the sake of argument, "Important Record Keeping and Supplies—IRS." We'll do everything on the former to avoid the wrath of the latter.

This list will contain only some of the supplies you'll need to get started and some of the records you'll need to keep in order to be in business for yourself. DISCLAIMER! I am not, nor have I ever been, an accountant or attorney, though I have played both on TV.

First thing on your list, therefore, is to schedule a talk with an attorney, or at the very least a good accountant, about your business. That's right, like it or not: the *business* of voice-over is exactly that, an honest-to-God business, full of niggling details and intimidating questions, from what tax records do I need to keep, to should I incorporate. Wanna-be, newcomer, or pro, this is a must-do first step.

Just for openers, you'll need the following supplies:

- A separate, business-only checking account and, if possible, a business-dedicated credit card
- Access to or your own computer with an Internet connection, an e-mail account, and a printer
- A fax machine or the ability to receive faxes on your computer
- Cell phone, beeper, or both
- An answering machine
- An adding machine
- A hundred or so voice demos
- Résumés
- Headshots, if you perform on-camera as well
- Business cards, thank-you cards, letterhead paper, and envelopes
- A date book—electronic- or paper-based
- A desk and a file cabinet
- A stopwatch—preferably one that doesn't beep—for practice and for use in sessions
- Some kind of voice recorder for practice

Now, with your basic setup in place, add a manual or computer-based system to invoice clients and keep track of whether or not you've been paid. Starting out, two folders marked "Unpaid" and "Paid" may suffice. As your business grows, you'll need "tickler" files to remind you if a payment is overdue. There are a number of small-business software programs than can help simplify these basic bookkeeping chores.

Be sure to keep a folder or envelope stuffed with every receipt for everything you spend in pursuit of work, from taxis to trains, buses to parking. Remember, your first and last trip of the day is not deductible. Keep receipts for classes, promotions, voice demos, and advertising, plus agent's commissions. All these receipts are needed to create a "paper trail" to prepare your taxes and in case you are audited.

Keep track of business-related telephone expenses, which are deductible. I have a separate phone line at home dedicated only to business. Years ago, I dialed (312) 427-5264 and found it was a disconnected number. I've had it ever since. This number—"312-HARLAN-H"—has served me well not only because it's easy for my clients to remember, but also because having this business-only telephone line makes it much simpler for me to account for business-related telephone expenses. Ideally, you'll also have a room, or at least a specific area, *exclusively* used for business if you want to take advantage of the home-office deduction on your taxes. Be sure you consult with your tax advisor because there are stringent Internal Revenue Service requirements. If you do qualify, by all means take the deduction.

Finally, you'll need to set up a database of some kind. That's a just a fancy term for a list of prospects and clients and maybe some information about who they are, if you've talked to them or promoted to them, and what the results were. That's information you can simply keep on another yellow legal pad. If you are more computer savvy, you may want to use one of the more sophisticated computer-based databases.

Starting out, you will probably just set yourself up in business as a sole-proprietor. Later, your business advisor may want you to incorporate for various tax benefits.

Do remember that the IRS does not allow you to deduct costs associated with a hobby—they expect you to be able to prove your deductions are reasonable and in pursuit of income. It's also smart not to get greedy or too imaginative in filing your taxes. Save the creativity for the studio.

A decade or more ago at an AFTRA-SAG panel discussion on tax strategies for actors, actress Daphne Maxwell-Reid, who went on to star as Aunt Viv on *The Fresh Prince of Bel-Air*, and Eartha on *Linc's*, was curious as to just what deductions the IRS would accept as career related. Daphne, who was gorgeous and the first black woman ever to appear on the cover of *Glamour* magazine, asked the accountants and tax lawyers, with a characteristic twinkle in her eye, if she could possibly deduct the cost of a trip to Mexico.

"Well, only if you can prove it's a necessary expense to seek work or further your career in some manner," was the reply.

"Here's the thing." she said. "I'm so light-skinned I don't get cast for many black roles, so I thought a week or two in Acapulco working on my tan might help." After some laughter and a brief consultation, the panel's advice was this: "Although you might justify that expense to the IRS, it'd be equivalent to tying a red helium balloon on your tax return labeled, 'Please Audit Me First!' so, we wouldn't recommend it."

One more personal tip. When I finish recording, I fill out the multipart union contract with a rubber stamp containing all my pertinent information: Corporation Name, Federal ID number, Social Security number, and so on. I've been teased unmercifully about it.

"Gee, too busy to fill out the forms, Harlan?" I've heard from other actors.

"Wow, you're working way too much Harlan!" I've heard from producers. I laugh, because the truth is so stupid and mundane they'd never believe me.

My handwriting stinks. There are deer tracks on our front lawn in the snow right now, which are far more legible. I've not only played a doctor many times, but have managed to replicate their handwriting. So I bought a rubber stamp after what I've come to call "The Harlan incident."

For the first ten years I was a voice-over actor in Chicago, most producers just picked up the phone and called us directly, saving themselves the 10 percent agent's fee. Hardly any voice-overs were exclusively represented by only one agent.

Slowly but surely, agents became more and more important, as more and more voice-overs entered the field. It was becoming necessary to choose one agent to sign with. And so, one particular agent was in a full-court press, wooing me. One day, as I was stopping by to pick up some money, she said she'd noticed that my checks were made out to "*Harian* Hogan."

"Yea," I said. "It's my fault. My handwriting is abysmal. I've called the ad agency, but they can't seem to get it corrected."

"Well!" she exclaimed. "I can fix that! You know, Harlan, no one exclusively represented here would ever have their name misspelled on their checks!" (Hint, hint, hint . . .)

"It's okay, I can cash 'em." I said.

"Hang on," she commanded while dialing the phone.

She proceeded to "straighten out" the accounting department at DDB Needham advertising, all for my benefit.

"The man's name is Harlan . . . got that? *Harlan* . . . H-A-R-L-A-N . . . *Harlan*!" Hanging up, she smiled demurely and said, "That's the way we handle our exclusive talents, Harlan. *We* solve problems, so *you* don't have to."

The next checks from DDB Needham were made out to "Harian *Harlan*"!

I could no longer cash the checks.

I spent hours on the phone with DDB Needham before I finally solved the problem.

I didn't sign with that agent.

I bought a rubber stamp.

I suggest that you add one to that ever-growing list of business essentials on your yellow legal pad—your Important Record Keeping and Supplies—the "IRS."

21

BEHIND THE SCENES—THE REAL WORK BEHIND VOICE WORK

"If you're going to be a bear, be a grizzly bear."—Richard M. Rodnick, Advanced Systems, circa 1976

"Talent Phone" was my first exposure to the potential convenience and power of the Internet as a casting tool, way back in 1976.

There was, of course, no Internet in 1976 that I was aware of, but the future was right there in Talent Phone's tiny offices on Michigan Avenue.

For a modest fee, Talent Phone would put your voice demo on a tape cartridge (essentially an 8-track, minus the other seven tracks) and clients could call in on the phone and hear your demo instantly. It worked well, as well as listening to voice demos today on talent agency and individual Web sites.

Over the Talent Phone door was a sign: PROMOTE OR DIE.

Technology put an end to Talent Phone, just as it did to Marietta's Answering Service, but not to the truth of that sign. "Promote or Die" is permanently etched in my head.

Due to my inherent shyness, I felt quite uncomfortable calling directly on writers and producers when I was starting out as a voice-over. So I put a lot of energy into direct mail promotional pieces, the kind I'd written and produced back at ASI. Once again, skills I never thought I'd use as an actor were becoming a real advantage. Voice demos of the day were universally reel-to-reel tapes in standard-issue five-inch white cardboard boxes. Voice-over actors usually just wrote their names on the edge with a felt-tip pen; instead, I printed up a simple self-stick label for my first tape. It was embarrassingly bright fluorescent yellow, but it seemed to work: it made me stand out from the crowd, if for no other reason than my garish color choice. Soon, I popped for a full-color custom-made box, and it more than paid for itself in increased business.

Over the years I experimented with ads in trade magazines and some public relations articles, but I always seemed to have the best results with direct mail pieces aimed directly at my clients.

Twice I had Harlan Hogan Stopwatches manufactured, and both times they were a hit with advertising creatives. I gave away more than a thousand over the years. Imprinted with my name and phone number, they provided "top-of-mind" advertising for me at the very moment a writer might be rough-timing his copy, reading it aloud before he had decided on casting.

Mouse pads have been a successful "'leave-behind'" promotional item the last few years as well. But the hands-down best, most talked about promotion I've ever done was the Harlan Hogan Calendars. In 1977 I decided that a calendar of some sort might be an effective promotion, so with the help of artist John Sandford, I created what I thought would be the first and only Harlan Hogan Production Calendar. One thousand copies were printed and distributed. Almost immediately, people began asking me what next year's calendar would be like. In ten years the circulation grew to four thousand, and to five thousand by the final calendar in 1994.

In seventeen years we had a lot of fun at the advertising industry's expense. Our parodies included everything from "The Discovery of Voice-Overs" to "Ad Stuffs," a snooty imaginary mail-order company. Advertising horror films, cable TV infomercials, top ten lists, even send-ups of old comic book ads like "I was a 97-word weakling 'til I took the Charles Adjective mail-order course . . . ." The Harlan Hogan Production Calendars developed quite a following, and I've included some of my favorite calendar illustrations throughout this book.

One of my favorite calendars happened almost by accident back in 1982. John and I were kicking around ideas for the next year's calendar (what screenwriters call "spit-balling"), bouncing ideas back and forth. We weren't getting anywhere and took a break. As John's wife Frances was pouring us some coffee, John started complaining about a multi-media startup company who'd "stiffed" him on some artwork. John held up this incredible, fanciful piece of illustration. It was a very different style for him, almost a woodcut, but done with pen and ink. The picture was of a grasshopper complete with video camera, clapboard, tape recorder, top hat, and a spaceship in the background. It was stunning, very much an illustrative style you'd expect to see in a high-quality children's book.

"I'll buy it," I said. "And eleven others in the same style. Now, let's do a rabbit as a producer."

"With a stopwatch?" John said, taking notes.

"Perfect. We'll do penguins for the account executives, dancing hippos for talent."

"A unicorn for the art directors," John suggested.

"Yes, John, a strange mythical creature just like you," I laughed.

And in less than five minutes we were done.

I'm still using much of this great artwork; it's that gorgeous. We added no captions or funny lines that year—letting the art stand on its own.

Shortly after the calendar was published, John used the artwork as samples to begin his now prolific career illustrating and writing children's books. He has illustrated over fifty books and authored four, including best-sellers like *Tales of a Tail*, *Moostick*, and *Happy Birthday to Me*.

Many other voice-overs, like me, give out small advertising specialties as a thank-you at sessions—coffee cups, memo pads, pens, candy, Koosh Balls, even a vibrator (but not *that* kind). Sometimes, however, busy recording studios begin to resemble my mom's living room on Christmas morning when we were kids, with all the gizmos, treats, and gadgets lying around. Chicago seems to have more of this kind of self-promotion than other markets. A Los Angeles voice-over coach once remarked that "Chicago voice-overs give away so many trinkets, it looks like they're running for election."

Walking into the control room at Avenue Edit one day, a fellow voice-over was overwhelmed by the junk left behind by the actor ahead of him. Facing a room of six people, each holding a pyramid of candy, pens, pads of paper, refrigerator magnets, and Slinkys, he was aghast. He was also empty-handed. Chuckling, he reached into his wallet and began distributing five-dollar bills to everyone saying, "Here, go buy yourself something you really *want!*"

Despite all the promotion we voice-overs do, we rarely include any photos of ourselves. It's not that voice actors are necessarily camera shy, or not photogenic, it's that we deal—like magicians—in illusion. The listener fills in our faces, our age, hair color, shape, and size in his or her imagination. Sometimes seeing a performer simply spoils the illusion.

Here's an experiment. You know those Little Caesar's Pizza spots, where the animated character says "Pizza Pizza"? That rough, tough, gravelly-voiced actor also created the voice of "Bluto" on all the *Popeye* cartoons, as well as "King Leonardo." Don't watch TV or cartoons? Well, if you've ever seen Woody Allen's films *Take the Money and Run*, *Bananas*, or *Radio Days*, you've heard this voice, not to mention scads of Paramount Pictures newsreels over the years.

Now, what do you think the person behind those deep resonating "pipes" looks like? Is he skinny or fat? Tall or short? Old or young?

In my mind's eye I'd always figured that voice belonged to a beefy, six-foot-four, forty-to fifty-year-old, weighing at least 250 pounds and most likely sporting a George Burns official-issue White Owl cigar permanently clenched in his teeth. But I was wrong—very wrong.

When I had the privilege of meeting the man behind that voice a few years ago, I was shocked to discover it belonged to a charming, energetic, and sophisticated gray-haired man, about five feet two, who didn't weigh more than 170 pounds soaking wet—Jackson Beck.

Enjoying a lobster dinner with fellow voice-over Reed Farrell and Jackson in Greenwich Village, I was fascinated by his wonderful war stories, and his wonderful voice. He told me what it was like to be a voice actor in the Golden Age of live radio shows like *The Adventures of Superman*. "Faster than a speeding bullet, more powerful than a locomotive, it's Superman!"

Discovering my interest in magic, Jackson recalled the time when—as the announcer on the popular radio mind-reading program hosted by mentalist Joseph Dunniger—he'd accidentally discovered one of Dunniger's most prized secrets. He also let Reed and me in on a secret of his own. He was born in 1912 and is still working, still sounding tough as nails, and still sounding fifty years old at best! So just because a voice-over sounds rough and tough, or soft and sexy, or old or young, doesn't mean he looks that way. For most voice-overs, the smart bet is to keep their appearance a bit of a mystery.

Occasionally, seeing a voice-over rather than just hearing a voice-over can affect a session even *after* it's cast. Jay Rose, a well-respected director and recording engineer of over ten thousand commercials tells a delightful story about his voice actress wife Carla in his book *Producing Great Sound for Digital Video*.

Carla, as both an expert with dialects and part Swedish, was booked as a Scandinavian spokesperson for Howard Johnson motels. As the session went on, the producer kept asking Carla to "sound more Swedish," but despite her adding more and more Swedish accent and even throwing in a few jokes and ad-libs in Swedish, he still wasn't happy.

In truth, the problem wasn't Carla's accent; the problem was that she didn't *look* Swedish. Somehow, the producer just couldn't *look* at this tall brunette and *hear* a Swede. Luckily, the recording engineer realized what was happening and moved Carla to a corner of the studio where the producer could no longer see her. He bought the very next take.

What you see is not always what you get when it comes to voice-overs. With that in mind, most of us remain just a bit camera-shy.

①Alarm clock goes off on producers' heads waking them up. They turn on console ② as racehorse, hearing sound of bells dashes into studio with copy. ③ He drops it on easel in exchange for carrots, ④ frightening vulture perched on easel who cues talent by nesting in his hair ⑤ Rabbits spot vulture and pull talent to easel as ⑥ Matilda connects cables and mops up.

DESIGNER _John Sandford_ APPROVAL _H² OK_ APPROVAL _Boss OK_ (_Let's take a look at it, rough, loose, drawing..._)
PROJECT TITLE _1980 HYGENIC STUDIO INITIATOR/STIMULATION SYSTEM_ PROJECT # _472-6550_

From the 1980 Harlan Hogan Production Calendar—John Sandford, Illustrator

Techniques of a Voice-Over: A Studio of Your Own—A New Opportunity, a New Convenience

"Everybody has his own theater, in which he is manager, actor, prompter, playwright, sceneshifter, boxkeeper, doorkeeper, all in one, and audience into the bargain."—Julius C. Hare and Augustus W. Hare, *Guesses at Truth*

What's tax deductible, convenient, saves you money, can make you money, and might also get you more voice work?

It's not a new agent. In fact, the odds are likely you already own a large part of this moneymaking, convenient magic device. It's a recording studio of your own, and if you have access to a computer, even an older, slower one, three-quarters of your in-house recording studio is right there in front of you. Assuming you're like most actors, you probably find the thought of recording at home either intimidating, expensive, or unnecessary. After all, aren't there enough recording studios in the world? And you have no desire to compete with them. Besides, as a serious actor, you likely feel confident discussing the subtleties of Meisner's versus Adler's approach to acting, but probably think "proximity effect" is a sci-fi movie and an "XLR" is a radio station in Jaurez.

However, recording at home in a studio of your own offers you many opportunities to save, and even make, money—and you don't need a Ph.D. in recording or computers to do it. Truth is, with modern audio software recording and basic editing is as simple as writing a letter in a word processor. All the basic functions of copying, pasting, and moving text remain the same, but now you're moving blocks of audio instead of blocks of words.

First, you'll save money producing your voice demos. Using an audio editing program, you can "rough-cut" your demo over and over again until you are ready to have it professionally finished by a top-notch audio engineer. The game of "what if?" is usually the most expensive part of creating a new demo, but by moving elements around at home until you and your agent are happy with it, you can greatly reduce your final studio bill. I do recommend you have a professional finish your demo and prepare it for CD-DVD mastering, but now you'll only be buying an hour or two of his or her time.

Secondly, assuming your agent is connected to the Internet, you can record auditions or even sessions at home or on location, never missing an opportunity simply because you're in North Carolina shooting a scene with Nicole Kidman. (It's my book, I'm allowed a minor fantasy.) Instead, back in your hotel room, you'll fire up your laptop, plug in the mike, read the script, and e-mail it back to your agent or client. If your computer has a CD-DVD burner, you can also record your tracks to it and just overnight the disc.

Thirdly, as your skills and confidence evolve, you may develop clients who want to record finished audio tracks with you, but who are on a tight budget. They'll cast you because (a) you're talented, and (b) you have your own studio, and that saves them time and money. Are you in competition with major recording studios? Hardly. You are, however, filling a "niche" market, and at the same time making the rent. By the way, this scenario has been in place in the United Kingdom for years; most voice-overs work from home studios, usually connected via ISDN phone lines.

Amazingly, the electronics and computer revolution means you need very little money to build your in-home studio. I already mentioned that you'll need a computer, but a fairly slow 200 megahertz or so "old" computer will suffice. I discovered that adding a second hard drive to my old computer worked wonders to speed up recording and editing. You install the recording software on one drive and record on the other, which improves performance remarkably. Here again, costs for gear have plummeted and hard drives are inexpensive.

Recording software not only gets better every day but also gets less and less expensive, with more and more professional features. "Lite" versions of many popular digital recording programs like Sound Forge, Cake Walk, Peak, and Cool Edit are less than $75, and there's even a free version of Pro Tools available on the Web. Most audio programs can save your auditions in the MP3 format, so you can simply e-mail them. Considering just the cost of parking in a major city for auditions, recording equipment can pay for itself in no time, let alone the wonderful convenience.

Before you buy any recording software, go online and download various trial versions and experiment with them to see what you find the easiest to use. Make a friend of a local recording engineer if you can and offer to pay him for his time in helping you choose equipment and set up your studio.

In addition to a computer, you'll need a fairly quiet room in which to record. You don't need a *totally* soundproof room, but the sound of busses, airplanes, and weed-whackers in the background aren't going to cut it. Walk around and clap your hands until you find an area where there aren't any obvious echoes. For simple auditions, almost any room will work. If you are recording finished tracks, then you'll need a more professional setup. I purchased a "Whisper Room" sound booth, but many voice-over actors, like Mike Matheson, have assembled great-sounding studios in their homes or apartments at little cost. Mike drove over to the local home center and picked up two dirt-cheap plywood doors to close off a portion of a small spare bedroom. He covered the area and the doors with acoustic foam, and voilà: a studio of his own. Three or four doors can also be hinged together, covered in foam, and turned into a portable booth.

Ask that friendly engineer for an old copy of *Mix Magazine* or *EQ Magazine*. Inside are lots of ads for sound equipment companies like Sweetwater and Full Compass. You'll also see ads for sound-absorption and sound-shaping supplies. Auralex Accoustics, for example, offers a readymade, inexpensive "studio in a box" and a free booklet entitled *Acoustics 101*.

Of course, some browsing on the Web will provide you with plenty of suppliers to choose from, and I've included some names and numbers in the resources section of this book. Jeffrey P. Fisher's *Profiting from Your Music and Sound Project Studio* has lots of tips on setting up a home studio and great promotional ideas as well—I recommend you pick up a copy.

You'll need a decent microphone, but again, the electronics revolution has made great-sounding microphones relatively cheap. For example, the AKG C-1000 cost well over $400 just few years ago and was a bargain even then; now you can buy one for as little as $200. The Rode NT3 is another excellent microphone in the same price range. Don't forget to purchase an inexpensive microphone stand as well. If you're on a really tight budget, browse *www.ebay.com* or *www.digibid.com* to bid on used audio gear.

For recording just auditions, the "sound board" already built into your computer may be sufficient. If you want better quality, you'll need an "interface," which converts analog signals like your microphone's into the digital format computers understand, and amplifies its signal. Interfaces are also called A-to-D converters, and they, too, have become much less costly. There are interface converter "boards" that you install inside your computer, and a there's a host of new "USB" (Universal Serial Bus) and "Firewire" audio interfaces that simply plug into your computer. Some interfaces even come "bundled" with free recording software, like Rolland's UA-30—a nice USB unit that's roughly the size of a paperback book and includes Cool Edit Lite software, all for less than $200. Midiman's USB Duo gives you professional quality sound, too, at only around $100. Now, you are all set to plug in your mike, put on your headphones, click on the record icon on your computer screen, and start talking.

If I could rewrite the curriculum for actors in college and universities, I'd add requisite courses not only in accounting and advertising but in basic sound recording and computer skills. I wouldn't eliminate the traditional "pretending to be a tree" and "the art of painting flats 101," of course—some things are sacrosanct.

If you take no other advice from this book, take this: Voice actors without recording facilities are already at a competitive disadvantage. A studio of your own will soon be a necessity, not a luxury. Personal recording is the only cost-effective way to compete globally on the World Wide Web, and that's the subject of my next Techniques section.

I almost forgot, proximity effect occurs during the winter solstice and an XLR is the leather-lined, luxury edition Audi Quattro.

Okay, okay, so I'm allowed at least one big, whopping lie in this book—maybe two. Actually, as you get closer to certain microphones the bass tones are magnified, resulting in a deeper sound—you are closer in proximity to the mike, and that's the proximity effect. XLRs are the type of audio connectors you usually see on the end of professional quality microphone cables.

We return now to the truth, the whole truth, and nothing but the truth.

22

MY SOON-TO-BE-FAMOUS ACQUAINTANCES—BEFRIENDED BEFORE THEY WERE STARS

"I'm not an actor, I'm a movie star!"—Norman Steinberg and Dennis Palumbo, *My Favorite Year*, MGM–United Artists, 1982

Before They Were Stars was one of my favorite TV shows. Sure, it was sappy, trite, and predictable, but for me—and many other voice-over actors—the program was a wellspring of unexpected income. When the show played old commercials featuring actors in their "prestardom" days, which included our voice-overs, we got paid—all over again!

Actors never know when the person sitting next to them at an audition is going to hit it big. I used to ride the 151 Clark Street bus with Jim Belushi almost every day. I recorded many radio spots with John Mahoney before he became Frasier's dad. I still remember giving George Wendt a ride to Union Station, a few days before he and his wife, Bernadette Birkett, headed west for "pilot season," the time roughly between March and May in Los Angeles when new television sitcoms and dramas are filmed and tested. Next thing I knew, there was George permanently perched on his barstool as the beer-swilling accountant Norm Peterson on *Cheers*. I always wondered if George's degree in economics helped him land that part. Coincidentally, I'd sat at Chicago's Boul-Mich bar with the other star of that show, Shelley Long, discussing her voice demo just the week before. She'd asked me to help her make a new one when she got back from pilot season. I'm still waiting.

Sometimes, even your writer or producer goes on to fame and fortune. Recording a series of commercials for a young Detroit-based copywriter, I never dreamed that I'd one day see his name in forty-foot-high letters on a movie screen instead of on my copy. Lawrence Kasdan's name appears as writer of four of the most successful films in history, from *Raiders of the Lost Ark* and *The Empire Strikes Back* to *Return of the Jedi* and *The Bodyguard*.

Deb Castellaneta and I were recording a spot playing a husband and wife when she casually mentioned that she was flying out to L.A. that afternoon to join her real-life husband, Dan. They'd decided to take their voice demo entitled "Deb and Dan" to the coast and give it a whirl. What a delight to see Dan as the silent divorce client of Danny DeVito in *War of the Roses*. But that was nothing, compared to the fun of hearing him weekly—as Homer Simpson.

I played a young film director on-camera in a Buick commercial with the late Walter Payton twenty-some years ago. In the background is an equally young William H. Macy, dressed as a mechanic polishing up the car, MOS. Bill was, and is, an amazingly generous actor. He once called me just to make sure that I would audition for a part in his friend David Mamet's radio play, *The Water Engine*. Its world premiere would be broadcast on National Public Radio's *Earplay* program.

"What part should I audition for?" I asked.

"Same one I'm auditioning for," he replied.

How many people would be that unselfish? As it turned out, we were both cast, in different parts. Bill went on to repeat his role in the stage version of the play, at the St. Nicholas and Goodman theaters, and in the made-for-TV movie.

About the same time, Bill applied for his Screen Actors Guild card and encountered the same name problem as I had. The nice "name lady" told him there was already a Bill Macy in the union. Remember him? He's probably best known for his role as Maude's husband on *Maude*, Norman Lear's spin-off from *All in the Family*.

So William Hall Macy chose "William H. Macy" as his official professional name. From *Fargo* to *E.R.*, *Oleanna* to *Boogie Nights*, it's refreshing to see someone as talented as Bill—whoops, sorry—"William," earn the recognition he deserves.

I also vividly remember the day I was booked with this really cute four-year-old kid in a McDonald's radio spot. The producer, Tony Vanderwarker, asked him if he could read, and he politely said, "Not too well, but if you'll just read it to me, sir, I'll remember."

I had visions of a session from hell, since the kid had most of the copy. He listened intently, and then proceeded to do take after take flawlessly. I knew right then, this kid was special. So did the rest of the country a few years later, as we watched Fred Savage every Wednesday night in *The Wonder Years*.

My wife Lesley is practically addicted to Home and Garden Television, so I have lots of opportunities to see my old friend Jim Parks hosting *New Spaces*. "Honey, have I ever told you how I once pushed Jimmy out of a snowbank?" Her usual response, "A thousand times!" seems a bit exaggerated to me.

Even my third-grade Whisper Room field trip partner Barbara Trent had her fifteen minutes of well-deserved fame when she won an Academy Award in 1992 for her compelling feature-length documentary, *The Panama Deception*.

But until last month, other than my family, close friends and other voice-overs, no one had ever recognized me for my voice.

Kraft Foods in Glenview, Illinois, has a very sophisticated automated telephone answering and expense account system. In addition to the usual "Thanks for calling . . . your call is very important to us" stuff, Kraft's salespeople phone in every night, and by simply entering data according to voice prompts, they can instantly file their expenses. The salespeople love the system because they are reimbursed much quicker. The voice they hear is mine.

I walked into the headquarters building to redo a number of these computerized messages and told the receptionist my contact's name. I chatted with her about the weather and the upcoming "Taste of Chicago," when she interrupted.

"You sound familiar," she said, looking at me quizzically.

"I've been here before," I said helpfully.

"Say something else," she said. I blanked, as usual, and just about reverted to, *Mary had a little lamb*, then it dawned on me: "Good afternoon and welcome to Kraft Foods," I managed.

"You're the guy!" she said. Another young woman passed through the office at that moment, and the receptionist said to her, "It's the guy!"

"What guy?" the woman responded.

"The guy on the phone!"

"You're the guy on the phone?" the second woman asked me, walking over to look at me. "I thought you'd have dark hair."

My client, Michael, came in the lobby at that moment and said, "Hey, Harlan."

"He's the guy on the phone!" the receptionist repeated.

"I know," said Michael.

"I thought he'd have dark hair," the second young lady repeated.

"You're famous here, you know," Michael said as we walked to the elevators. "There are thousands of employees who talk to you on the phone every night."

Sitting in Mike's cubicle before we started recording, person after person popped their head over the wall to say "Hi," or get a glimpse of "the guy." It seemed so ironic that I'd be a recognized celebrity to the Kraft Foods sales force, while no one ever remembered hearing my voice on all the Kraft Singles, Velveeta, and Kraft salad dressing commercials I've done over the years.

Later, while I was walking out of the lobby, the receptionist said, "Excuse me?"

I had an inkling she was going to . . .

" . . . can I have your autograph?"

I laughed, then realized she was serious.

"Sure," I said awkwardly.

"Make it out to Mary Ann."

Scribbling something, since my handwriting, as you know, is not a strong point, I can honestly say I've never felt so silly in my life.

My wife and kids do, of course, treat me like a famous celebrity. Waiting on me hand and foot, I bask in the light of my well-deserved adoration. Whoops, sorry, my mind wandered there for a minute. Actually, I think Lesley, Jamie, and Graham are ever-so-slightly embarrassed when my voice comes on the radio or TV—God knows our dogs and cats are mortified.

After leaving the talent agent business, Lesley turned her attention to her first love, design. She has an eye for fashion, an eye for fastidious detail, an eye for decorating. She does not, however, have an eye on the clock. There are no alarm clocks on her side of the bed. Mornings are a time for silence. Mornings are a time for me to stifle my incessant babble. Mornings are a time for weak coffee and very little talk.

One sunny Saturday, it became my delicate duty not only to engage my lovely bride in morning conversation but to wake her up as well. Wake her up, so she could attend traffic school at 8:00 A.M.

Figuring it was best to get this over with. I decided on the "Pull the Band-Aid off the cut as fast as possible" approach. I strode to the damask curtains, and in one smooth yank whisked them open.

"Shhhhhh!"

She rose from the bed, quite beautiful even without her makeup, and raised a finger to her lips. Half smiling, half still asleep, she bargained, "I'll get up, but no talking!"

"Okay," I said.

"What part of 'No talking' did you not understand?"

I put my finger to my lips, pointed to the clock, and with exaggerated mime movements went downstairs. No words were spoken. Lesley pulled her black leather baseball cap low over her forehead, and drove the mile-and-a-half to the Bannockburn City Hall, to do penance for her traffic offense.

Even though she'd be spending the next four hours being lectured on improving her driving skills, at least she'd had a peaceful morning. A morning free of my maniac prattle on how she shouldn't be late, and how important it was to attend class so our insurance rates wouldn't go up, and blah, blah, blah, blah.

Settling into her chair, along with the twenty or so other transgressors, the instructor greeted them.

"Good Morning! Let's get started with an educational video called *Street Smarts* from the National Safety Council."

As the teacher dimmed the lights and the opening music swelled, the narrator enthusiastically began thirty-five minutes of safe driving tips.

"Safe driving is everybody's responsibility," he intoned.

"Oh for Christ's sake!" Lesley thought, as she recognized the voice. "It's Harlan!"

From the 1990 Harlan Hogan Production Calendar—John Sandford, Illustrator

Techniques of a Voice-Over: Virtual Voice-Over—The New Business Model

"Pay no attention to that man behind the curtain."— Noel Langley, Florence Ryerson, and Edgar Allan Woolf, *The Wizard of OZ*, MGM, 1939

There's nothing terribly unusual about this e-mail, except for the fact that it came from a casting director in . . . Amsterdam.

> Hereby I send you the script of Tommy Hilfiger. I hope you can do the recording of the script A.S.A.P. The customer wants it to sound like it's a trailer of a movie. Please send the final recordings to us as MP3 files. *Met vriendelijke groet,* Lilliane.

The business model for our industry has already begun to change. Like so many other industries—from banking to retailing—the Internet has affected traditional "bricks and mortar" businesses, and we are no exception. We are beginning to be "virtual voice-overs," perhaps represented by virtual agents, protected by virtual unions, and paid by virtual banks, anywhere in the world.

Already, I do the vast majority of my auditions from my home studio and e-mail them to Chicago, New York, or California. More and more, I'm recording the finished tracks here as well, converting them to MP3—which compresses, or "squeezes," the size of the file being sent over the Internet. We discussed ISDN phone lines earlier, and when I use my ISDN codec, the producer can not only direct me in real time—he or she can instantly go on the air with my broadcast-quality voice-over tracks.

High-speed phone wires and the Internet have conspired to reshape the *way* we do business and *where* we do business. These wonderful technological breakthroughs have also leveled the playing field, and you can now compete with voice-over actors around the world, as they compete with you. Plus, the Internet itself has created still another medium that needs voices. Ignore this new scenario at you own peril.

So, armed with the studio of your own we discussed in the last Techniques section, you are almost ready to sally forth onto the World Wide Web and discover a brave new world of opportunities. Naturally, that new cyber-world is also fraught with difficulties—from the expense of a high-speed Internet connection to creating a Web site to getting paid properly. If you are a SAG or AFTRA member, please don't forget that not long ago we endured a heart-breakingly long strike, and that one of the biggest sticking points was our demand that SAG and AFTRA have jurisdiction over our performances used on the Internet. We won that battle, so we need to be sure that we follow our unions' Internet rules. Make certain you and your agent have done, as the lawyers say, your "due diligence," ensuring that your employer—live or cyber—is signatory to the appropriate union contracts.

If you are not a union member, you need to be extra careful. Without a union contract and guarantees, once you e-mail out a voice track, you have pretty much lost any control over it. Getting payment up front and some kind of signed memo of agreement as to the use of your work is essential. That quick and easy announce track for an auto dealer's' Web site, for example, might suddenly show up on radio and TV commercials, and you might be paid nothing for that additional use and exposure—so beware.

If you have friends who are computer whizzes, now is a good time to treat them extra special. You'll likely need some help setting up the fundamental necessity of a virtual voice-over—a Web site.

Your Web site does not have to cost a fortune or be filled with the latest Java applets. But it does need to be sophisticated enough to host your audio demo and some promotional facts about you. In fact, many Internet service providers include "cyber space" for a personal Web site free with your monthly subscription. You may also want to set up a download area so you can send— usually using a simple FTP program (file transfer protocol)—the audio tracks you've recorded to your site. Audio files—even compressed ones like MP3s— are large and frequently too big to simply be e-mailed to your client or prospect directly. Instead, FTP the files to your site, and the producer can download them later at his convenience. An added value is that this makes your client revisit your Web site, a chance for further promotion.

Virtual voice-over is already a reality, and an exciting one. You don't have to live in a large city to pursue voice work anymore. Squandering thousands of dollars on duplicating and mailing voice demos that get tossed in the trashcan soon become a distant memory. Instead, you can invest that money in promotions that "drive" prospects to your Web site where your latest demos—easily and constantly updated—are waiting.

Web-based casting services such as Voicebank.net are proliferating, and it wouldn't surprise me to see clients posting auditions directly onto their own organization's Web sites the same way they do traditional job openings. Voice-overs could read the requirements and direction and e-mail their auditions in directly.

Most exciting is the reality that you can perform globally. One thing, though: Get used to being called a "Voice Artiste" and being asked for a copy of your "Show Reel" by those foreign producers. And, by the way, *met vriendelijke groet* means "best regards," in English.

23

RIDING THROUGH THE STRIKE ZONE—A FORCED VACATION, FOR A CHOSEN VOCATION

"Teenagers: They think they know everything. You give them an inch, they swim all over you."— John Musker and Ron Clements, *The Little Mermaid*, Buena Vista, 1989

You can count on some things in life, like the fact that Wisconsin always has been and always will be the Dairy State.

Or is it?

As two adults and two teenagers settled into the well-worn burgundy vinyl booth in the brightly lit fluorescent dining room of the American Inn of Reedsburg, Wisconsin, we checked our menus for that evening's specials.

This Saturday night in Wisconsin was no different than any other. Saturday night offers a statewide orgy of prime rib and salad bars. Sunday's special? *Grilled* prime rib, of course, and come Monday, cold prime rib sandwiches adorn the menu of more than just a few Wisconsin restaurants and bars.

Our waitress-hostess-cashier-manager's name tag read KATHY.

"But you can call me Georgia," she said with a certain breathy air of intimacy, tempered a bit by the presence of the teenagers.

"Which do you prefer?" I asked as sincerely as I could muster.

"Which do you like better?" she rejoined.

"Both," I replied. And after a long silence, I added, "You know, Georgia/Kathy, according to the sign we passed as we motored into town, Reedsburg here is the butter capital of the world." I was trying in vain to make even this tiny portion of our trip ever so slightly educational for my sixteen-year-old son, Graham.

Graham and his buddy Dan seemed appropriately uninterested, and in light of the good day we were having so far, I didn't elicit any comment from them on my question. Secretly, I was just happy they didn't burst out laughing. Like most grown-ups, I know when I'm sounding stupidly parental, but I just can't help myself sometimes.

As I glanced at Georgia/Kathy I thought I detected a slight blush, or maybe that was her natural skin hue, Wisconsin being full of generations of Scandinavians. Or perhaps it was the God-awful restaurant lighting. No, that *was* a blush, I decided.

"Well kinda, kinda," she said.

"Kinda?" I repeated, fighting off the urge to add just a touch of her Wisconsin lilt to my words.

"Well, Georgia/Kathy, are we in the butter capital or not?" chimed in the other adult, Al Mitchell, voice-over and motorcycling buddy whose talent is just as tall as he is.

"We were," Georgia/Kathy said quietly.

"But . . . ?" Al prompted.

"Some town in California is the capital now," she confided. "I guess Reedsburg never bothered to change the sign."

"California?" I said, surprisingly indignant, since I cared about the butter capital competition about as much as I care about the World Series. "Figures." Even on vacation, advertising half-truths were plaguing me, as was California, home of the celebrities who had gobbled up much of our voice-over work; the same way the town of Whatsitsname, California, has dethroned the good citizens of Reedsburg as the fiefdom of butter. We had ridden into the now former butter capital because it was, frankly, a lot cheaper to stay in Reedsburg than twenty miles east in the Wisconsin Dells proper.

Al and I were not only on vacation—we were also on strike. The strike proved to be the longest in entertainment history, and saving a bit of money on our motel bill turned out to be a wise decision. I found it ironic, too, that our union, the Screen Actors Guild, was based in—where else?—California.

Graham, age sixteen and change, was still in the throes of "Early Driving Fever," that brief and exhilarating time, just after muddling through your driver's license exam, when driving to the drugstore is as exciting as a spin around Le Mans in a Ferrari. I remember it well, being thrilled to speed across the Illinois cornfields to visit Eureka College. He'd surprised me with his idea for a summer vacation.

"How's this? Let's take a road trip. Dan and I will drive your Beetle, and you and Al can ride your motorcycles, and we'll go to the Dells."

The Dells is tantamount to Las Vegas for kids, with an unbelievable concentration of water slides, go-kart tracks, wax museums, and attractions. For adults, particularly motorcycle enthusiasts like Al and I, the area just west of the Dells is simply motorcycle heaven. Mile after mile of twisty, hilly roads, and the only traffic is an occasional Amish horse and buggy.

Ride the bike, actually *see* my sixteen-year-old, and get out of town and picket duty? This was truly a no-brainer.

"Let's do it!"

So, with the strains of *Evergreen* wafting its simpering way in from the Raven's Cocktail Lounge next door, we all ordered—ordered anything other than prime rib.

After a mediocre meal that didn't dampen our spirits a bit, Al and I began to do what two guys in their mid-fifties always do, we began to tell our obligatory war stories.

"Did I ever tell you about the time I was doing this narration and they wanted me to say 'At Northrop Defense Systems, we're rewriting history'?"

Al and Graham immediately said, "yes," in unison. I looked at Dan, who tried to appear interested out of sheer courtesy, but I knew it was time to let that story go.

Al picked up, "So just before the strike started, I'm over at Bosco Productions, and the producer, who's about twenty-two, is stopping me every other word. It's becoming a regular Blooper's Soap."

"Dan," I interjected, "do you know what a 'Bloopers Soap' session is?"

Dan smiled wanly as his pal Graham rescued him from another of my lengthy explanations.

"I'll fill him in tomorrow at the Dells," Graham said. "Anyway, Dad, it's probably time for us to hit the hay. We're buying all-day tickets at the Big Chief go-kart track, so we need to get up early."

"Sounds good," I said, amazed that this was my son, actually talking about getting up before one in the afternoon. "Breakfast here at 8:00?" I asked.

"How about 7:30?" Dan suggested. "You guys want to get out riding, don't you?" I glanced at Al, who smiled and nodded to the boys.

"Sounds good. Nightcap?" he said to me.

"Sounds even better," I agreed as I started to get up. "Al, don't let me forget to tell you about my session with this guy from Minneapolis last week. It was insane. Every time he didn't like a line reading, he'd punch the talkback and say, 'Harlan, Harlan, Harlan,' and slowly shake his head back and forth, I wanted to kill him."

"Puleeze," said Graham, as he and Dan started toward their room. "You know you guys have the easiest job in the world."

Dan grinned in agreement. I wanted to point out that they were hardly experts on the subject, since their combined job experience consisted of after-school counter duty at the La Grange Boy Scout Store and the Western Springs Oberweiss Dairy.

I wanted to, but couldn't. I looked at Al, father of three grown daughters, for help, but he too was silent. As the boys left for their room, and Al and I walked into the cocktail lounge, we smiled at each other. We both knew better than to argue with teenagers, especially when they're right.

Less than a year later, Al and I were once again on a motorcycle trip, in a slightly more exotic location—Spain. We'd actually planned a motorcycle trip in Spain's Andalusia region the year before. According to the guidebooks we'd read and reread, the area enjoyed an average of three hundred days of sunshine a year, making it at least 3 million percent sunnier than the Midwest. But the impending commercials strike convinced us to postpone the trip and make do with the Wisconsin Dells. Now, with the strike behind us, we were joined by film director Robin Rutledge and our significant others on an adventure that took us from the palm-tree-lined Costa del Sol to the snowcapped ten-thousand-foot Sierra Nevada mountaintops.

Along with all our requisite motorcycle gear, we brought along a self-powered AKG microphone, a USB audio interface, and a three-pound laptop computer loaded with recording software. We were all set to record tracks, edit them, and upload them to my Web site.

About now you may be asking yourself, why would anyone want to work while on vacation? Isn't *not* working the whole point of a vacation?

That's a rational question, but being a voice-over actor is hardly a rational vocation. In many ways, we are always on a perpetual vacation. As you know by now, the odds of getting each job can be astronomical. Realizing that you might miss a session, or even an audition, makes relaxing on vacation problematic. That's why I bring my little portable studio along.

As we meandered the twisting roads of southernmost Spain, our agents could e-mail scripts to Al and me, which we'd record in the hotel that evening. Spain uses the same phone connector we do in the United States, so it was easy to plug in the modem, dial an Earthlink local telephone number, and upload our voices back to the states.

The maid who interrupted me at the Paradore Ronda is probably still wondering why I had taken all the fluffy quilts off the bed and hung them up over the windows. I did it to quiet down the street noise echoing up from the Puente Nuevo bridge that spans the three-hundred-foot Tajo Gorge, upon which our hotel was perched. Since my Spanish is about as good as my handwriting, I'm sure my explanation and gesticulations made no sense to her at all.

At the end of our trip, basking in the warm Spanish sun and happy to be freed from the confines of our helmets and leathers, I asked, "Hey, Al, remember how Graham and Dan accused us of having the easiest job in the world last summer?"

Al smiled and said, "Yeah, and don't you just hate it when they're right."

Hold the *Magic Talent Indicator* over any piece of Advertising copy and instantly it moves in a straight line, backwards and forwards showing the copy is ok.. **BUT** . . . hold it over a piece of drek and it begins spiraling around and around **faster and** faster until it dive bombs right into the copy. **Its fascinating** . . . its *baffling* . . . We have never been able to figure out how it works but we've *never seen it fail*.

Forget focus groups, copy testing and headhunters! *Magic Talent Indicator* does it **ALL**!

No more costly mistakes . . with *Magic Talent Indicator* you'll hire the RIGHT people who can write the RIGHT ads. *Magic Talent Indicator* can also be used to determine the sex of chickens and birds.

Available at all **Walgreed**, **Ribaldy** and **Wolfstein** drugs stores

From the 1980 Harlan Hogan Production Calendar—John Sandford, Illustrator

Techniques of a Voice-Over: Kaizen for Voice-Overs—One Lesson, One Session at a Time

"It is better to know some of the questions, than all of the answers."
—James Thurber

Fear is the enemy of creativity.

If you are afraid—afraid of the producers, the writers, your agent, or coaches—you can't be creative. If you are afraid to ask questions, you are doomed.

I've encouraged you throughout the Techniques sections of this book to constantly ask questions. Who is the audience I'm talking to? Will this promotion piece delight the recipient? Do I have the right agent for me? What does this humungous wheel of cheese sound like and how will he escape destruction in the Velveeta melting pot? But asking questions always carries the implicit risk of a "wrong" answer. So it's only human that we often settle for the tried-and-true no-risk approach to performance, promotion, and business. Safe, perhaps, but not much fun, and certainly not very creative.

Most of us, though—particularly Americans—have been taught to ask the big, bold, breakthrough kinds of questions. How will I make a living at this? How can I get that new agent to sign me? How can I make this audition so good they'll send everybody else home right now? How can I make my voice demo break through the clutter? How can I get rich by tomorrow? These kinds of questions are self-defeating and downright depressing. They are ends, not means.

The ancient Zen philosophy of Kaizen (pronounced in "Harlan-phonetics" as "Kigh-zen") suggests a different approach and different kinds of questions. Instead of seeking "breakthroughs," Kaizen teaches small, constant improvements by taking tiny steps and asking easy questions to achieve large goals. The philosophy advises you to look closely at small, seemingly inconsequential details to learn big lessons.

Instead of, "How can I make a living at this?" ask, "What one producer could I call or write today?"

"How can I get that new agent to sign me?" becomes, "Have I told my present agent I appreciate her efforts?"

"How can I make this audition so good they'll send everybody else home right now?" might be, "Can I make a newcomer feel welcome in the waiting room?"

"How can I make my voice demo break through the clutter?" could become, "Have I gotten around to joining SAG's Book Pals and volunteered to read to school children?"

"How can I get rich . . . tomorrow?" might be more productive as, "Can I put aside $5 or $10 today toward a postcard mailing next month?"

Big questions send your brain into the "fear zone." Little questions—and little steps—are easy, comforting, and attainable. When I started to write this book, I was fortunate not to know that I'd need roughly eighty thousand words before I'd be through. My ignorance was Kaizen in action—I never once worried about that daunting task and instead just wrote one word at a time.

If this sounds a little ethereal and unbusinesslike, you're wrong.

After World War II, Japanese auto manufactures used the principles of Kaizen first to rebuild, and then to perfect, their auto industry. While American manufacturers were busy cranking out the same old land yachts loaded with chrome, whitewalls, and mediocre quality, the Japanese encouraged their workers to ask small, easy questions every single day to find small, manageable ways to improve their cars—over the long term. By the 1980s Japan had the United States automobile industry on the ropes.

Ask yourself what one, tiny thing can I do to further my voice-over career today? The so-called "right" answer is, as always, up to you. Read a book, lunch with a friend, or play with my kids is just as good an answer as pitch a new agent, make a new demo, or mail out a promotion—maybe even better.

Advocates of Kaizen strength training recommend adding only a small amount of weight in each workout to build their strength slowly and surely; improving your voice-over career is also a step-by-step, one-day-at-a-time time project. Keep acquiring and improving the Four Ts of voice-over—Training, Talent, Tools, and Technique—by asking the small questions, taking the small steps, learning each lesson, and enjoying the long journey—one session at a time.

24

ACTING UP, CRACKING UP—CONDUCT UNBECOMING

"It's such a fine line between stupid . . . and clever."— Christopher Guest, Michael McKean, Harry Shearer, and Rob Reiner, *This Is Spinal Tap*, Embassy, 1984

There are a few "givens" when you're entering a recording session. Everyone knows studio time is expensive. Everyone knows that this is not play but work time. Everyone knows that giggling, laughing, and becoming hysterical is unprofessional. And everyone knows that sometimes, you just can't help yourself.

Another performer's wonderfully funny reading, the subject matter itself, or even a well-intentioned direction that contains unplanned double entendres, can send even the most seasoned performers into spasms of laughter. Voice-over Pete Stacker was reading a spot for a new roller coaster ride in his most gripping, energized, and dramatic tone of voice, when the young woman producer told him, "Don't get me wrong, I love it hard, but," she softly whispered into the talkback mike, "what I really want is your nice warm Peter."

Everyone in the room, from Chicago Recording Company engineer Mike Mason to the client, art director, and writer, burst out laughing— except, of course, the producer. "Wha?" she said, as her mind did a quick rewind, and then fast forward, of what she'd just—so innocently—said. "Blush" isn't a strong enough shade of red to describe her face.

For the record, I've had a few out-of-control giggle fests myself.

Writer and producer Bruce Skinner flew into Chicago from Louisville to record an agency presentation with me for Indoor Advertising of America. Nothing intrinsically funny about that, except that this company was formerly known as Johnny Boards. That's right, this was supposed to be a serious video selling the benefits of washroom advertising.

Bruce was laughing as he handed me the script. By the time I'd read lines like, "Now, let's look at Indoor Advertising's gross impressions . . . ," "Here's your opportunity to reach consumers in an undisturbed, intimate setting," and finally, my favorite, "Did you know the average employee goes to the washroom 3.5 times each day?" Bruce was totally out of control.

Stan Oda, our engineer, was laughing so loud I could hear him through the studio glass.

"Uhhh, just a question, Bruce," I said. "What happens on the point five visit to the bathroom? Do they only make it to the sink?" And at that point I, too, convulsed into laughter.

After three or four false starts, we managed to get through the script. Bruce sat on the floor under the control room console so I couldn't hear him giggling, while I pulled the copy stand up high enough that I couldn't see Stan.

Not long after, I was blindsided at the end of a narration for Simplot Corporation, suppliers of potatoes to McDonald's. I was cold-reading my way through the Simplot Man of the Year Award in my most sincere tone of voice. The script read:

> **Our honoree is a man we can all be proud of. He's a family man—a foster parent who's adopted three homeless children. A man of God, active in the Evangelical Lutheran Church. A man you'd be proud to call your friend. A man always willing to help not only friends, but strangers. A man who personifies what it means to be a good neighbor. But most important of all: He's a man of . . . Potatoes.**

Visions of Mr. Potato Head, Mrs. Potato Head, and their three little adopted sweet potato children swam through my head. Wow! This guy must have starch running through his veins, I thought. It took me twelve takes to finally do the "big potato man conclusion" without laughing.

From the 1986 Harlan Hogan Production Calendar—John Sandford, Illustrator

Techniques of a Voice-Over: The Simple Truth—A Conversation Peer to Peer

"The work, the work, the work. Who among us throw themselves into work with more whole-hearted passion, more commitment, more disregard for practical concerns, and more undiminished, ever-optimistic hope than an actor?"—David MacFarlane, Canadian Theater Critic, 1999

Let me share some advice once given to me by an advertising genius: "Don't work too hard." That may sound like a contradiction, but stay with me.

You can't work too hard at promoting.

You can't work too hard at being professional.

You can't work too hard at cementing long-term business relationships.

You can't work too hard at being fun to work with.

But . . . you *can* work too hard in the studio.

Remember, we deal with only one sense in our performances—sound. Everything we do is wrapped up in just our voices, so it's only natural to try to put a little "too much" into that one sense. We are so tempted to work too hard, which is a nice way of saying "overacting."

I was mugging my way through a *Playboy* magazine radio spot early in my career, trying desperately to be funny and cute, and impress those wonderful writers and producers of radio comedy, Dick and Bert. Dick Orkin and Bert Berdis, before they moved to Hollywood and eventually split up, were the creators of the *The Tooth Fairy* and *Chickenman* radio series, in addition to thousands of award-winning comedy radio spots. Totally impressed to be working with them, I was working too hard, trying to prove myself and confirm their decision to hire a young upstart.

Working too hard is not a strong enough description, really. I was toiling in the salt mines of Siberia for a laugh, a smile, a nod of approval.

Dick Orkin, during a break, quietly said to me, "Don't work so hard. You've got the gig."

Great advice. Author-musician Kenny Werner agrees. In his book *Effortless Mastery*, he says, "Effort and/or lack of preparation blocks true mastery."

It's so easy to push it a bit and try a little too much. Like all performers, we're grateful for the work, and we want to show them how good we are. Because we perform in a glass-encased box instead of a stage, we never hear applause, or the accolades of fans waiting for an autograph. Often, it seems that producers take our performances for granted. That is, in fact, the best compliment.

If you've done your job, really done your job, and created a real believable character, it should sound—and be—simple. No cheers and no praise are necessary.

If the producers are unaware of what you've just managed to create within the confines and constraints of thirty or sixty or even—God forbid—fifteen seconds, then that's your own silent, wonderful applause.

You don't need, nor will you ever get, histrionics, curtain calls, or gasps of wonder at your prowess. Your standing ovation is just a signed contract, a check in the mail, and in the best-of-all-possible worlds, an opportunity to work for that producer or writer again in the future—that's the best affirmation of all. Remember, once you're booked, the hard work is over. Now it's time to have some fun. Show your stuff and revel in the moment, with no reason ever to work too hard.

Most of the time, though, it's not working too hard that's the problem for voice-overs—it's working at all. A friend's wife once secretly needlepointed a tapestry for him as a present; it read: YOU HAVE WORKED IN THE PAST . . . YOU WILL WORK IN THE FUTURE.

She clearly understood how crazed and depressed we actors get when times are slow. On the other hand, we chose this ride, and we knew, intellectually, that it would have plenty of ups and downs—we just didn't believe it emotionally.

We are not alone. Writers, directors, musicians, everyone in the entertainment business is riding the same coaster. Don Barrett, writer, producer, and director of more than two hundred hours of television programming, tells his workshop classes this story.

Prior to the release of *Star Wars*, George Lucas had to borrow 35 cents from actress Cindy Williams just to catch a ferry across San Francisco Bay to Marin County. Today, Lucas is the largest property owner in Marin County.

In the motion picture *Parenthood*, the grandmother, played by actress Helen Shaw, describes the thrill she got as a young woman riding on a roller coaster. It's as apt a metaphor for parenting as it is for the life of an actor:

> It was just interesting to me that a ride could make me so . . .
> so frightened, so scared, so sick, so . . . so excited, and, and so
> thrilled, all together. Some didn't like it. They went on the
> merry-go-round. That just goes around—nothing. I like the
> roller coaster. You get more out of it.

Wanna-bes and new-bes may think that eventually it all gets easy: The phone starts ringing and never stops. I wish that were true. It's not. Still, the ride is worth it, believe me.

Meanwhile, your work continues, if not in a studio doing a paying gig, then in a class, with a coach, or practicing at home. If you're not working to get better, you're working to get worse.

Surround yourself with positive people, from many different walks of life. Keep your momentum going, never waiting for the phone to ring. Author Ray Bradbury writes, in his book *Advice to Writers*, "You have to know how to accept rejection and reject acceptance." That's damn good counsel for voice actors, too, whether you are at the top or bottom of your career.

Remember, auditions are simply a numbers game. You don't win and you don't lose, as long as you at least get up to bat. I try to keep this quote from Robert Heinlein's sci-fi masterpiece, *Time Enough for Love*, in mind— "Certainly the game is rigged. Don't let that stop you, if you don't bet, you can't win."

And, if you are just starting to pursue a career as a voice-over, and you end up having to change your name, the Hogan clan still has a spare "Bob" floating around our genealogical chart. It's yours for the taking.

25

FAST-FORWARD TO FUTURE TENSE—WHERE VOICE-OVER ACTING GOES FROM HERE

"Skate to where the puck is going to be, not where it has been."
—Wayne Gretzky

So where does the career of a voice-over actor go from here?

This chapter is quite personal, and first of all I've got to admit two things. One, I'm very opinionated. Two, I've proven myself to be a pretty lousy fortuneteller over the years, despite knowing most of the tricks of the trade.

In 1927, novelist J. B. Priestly was asked to write about the future. I'll have to say I agree with his conclusion that "solemn prophecy is an obviously futile proceeding, except insofar as it makes our descendents laugh." So, with my misgivings and J. B.'s warning, here's what I see happening to the voice-over business for the journeyman actor or actress.

First, the bad news—everything has changed.

Now, the good news—that's not necessarily bad, only different.

Creativity, Celebrities, and Selling Products

"We figured out that a customer base with a salary was better than a customer base with an allowance."—Michael A. Weiss, President, The Limited

After years of advertising full of "loose bricks" and "Huh?" advertising we seem to be seeing a return to sales-oriented creativity. Legendary adman David Ogilvy once said, "If it doesn't sell, it isn't creative." John Hancock Funds retail analyst Steve Paspal agrees, stating that advertising has been failing to fulfill its primary purpose lately: "Consumers are clearly buying less," he said, "but it's not because they're afraid to spend. There's nothing drawing them into the stores."

Jonathan Kirshenbaum, cochairman of Bond & Partners Advertising in New York, agrees that advertising will have to become more frugal and accountable. "I think long-term, this economy is good for the industry . . . the cutbacks force everyone to be more accountable. That is fine with us. Playtime is over."

Economic conditions seem to point to possible good times within the bad times. The American Business Institute trade group recently reminded its business-to-business members that (just as in the "Golden Age" of advertising of the 1980s) "when times are good, you *should* advertise; when times are bad, you *must* advertise."

If advertising returns to bottom-line accountability, and has to sell products and services within its budget, it's good news for the journey-men voice-over actors and local postproduction facilities. As for celebrities, as long as they are "bankable," clients will be willing to pay the tariff. Frank Sinatra earned over $6 million last year, and he's dead—so the value of celebrity is very real. But in an era of new media like the Internet, where advertising results are clearly measurable, even celebrities will most likely have to pull their weight and bring in sales, or the bean counters will find a more economical option.

Everything has changed.

That's not necessarily bad.

New Media Venues

"What is certain about the future is this: The networks can never recapture their monopoly . . . having tasted the power to choose, viewers will continue to insist on programming for themselves."
—Ken Auletta, *Three Blind Mice*, Random House, 1991

Despite the fact that cable TV talent fees are still too low for the amount of exposure given to a performer, we still may be entering a new advertising Golden Age.

This Golden Age will be different. With the emergence of a multitude of new technologies, our opportunities and incomes as voice-over performers will more likely be based on the sheer *volume* of the work we do, unlike the 1980s, when the residuals from just one network commercial might pay the rent.

Internets, Intranets, Web sites, CD-DVDs, telephony, wireless, voicemail, all can—and will—"talk." Until synthesized speech is really perfected, we have a vast opportunity ahead. DDB Needham Advertising agency chairman speculates that, "Eventually there will be entire channels devoted to commercials."

Radio, like the telegraph before it, began as one-to-one medium. In 1910 inventor and scientist Lee DeForest had a thought. He put a crude microphone in front of an opera singer at the Metropolitan Opera House in New York and turned on the transmitter. At that moment, broadcasting—a farm term originally meaning sowing a wide circle of seeds—began. Many people heard the singer's voice instead of just one. No longer was radio only a one-to-one means of communication. Just twelve years later, the first commercial was broadcast over radio station WEAF New York.

Now, the cycle is beginning to come full circle. As radio, TV, and the Internet get smarter and faster, we'll return to one-on-one communication by choosing what programs we watch or listen to, and when. Already, between 5 and 6 million households in the United States have high-speed cable or DSL access, a fivefold increase in one year. Projections say that number will be 27 million in just five years, according to *Digital TV* magazine. High-speed access makes broadband or "streaming" media possible. All those "silent" sites will be talking, and that's what we voice-overs do best. And now, satellite radio is capable of changing the way people listen to radio, in the same way cable changed television.

Right now, your TV is the dumbest appliance in the house, but not for much longer. Some call it convergence, others interactive television (iTV), but whatever the name, the blending of computer intelligence with television and radio will lead to far more sophisticated ways of advertising and selling products. For example, you may soon be able to instantly buy almost any product on TV just by clicking your remote on it, or even an actor's sweater or shoes. Dubbed "Television commerce" (T-commerce), it takes impulse buying to a whole new level.

More intelligent media like T-commerce means more targeted marketing and tracking of results. This, I believe, will lead to more, not less, commercial work being created.

More than likely, the TV networks will still be our national "meeting hall" for the hot TV show of the season and major sporting events. Brand image advertising will still be plentiful there. As ad legend Jay Chiat said in *Time* magazine, "People who watch the Superbowl are interested in the game, but even more interested in the advertising."

But the trench work of moving products will more likely be the purview of the new media, born of convergence. High-definition digital TV will allow targeted commercials to reach specific homes. If you are the parent of an infant, for example, your smart TV will pass through commercials for disposable diapers, while Lesley and I are viewing a spot on investing our retirement funds at the exact same moment. End result? More commercial production, but less exposure for an actor. The sheer volume of commercials created by these new delivery systems will, hopefully, offset the possibly reduced per-use payments to actors.

The Internet has been fairly quiet, but it is already singing, moving, and talking. Andrew Lubman in *Internet Audio* magazine points out, "We've been raised on media, such as radio and television, where music and sound are always there to help add realism, paint a sonic picture, or evoke a certain mood. And, on the Internet, audio can be even more at the forefront of the experience."

Meanwhile, the voice market for corporate and long-form narrative voice-work, interactive games, and animation shows no indication of slowing down in the near future. So I'm confident the opportunities for voice-overs will increase, not diminish.

Everything has changed.

That's not necessarily bad.

Casting

"A believable synthesized human voice that can read from a script with proper emotion is well beyond the reach of current technology, and is likely to remain so for several decades at least."
—Bill Machrone, PC *Magazine*, 1999

Well, I hope so.

Especially since right now, there seem to be more and more performers for fewer and fewer jobs. I'm sure we'll hear synthesized voices on a spot or two before long, but for the foreseeable future, casting will still involve humans—those looking for work and those looking for us. Today, however, there are far more filters between us voice-overs and our potential employers.

In the Seventies and Eighties voice actors made rounds—sales calls—and met with creatives face-to-face. Those meetings frequently led to auditions almost always held at the ad agencies. We were directed by the writers and producers themselves and had a chance to perform at our best. Meanwhile, creatives had an opportunity to build a knowledge base of the local talent who could do the job and whom they wanted to work with.

Now we are cast, long distance. General descriptions are e-mailed or faxed to our agents or to casting directors. Unfortunately, auditioning has become more like a lottery than a creative exercise. The performer who guesses right, and comes closest to what the writer had in his or her mind, gets the job. Voice-overs are now more of a commodity like sound effects, stock music, and typography.

But agency people are nothing if not smart, and at least in Chicago we're seeing more and more "live" auditions being held back at the ad agencies. That's very encouraging, because talent and creatives both benefit. I know as a writer myself that my best ideas have come from my knowledge of the talent pool. I heard the offbeat sound of voice-over Chris Harlan in my head as I wrote a "fish-out-of-water script" of a salesman writing home to his wife from a sales meeting. *Letters from Appleton* was a breeze to create for Miller Electric, because I knew how much Chris would bring to the party with his unique style.

When I envisioned a slightly ditzy wife for a Nokia commercial, chastising her husband for his lack of observation, I heard voice actress Marie Burke in every line I created. The versatile Mindy Bell's voice was also firmly planted in my "mind's ear" when I imagined a lone woman walking along windswept Navy Pier on a Halloween night—one minute frightened, the next minute just a suburban-sounding mom.

Writers and producers who don't have knowledge of the talent pool are robbing themselves of a great source of inspiration and creativity. As much as I embrace new technology, nothing takes the place of a one-on-one audition, with the performer and creative working together to find just the right sound and approach.

New technology is beginning to eliminate the need for traditional voice demos, though. From a talent's perspective, that isn't necessarily a bad thing. It's becoming unnecessary to send out thousands of voice demos to uninterested producers. Instead, talent agencies and individual talents' Web sites have our demos available on demand "24-7."

I'm also seeing a voice-over version of one-stop shopping cropping up. Some audio studios and production centers like Studio Center in Norfolk, Virginia, and Chicago Recording Company are now providing casting, as well as recording, services. As long as there isn't a conflict of interest between the talent, studio, and clients, I can see how appealing, and potentially timesaving, this approach can be.

I mentioned I'm a pretty lousy fortuneteller, and here's proof. By the time I had finished this chapter, AT&T announced that they had developed "software capable of copying any human voice!"

In a subsequent article, the *Wall Street Journal* cited a market for text-to-speech of $1 billion in the next five years. It also revealed that "cloning" celebrity voices—dead or alive—had many legal implications, and that to produce smooth, realistic sound required a "voice donor" willing to contribute ten to forty hours of reading into their computers.

Just as movies have embraced digital actors for background scenes, replacing extras, I can see how digitized voices might make sense for walla groups and short audio bits like "Please press one," or, "Will that be all, sir?" But to struggle through the programming necessary to create even a thirty-second radio commercial, let alone a sixty-minute documentary narration, makes no sense, economically or artistically. Listen to the National Weather Service radio reports some time and chuckle as their computer-generated voices (named, by the way, Paul, Craig, and Donna) stumble over even simple words. River sounds like "'rye-ver,'" forty degrees comes off "'four-dee-dee-greez,'" and cloudy becomes "'clouuuuuuuuuudee.'" As synthesized voice technology improves, I'm sure some small parts may indeed go cyber, but overall it seems there's still life in this career for humans. But it does mean . . .

Everything has changed.

That's not necessarily bad.

Call me optimistic, but I'm sticking with Barbra Streisand. Back at WIOK radio I still remember that it was her voice on the station loudspeakers as I frantically searched the United Press International Teletype for my first five-minute newscast. She was belting out "Happy Days Are Here Again," and I noticed it was the last song she sang on her farewell TV concert. Well, even after all these years, I'm still betting Barbra's right.

Questions from a Teenage "Wanna-Be" Voice-Over

Here we are back where we started. This e-mail from a high school student got me thinking, and reminiscing. I hope I've at least partially answered her questions. If she decides she'd like to do voice-overs, maybe someday we'll meet and, even better, work together.

Dear Sir:

1. So how did you become a voice-over?

Through a twisted career path, peopled by wonderfully bright and generous people.

2. How much do you make?

It varies, but I'm comfortable, and more importantly, happy.

3. Did you need any training?

Yes, theater, broadcasting, advertising, computers, and loads of trial and error.

4. How can I get to do voice-overs?

I've given you a lot of suggestions and opinions through-out this book's Techniques of a Voice-Over sections, and some other books to study, in the resources section. But above all—as Dick Rodnick once cautioned me—just be sure that being a voice-over actor really is your heart's desire.

Postscript: The Unremarkables

"I submit this to you. If one night you were to be introduced at a party to some of our most successful voice actors, say Joel Cory or Harlan Hogan or Russ Reed, it would never enter your mind to gasp, 'What stentorian timbre! What silky intonation! What irre-proachable diction!' Fact is, like a lot of other first-rate narrators, their voices are remarkably unremarkable.

"So, what's their secret? They are actors and interpreters first, announcers last. They have managed the virtuosity of taking a stiff, unventilated script and through some magic force, in one cold read, resuscitating it into a breathing, moving, limbed body of language that somehow resembles human conversation. Each in his own peculiar style has mastered the seemingly simple, yet subtly demanding, art of sounding like one human being talking to another human being."—Jack Badofsky, Executive Creative Director, K & R Marc Advertising

Sometimes, late at night, watching the umpteenth rerun of *St. Elsewhere,* or *NYPD Blue,* I see them. A flitting moment of *almost* recognition. A face, a look, or a voice that deep in my memory rings a soft almost silent bell. I smile in recognition of fellow "unremark-able" actors. They are the journeymen in the acting craft, not celebri-ties by any means, and not even one of those semirecognizable character actors.

No, these are the actors in movies, training films, and TV shows who aren't noticed—actors who never lure the spotlight away from the star. They're cast because they always seem to look right and sound believable. I've been privileged to be one of those unremarkable, journeyman actors.

Who knows, maybe sometime you'll recognize me, or one of my peers, when you listen to the radio, or attend your company's annual sales meeting, or even when you're put on hold at your favorite restaurant. We'd love that, but we love our anonymity too, because for us, being unremarkable is precisely what makes us—remarkable.

~ May the
Wind be ever
At your back,
Your editing
Behind you.
And may you be
In heaven's studios
An hour before
The client knows
You're dead.

From the 1980 Harlan Hogan Production Calendar—John Sandford, Illustrator

RESOURCES

Books on Voice-Over

Alburger, James. *The Art of Voice Acting: The Craft and Business of Performing for Voice-Over* (Woburn, Mass.: Focal Press, 1998).

Apple, Terri, and Gary Owens. *Making Money in Voice-Overs: Winning Strategies to a Successful Career in Commercials, Cartoons and Radio* (Los Angeles: Long Eagle Publishing, 1999).

Blanc, Mel, and Phillip Bashe. *That's Not All Folks* (New York: Warner Books, 1988).

Blu, Susan, and Molly Ann Mullin. *Word of Mouth: A Guide to Commercial and Animation Voice-Over Excellence* (Beverly Hills: Pomegranate Press Ltd., 1996).

Cartwright, Nancy. *My Life As a 10-Year-Old Boy* (New York: Hyperion, 2000).

Clark, Elaine A. *There's Money Where Your Mouth Is: An Insider's Guide to a Career in Voice-Overs* (New York: Backstage Books, 1995).

Cronauer, Adrian. *How to Read Copy: Professional's Guide to Delivering Voice-Overs and Broadcast Commercials* (Chicago: Bonus Books, 1990).

Douthitt, Chris, and Tom Wiecks. *Voiceovers: Putting Your Mouth Where the Money Is* (West Linn, Oreg.: Grey Heron Books, 1997).

Quinn, Sunny. *Put Your Mouth Where the Money Is: Get Your Voice on Radio and TV Commercials* (Jupiter, Fla.: Airwaves Publishing, 1998).

Thomas, Sandy. *So You Want to Be a Voice-Over Star* (Wantagh, N.Y.: In the Clubhouse Publishing, 1999).

Books on Acting in Commercials

Berland, Terry, Deborah Ouellette, and Jason Alexander. *Breaking into Commercials* (New York: Plume Books, 1997).

Dameron, Steve. *Star Quality: How to Make It in Commercials, TV and Film Acting* (New York: Magnetic Press, 1998).

Dougan, Pat. *Professional Acting in Television Commercials: Techniques, Exercises, Copy, and Storyboards* (Portsmouth, N.H.: Heineman Publishing, Portsmouth, 1995).

Fridell, Squire. *Acting in Television Commercials for Fun and Profit* (Jackson, Tex.: Crown Publishing, 1995).

Hunt, Gordon. *How to Audition: For TV, Movies, Commercials, Plays and Musicals* (New York: HarperCollins, 1995).

Johnson, Batt, and Richard Lewis. *Rich and Famous in Thirty Seconds: Inside Secrets to Achieving Financial Success in Television and Radio Commercials* (Lincoln, Nebr.: iUniverse.com, 2000).

Searle, Judith. *Getting the Part: Thirty-Three Professional Casting Directors Tell You How to Get Work in Theater, Films, Commercials and TV* (New York: Limelight Editions, 1995).

See, Joan. *Acting in Commercials: A Guide to Auditioning and Performing On-Camera* (New York: Watson-Guptill Publishing, 1998).

Steele, William. *Stay Home and Star! A Step-by-Step Guide to Starting Your Regional Acting Career* (Portsmouth, N.H.: Heineman Publishing, 1991).

Wolfe, John Leslie, and Brenna McDonoguh. *You Can Work On-Camera! Acting in Commercials and Corporate Films* (Portsmouth, N.H.: Heineman Publishing, 1999).

Other Books

Arlen, Michael J. *Thirty Seconds* (New York: Farrar, Straus & Giroux, 1980).

Barr, Tony. *Acting for the Camera.* (New York: HarperCollins, 1997).

Fisher, Jeffrey P. *Profiting from Your Music and Sound Project Studio* (New York: Allworth Press, 2001).

Fisher, Jeffrey P. *Ruthless Self-Promotion in the Music Industry* (New York: Hal Leonard Publishing, 1999).

Hanssen, Deirdre, and Jodi F. Gottlieb. *TV: Sex, Lies and Promos* (Los Angeles: The Promo Zone, 2000).

Henry, Mari Lyn, and Lynne Rogers. *How to be a Working Actor* (New York: Back Stage Books, 2000).

Levinson, Jay Conrad. *Guerrilla Marketing Excellence* (New York: Houghton Mifflin, 1993).

Levinson, Jay Conrad, and Seth Godin. *The Guerrilla Marketing Handbook* (New York: Houghton Mifflin, 1995).

Ries, Al, and Jack Trout. *Positioning: The Battle for Your Mind* (New York: McGraw-Hill, 2000).

Ries, Al, and Jack Trout. *The 22 Immutable Laws of Marketing* (New York: HarperCollins, 1993).

Rose, Jay. *Producing Great Sound for Digital Video* (Gilroy, Calif.: CMP Books, 2000).

Werner, Kenny. *Effortless Mastery* (New Albany, Ind.: Jamey Ambersold Jazz, Inc., 1996).

Periodicals

Voice Over Guide (published quarterly): Dave & Dave Inc. 4352 Lankershim Boulevard, Toluca Lake, California 91602.

Backstage, Backstage West, and Backstage Handbook for the Performing Artist: 1515 Broadway, 14th Floor, New York, New York 10035.

Hollywood Reporter: 5055 Wilshire Boulevard, Los Angeles, California 90036.

Variety: 5700 Wilshire Boulevard, Los Angeles, California 90036.

Screen Magazine: 222 West Ontario Street, Chicago, Illinois 60610.

Adweek Magazine: 770 Broadway, 7th Floor, New York, New York 10003.

Advertising Age: 360 Michigan Ave., Chicago, Illinois 60601.

Internet Audio: www.mixonline.com/internetaudio/intaud.cfm

Ross Reports (monthly): P.O. Box 5018, Brentwood, Tennessee 37024.

Organizations and Mailing Lists

Audio Publishers Association
627 Aviation Way
Manhattan Beach, California 90266
www.audiopub.org

Bob Paquette's Microphone Museum
107 E. National Ave.
Milwaukee, Wisconsin 53204
CALL FIRST! (414) 645–1672

H.E.A.R.
P.O. Box 460847
San Francisco, California 94146
www.hearnet.com

Promax
2029 Century Park East, Suite 555
Los Angeles, California 90067
www.promax.org

National Association of Television
Program Executives (NAPTE)
Station Listing Guide
2425 Olympic Boulevard, Suite 600E
Santa Monica, California 90404
www.napte.org

Standard Rate and Data Service (SRDS)
1700 Higgins Road
Des Plaines, Illinois 60018
www.srds.com

Recording Software

Cool Edit
Syntrillium Software
P.O. Box 62255
Phoenix, Arizona 85082
www.syntrillium.com

Sound Forge
Sonic Foundry, Inc.
1617 Sherman Avenue
Madison, Wisconsin 53704
www.sonicfoundry.com

Pro Tools
Digidesign
3401-A Hillview Avenue
Palo Alto California 94304
www.digidesign.com

Recording Equipment and Supplies

Markertek Supply
P.O. Box 397
Saugerties, New York 12477
www.markertek.com

Sweetwater
5335 Bass Road
Fort Wayne, Indiana 46808
www.sweetwater.com

Full Compass
8001 Terrace Avenue
Middleton, Wisconsin 53562
www.fullcompass.com

B&H Pro Audio
420 Ninth Avenue
New York, New York 10001
www.bhphotovideo.com

Digifon ISDN Services
20 Deepwood Road
Fairfield, Connecticut 06430
www.digifon.com

Auralex Acoustics
8851 Hague Road
Indianapolis, Indiana 46256
www.auralex.com

Acoustics First
2247 Tomlynn Street
Richmond, Virginia 23230
www.acousticsfirst.com

Silent
58 Nonotuck Street
Northampton, Massachusetts 01062
www.silentsource.com

Whisper Rooms
116 Sugar Hollow Road
Morristown, Tennessee 37815
www.whisperroom.com

Vocal Booths
1631 South East Riviera
Bend, Oregon 97702
www.vocalbooth.com

Unions

American Federation of Television and
Radio Artists (AFTRA)
New York National Office
260 Madison Avenue, 7th Floor
New York, New York 10016
(212) 532–2242
www.aftra.org

AFTRA: Chicago Branch Office
One East Erie, Suite 650
Chicago Illinois, 60611
(312) 573–8081

AFTRA: Los Angeles National Office
5757 Wilshire Boulevard
Los Angeles, California 90036
(323) 634–8100

Other AFTRA branch offices are
located in California, Colorado, Florida,
Georgia, Hawaii, Massachusetts,
Maryland, Michigan, Minnesota,
Missouri, Nebraska, New York, Ohio,
Oregon, Pennsylvania, Arizona,
Tennessee, Texas, and Washington State.
Call an AFTRA national office or visit
www.AFTRA.org for addresses and phone
numbers.

Screen Actors Guild (SAG)
National Office
5757 Wilshire Boulevard
Los Angeles, California 90036
(323) 954–1600
www.sag.org

SAG: Chicago Branch Office
One East Erie, Suite 650
Chicago, Illinois 60611
(312) 573–8081

SAG: New York Office
1515 Broadway, 44th Floor
New York, New York 10036
(212) 944–1030

Other SAG branch offices are
located in Arizona, California, Colorado,
Florida, Georgia, Hawaii, Massachusetts,
Washington D.C., Michigan, Minnesota,
Missouri, Nevada, North Carolina,
Ohio, Oregon, Pennsylvania, Puerto
Rico, Tennessee, Texas, and Washington

State. Call the SAG national office or
visit *www.SAG.org* for addresses and
phone numbers

Alliance of Canadian Cinema,
Television, and Radio Artists
(ACTRA)
2239 Yonge Street
Toronto, Ontario M4S 2B5
Canada
(416) 489–1311
www.actra.com

Author Contact Information

Harlan Hogan can be reached via
e-mail, through his publisher and
agents, or on the Web:
E-mail: *Harlan@HarlanHogan.com*

Publisher:
Allworth Press
10 East 23rd Street
New York, New York 10010
(212) 777–8395
www.allworth.com

Agents:
Access Talent
37 East 28th Street, Suite 500
New York, New York 10016
(212) 684–7795
www.accesstalent.com

Stewart Talent
58 West Huron
Chicago, Illinois 60610
(312) 943–3131
www.stewarttalent.com

William Morris Agency
151 El Camino Drive
Beverly Hills, California 90212
(310) 859–4000
www.wma.com

Web Presence:
www.HarlanHogan.com
www.StudioCenter.com (Norfolk)
www.SoundOfTheWeb.com (London)
www.intervoice.nl (Netherlands)

From the 1994 Harlan Hogan Production Calendar—John Sandford, Illustrator

Alice's Adventures in Adland

I've collected lots of outtakes and parodies over the years. In addition to "Blooper's Soap" and the Orson Welles session, I have a purloined copy of an ill-fated—and never finished—narration on penile implants that degenerated into a sniggering, giggling disaster. Another favorite of mine is a classic New York Telephone radio spot. A pontificating announcer tells us, "We know getting an obscene phone call can really piss you off . . . but offenders have learned that a ten-cent phone call can jam their ass in prison for a year . . . after all, at New York Telephone the service we give you is obscene enough."

So, I guess it was only natural that I'd want to try my hand at an advertising parody of my own. In 1997, with lots of help from my friends, I wrote and produced *Alice in Adland*. It's the story of Alice Lidell, a seemingly ordinary thirteen-year-old who has an extraordinary dream after dozing off during career day at McClure Junior High.

> **NARRATOR:** Once upon a time, Alice Lidell, a seemingly ordinary thirteen-year-old, had an extraordinary dream. You see, it was career day at McClure Junior High, and as Paula Prang, Creative Director of the Wheedle, Wheedle, Jaberschlock and Prang Agency was extolling the joys of a career in Advertising, Alice began to doze . . .
>
> **PAULA:** (Delivering speech in background)
> . . . and then there's the lunches! sushi, huge steaks, dry martinis . . . Oh, did I mention the celebrities? Just last week—out to the coast, quick casting session, then Spago with Demi.

Of course, children, the ad biz isn't all fun and games!
Sometimes you actually have to eat with the client! But that's
rare at my level . . .
(Paula's audio tails off . . .)

ALICE: (soft snoring over Paula)

NARRATOR: Chapter 1: In which Alice free-falls into freelance.

MUSIC/SFX: SPINNING/FALLING MUSIC, WITH VOICES
IN BACKGROUND.

VOICE 1: Résumé, please . . .

VOICE 2: We'll let you know . . .

VOICE 3: Leave your book . . .

VOICE 4: Too young . . .

VOICE 5: Check back next week . . .

VOICE 6: Too pretty . . .

VOICE 7: Don't call us . . .

VOICE 8: Too blond . . .

VOICE 9: Check the mailroom . . .

VOICE 10: Check next millennium . . .

ALICE: (Dreamily at first . . .)
Falling, falling . . . Down I go. Will I find work? I just don't
know.
Floating, floating . . . Past each place . . .
Door after door slammed in my face.
Dropping, dropping . . . On a summer's day, please give me a
chance, I don't need any pay.
Drifting, drifting . . . Will this stop?
I'll take any old job at any old shop.

VOICE 11: Well, there is one job open . . .

ALICE: Gliding, gliding . . . I think I see—an intern job! That's
perfect for me!
Landing, landing . . . My feet touch the earth . . .

VOICE 12: You're hired . . .

ALICE: Let's get to work—I'll show you my worth!

SFX: OFFICE NOISE, A CACOPHONY OF PHONE BUZZES & RINGS WITH THE AUTOMATED ATTENDANT'S VOICE IN BG UNDER NARRATOR, THEN SFX OF DOOR SWINGING OPEN.

ATTENDANT: Not in, try later . . .
. . . she's gone,
. . . he's gone,
. . . gone to lunch,
. . . gone freelance,
. . . I'll leave word.
. . . On vacation,
. . . on the coast,
. . . still in a meeting,
. . . on location.
Please hold, please hold, please hold . . . !

NARRATOR: Chapter 2: Alice meets the automated attendant and learns why no one is *ever* in.

ATTENDANT: (sung)
Out to Lunch! Out to Lunch! Yes, that's right, the whole damn bunch!

ALICE: S'cuse me . . .

ATTENDANT: Oh? You're the intern? So? Big deal!
Cause they're all out at a fancy free meal!
How 'bout some Muzak? Nice and boring?
Stop that, young lady!

ALICE: Sorry!

ATTENDANT: . . . I saw you yawning!
Just leave a message at the tone, then we'll play tag-on-the-phone!
Now, be a good girl, young and thoughtful. See, Mr. Jabberschlock—
He's downright awful! (Sung)
Out to Lunch! Out to Lunch! Yes, That's right, the whole damn bunch!

NARRATOR: Chapter Three: Alice gets the lowdown on her new boss.

SFX: FOOTSTEPS TO DOORWAY—DOOR OPENS AS WE HEAR TWO CREATIVES KICKING AROUND COPY PLATFORMS.

TAMMY: How 'bout cabbage—it's better for you than it looks.

ERIC: Ahhh . . . Sometimes things that are green and slimy are actually good for you . . .

TAMMY: . . . Cabbage, it's not just for breakfast any . . .

ALICE: Excuse me . . .

ERIC: . . . 9 out of 10 people prefer cabbage over brussels sprouts . . .

ALICE: Hello?

TAMMY: . . . Where would corned beef be without cabbage . . .

ALICE: I think I'm lost . . .

ERIC: Can we help you?

ALICE: I'm Alice, I'm supposed to see a Mr. Jabberschlock?

TOGETHER: (slight laughter)

TAMMY: Should we warn her, Eric?

ERIC: Common decency dictates, Tammy.

TAMMY: Beware the Jabberschlock, my friend, with Armani suit and Mont Blanc Pen.
Those A.E. lies, those Italian ties, those exaggerated media buys.

ERIC: Mr. Jabberschlock, Mr. Jabberschlock.
With warm-up suit and diet pop.
He's never on time, it's the *client's dime*, he's got a Rolex, so that's a crime.

TAMMY: Beware the Jabberschlock, hon. He wheels 'n' deals with gilt-edged tongue. He'll trash your script, says it's too hip, but don't complain or you'll get a pink slip!

ERIC: Mr. Jabberschlock has a limousine—the way he spends, it's just obscene.

No taste, no class, no sense of style.
Just fixed, glazed eyes and phony smile.

TAMMY: Take heed of the Jabberschlock, my girl.
He'll take you on a tilt-a-whirl.
Of sleepless nights on presentations . . .
Of pencil tests for animation . . . just praying for account salivation.

ERIC: Mr. Jaberschlock, Mr. Jabberschlock.
He's always gone by five o'clock . . .

TAMMY: "Create! Create! Create!" he'll yell. "We've got exciting things to sell!"

TOGETHER: Alice, tell him to go to hell.

NARRATOR: Chapter Four: Alice is assigned to the "Cabbage Fit for Kings" account and meets Wheedle Dee, Wheedle Dum, and the client!

CLIENT: The Time has come.

NARRATOR: The client said.

CLIENT: To Talk of Many Things, of GRP's and Focus Groups and such creative things.
Of Budgets, Bids, and estimates of billboards by the dozens.
Of deals, free meals, and other perks, since you boys are my cousins.

WHEEDLES: Yes, now's the time!

NARRATOR: The Wheedles declared.

WHEEDLES: For numbers and statistics . . .

WHEEDLE DEE: We'll maximize your market share . . .

WHEEDLE DUM: We'll handle the logistics.

WHEEDLES: Right! Right! Right! And right again!

NARRATOR: The little suitees shouted.

WHEEDLES: When it comes to selling things, we know all about it!

CLIENT: The time has come . . .

NARRATOR: The client said.

CLIENT: To think of brand new things. Of coaching each new customer to buy our *Cabbage Fit for Kings!*

WHEEDLES: Oh Yes! Oh Yes! Oh Yes! Yes, Yes.

NARRATOR: The tiny Yes Men squealed.

WHEEDLES: We're the city slickers . . .
Who can do the deals!

WHEEDLE DEE: We'll buy the time, we'll place the space, all at a bargain rate . . .

WHEEDLE DUM: The broadcast and the FSI's run on their scheduled dates.

CLIENT: That's it then, boys, the game's afoot!
Our spots will pull—they'll have the look!
Sooooo, the time has come.

NARRATOR: The client said:

CLIENT: To *MAKE* some advertising. Some Stealomatics and storyboards, show me something surprising!

WHEEDLES: Present! Present! Present! Right now!

NARRATOR: The Duo A.E.'s canted.
WHEEDLES: With Alice and her overheads, he's sure to be enchanted.

ALICE: (Clears throat)
"ERRRRRR . . . The Time Has Come."

NARRATOR: Alice said.

ALICE: To let our Jingle sing . . .
(sung)
"C'mon America Sit Right Down, Taste Our *Cabbage Fit for Kings!*"

CLIENT: Stop! Right there!

NARRATOR: The client said.

CLIENT: That's the best you can do?!
I'll make some calls across the land, for an agency review.

WHEEDLES: Oh no! Oh no! Oh not again!

NARRATOR: The teeny suitees sobbed.

WHEEDLE DUM: It's all *HER* fault . . .

WHEEDLE DEE: She's not creative!

WHEEDLES: Fact is we've been robbed!

CLIENT: Now, Alice, come here . . .

NARRATOR: The client said.

CLIENT: Let's talk of *important* things.
Of Golf, fine food, and *your* good looks, and my giant pinkie ring.

ALICE: Yes, the time *has* come.

NARRATOR: Alice said.

ALICE: To talk of *important* things. Of life, and love, and brother-hood . . .
Not Your *Cabbage Fit for Kings!*

CLIENT: What Ho! What Ho! What *you just* said . . . that's what our product needs.
We'll beat the drums for *brotherhood* . . .
And take in all the dweebs!

ALICE: Enough! Enough! I've heard it all!

NARRATOR: Alice angrily shouted.

ALICE: This game's no fun, no fun at all!

NARRATOR: She turned, and then she pouted.

CLIENT: All right! All right! We'll try your spot.

NARRATOR: The client quickly agreed.

CLIENT: We'll market test and interview, see if it meets our needs.

WHEEDLES: (Clearing throats)
Then the time has come . . .

NARRATOR: The Wheedles said.

WHEEDLES: To make our reservation . . .

WHEEDLE DEE: C'mon let's eat . . .

WHEEDLE DUM: And let's eat big . . .

WHEEDLES: Then we'll go on location!

CLIENT: Hawaii's nice . . .

NARRATOR: The client said.

CLIENT: But tell me what *you* think.
We'll plan campaigns all afternoon, over juicy steaks and drinks.

ALICE: The time has come.

NARRATOR: Said Alice . . .

ALICE: For me to move along. If that's what you call advertising, it isn't where I belong.

NARRATOR: Chapter Five: In which Alice attends the Gladhander reps' not-so-free party.

SFX: RESTAURANT BACKGROUND

GLADHANDER: (sung)
Twinkle little spot . . . Oooooo ya know I like it a lot!
My director's reels, as you can see . . .

WAITER: Anything else, sir?

GLADHANDER: . . . can be taken literally.
Every job—they've actually done. Every spot—has actually run.
As for cost, we'll never fudge it!
Every job was under budget!
Twinkle, twinkle, night and day, Alice, join us in L.A.!

NARRATOR: Chapter Six: Alice relaxes at the shoot.

SFX: CROWD NOISE ON SET

SPIKE: . . . And action!
Big cabbage bite, smile . . . it's real good, real good . . . c'mon, act, act, act,
good, good, good!
Cut, print, let's take five.
So, Alice, your first shoot. Having fun?

ALICE: Yes, Mr. Spike, but aren't we going into overtime?

SPIKE: (Devilish laugh, then sings)
Overtime? Overtime? Little Alice, that's just fine.
What the heck, *it's the client's dime.*
Forget the bid, the budget too.
It's the perfect spot I'm creating for you.
So just kick back. I'll teach you what to do:
(Sung, new tune)
There's margaritas everywhere, tacos too, they're over there.
There's time for work, but now it's play . . .

ALICE AND SPIKE: (Sing together)
. . . 'Cuz that's the way it's done here in L.A.!

SPIKE: Ohhh, I'm digging this, Alice.

NARRATOR: Chapter Seven: In which Alice finds herself way over budget.

SFX: ADDING MACHINE CLICKS AND TOTALS

ALICE: Of bids and budgets I've had my fill!
Numbers, percentages, stacks of bills.
Carry one . . . divide by two . . . I simply don't know what to do!
I've spent too much for this silly commercial,
on actors, extras, and dress rehearsals.
Too many lunches, too many trips.
Look at the cost, it just makes me sick.
I've got no excuse, I've got to admit.
(sighs)
But the Queen of CDs will just have a fit!

NARRATOR: Chapter Eight: Alice's Creative Review.

PAULA: (sung)
Creative review! Creative review!
Oh how I love a creative review.
Look at your spot!
The color's not true . . . Good thing I called this Creative Review.
Creative Review! Creative Review!
When you're a CD, you can schedule them too.

Your spot would look awful if left up to you . . .

ALICE: Really?

PAULA: . . . Thank God we had this creative review.
Creative review! Creative review!
If you're over budget our client might sue.

ALICE: (Gulps)
Really?

PAULA: Trash all your work, go edit anew.
Gee I just love this creative review.
Creative review! Creative review! I know what I like, and I like very few.
That cabbage looks black, black as my shoe, go book a paintbox see what they can do . . .
Creative review! Creative review!
I'm judge and I'm jury, at creative review!

NARRATOR: Chapter Nine: Alice encounters the Cheshire Mac.

SFX: MOUSE CLICKS

CHESHIRE MAC: Cabbage *SHOULD* look rich and green steaming in that hot tureen . . .

ALICE: I know you're right, and I see what you mean . . .
But will it read on a TV screen?

CHESHIRE MAC: A tweak here, a tweak there, I'll colorize it everywhere . . .
Beeeautiful cabbage, beeeautifully shot.
Gee . . . I'm a genius at selling this slop.

NARRATOR: Chapter Ten: Alice attends the awards.

SFX: CROWD AND APPLAUSE
PA ANNOUNCER:
Ladies and Gentlemen, welcome to the twelfth annual Ronco awards for excellence in package goods advertising run in non-weighted markets on alternate Thursdays during the summer solstice . . .
(fade under Alice)

ALICE: Glittering trophies, all in a row, will I win one? I just don't know. But with a "Ronnie" my career would grow.

Award, statues, plaques galore, purchased at the trinket store . . .

But what in the world are they really for?

(yawns)

Suddenly I'm feeling drowsy.

Truthfully, a little lousy.

Oh dear, so sleepy, was it that wine? Or have I just—run—out—of—time?

SFX: SPINNING MUSIC FROM OPENING—WE HEAR PAULA'S SPEECH IN BACKGROUND AS ALICE BEGINS TO WAKE UP

ALICE: (yawning)

I liked advertising, I might have known.

But it can wait . . .

Until I'm grown.

PAULA: (reprising her opening speech under)

Of course, children, the ad biz isn't all fun and games! Sometimes you actually have to eat with the client! But that's rare at my level.

Then there was that one fabulous shoot where Wolfgang actually catered right on location! We scouted for almost six months and found this incredible place in the Caymans that looked for all the world like Cincinnati. It was heavenly and warm and 50 below back home. Anyway, Spike and Martin were codirecting this 15 for United Bank of Ohio, and what a shoot it was. Let me tell you I really earned my keep for Wheedle, Wheedle, Jaberschlock and Prang (she trails off . . .)

ALICE: (soft snoring . . .)

Oh no, not again . . .

(waking up, talking to herself)

Geez . . . After Wheedle, Wheedle, Jaberschlock and Prang, working at the Gap is sounding better and better . . .

NARRATOR: Thanks for joining us for Alice's Adventures in Ad Land.

ORIGINAL CAST: Narrator—Harlan Hogan
Alice—Marie Burke
Paula and The Queen of CDs—Linda Kimbrough
Automated Attendant—Fern Persons
Tammy—Margaret Travolta
Eric—Al Mitchell
Wheedle Dee—Mike Matheson
Wheedle Dum—Chris Harlan
Client—Chelcie Ross
Gladhander Film Rep.—Joe Guzaldo
Mr. Spike—Tab Baker
Cheshire MAC—Pam Hoffman
Ronnie awards announcer—Ron Rolland
Sound design—Richard Hawksworth
Original music—Marty O'Donnel.

I'll never be able to thank everyone involved in my pet project adequately. As for me, I learned so much sitting on the other side of glass for a change. That experience confirmed my belief that 99 percent of the success of a voice project is in the casting.

I had the luxury of casting the absolute best, and interestingly, during the entire production, we never had to record more than two takes per talent. That's just how good these voice actors are!

"Alice" has won several awards, and is in the audio archives at Bowling Green University, nestled right up next to the Steve Allen Collection and countless other comedy audio tracks.

Once again, you can hear the original recording by clicking on the "VO: Tales and Techniques of a Voice-Over Actor" button at *www.HarlanHogan.com.*

Index